A lifetime of Big Ships & Little Ships

Roy Waters

Pen Press Publishers Ltd

Copyright © Roy Waters 2003

All rights reserved

No part of this publication may be reproduced, stored in a retrieval system, or transmitted in any form or by any means, without the prior permission in writing of the publisher.

First published in Great Britain 2003
by Pen Press Publishers Ltd
39-41, North Road
Islington
London N7 9DP

ISBN 1-904018-47-5

Printed and bound in the UK

A catalogue record of this book is available from the British Library

Cover design Jacqueline Abromeit

To my wife Susie, who while far too busy with almost full time employment and a family to look after, to assist with checking the text, gave me every encouragement to write this book and indeed urged me to do so.
And to Geoffrey and Robert

CONTENTS

Foreword

1.	Early Days	1
2.	An Apprenticeship in Shell Tankers - My First Ship	12
3.	Two More Ships	27
4.	An Officer at Last	38
5.	Up the Ladder. Promotion to Second Mate	50
6.	Exam success	63
7.	Departure from Shell...	73
8.	...And Quicker Promotion	80
9.	Drama on Land, Then Back to the "Hamilton"	96
10.	Thirty Years a Civil Servant - The Early Days	107
11.	London Outport	121
12.	Later Days	135
13.	Marine Pollution and Other Accidents at Sea	148
14.	Decline and Change	162
15.	Sailing Days, 1965 to 1968	175
16.	Sailing Days, 1969 and 1970	184
17.	1971 to 1976 - Some Serious Racing	192
18.	A New Boat nd More Serious Racing	209
19.	Twenty Years with "Melandy"	220
20.	"Sundowner", a Comfortable Cruising Yacht	240
21.	An Ambitious Cruise	252

Appendices

1.	The British Merchant Navy. Then and Now - Some notes	260
2.	Yachts and Yacht Racing. Then and Now - Some notes	271

Glossary	276
Epilogue	280

FOREWORD

In about 1947, when I was 15 years old, a girlfriend at school gave me a pocket diary for Christmas. I started to write a few words in it each day and ever since then I have kept a diary in one form or another, but mostly in the 'two-or-three-days-to-a-page' format.

As a Government marine surveyor, extensive written reports, especially in connection with marine accidents, were part of one's life and so I got plenty of practice writing about my various experiences. In recent years I have written up each season's main sailing and cruising activities in the form of a 'log' and some of these are quite bulky volumes. Some have even won prizes in yacht club cruising competitions. Also in recent years I have produced a number of articles for local yacht club magazines such as the 'Spreader' and the Irish Cruising Club's Annual Journal. The Belfast Master Mariner's Club has lately produced an Annual Journal called the 'Seamew' and some of my experiences both at sea and as a Government marine surveyor have appeared there.

In later years, especially after retirement, one tends to look back and wonder 'what if'? Well, I didn't become a successful businessman or make a lot of money on the stock exchange but I am lucky to have led an interesting and enjoyable life in a marine environment, both as a career and a pastime, and I have no regrets there!

With the encouragement of my wife I decided to go through all my records and produce a volume of memoirs, which should at least be of interest to my immediate family and some of my contemporaries.

This book is the result.

CHAPTER 1: EARLY DAYS

In later life, what can one remember about one's early days? All I remember of mine is that they were largely untroubled and full of interest, despite the interruption of the Second World War.

My mother was born in Warminster, Wiltshire, and my father in Nottingham. I cannot remember how my parents met but they were married in 1919 and lived in a house in West Bridgeford, Nottingham. After the First World War, Dad was redundant for a while until he got a job with the British Petroleum Company and was posted to their oil terminal at Avonmouth. BP was expanding and they opened an oil terminal in Belfast. Guess who was sent over with the advance party in 1926 as a temporary transfer until the new terminal was established. Dad lived in digs until he found rooms in a house in Sydenham Gardens, off Holywood Road, and mother came over to join him. It must have been traumatic since the early "Troubles" were at their height. I remember stories such as the one about the tram conductor shouting "Everybody down!", whereupon all passengers hit the floor while bullets flew past nearby. During this period my older brother Geoffrey was born but tragically died of meningitis at the age of three before I was born, and I remained an only child.

Around 1930 my parents rented a house in nearby Denorrton Park, where I was born in 1932 and which remained home for me until 1970. They expected to move back to England one day; even when Dad retired in 1957 it was still on the cards, but they never did.

I well remember when war was declared in 1939, and the events that followed. Everyone was issued with gas masks and I remember going to a special container where they were demonstrated, fitted and tested. We had a "stirrup" pump at the house in case of fire and soon also a "Morrison" air raid shelter. This was a very heavy steel "table" which had to be carried into the house in bits and bolted together on site. It took up about half the space in our small dining room but had a steel mesh underneath on which we were supposed to lay mattresses and blankets. In fact when the air raids did start we usually spent the night in the basement of one of the adjacent houses, the best being the Mahoods'. A good many years later I actually built a 20-foot pocket sailing cruiser in this very basement, with Dad's help. Air raid shelters of brick and concrete were built in

1

the road in two places in Denorrton Park and, of course, all over the city. They were great places for children to play. There were some quite heavy air raids on Belfast, the shipyard and the aircraft factory of course being the targets. An incendiary bomb once even landed in our back yard and it was dealt with by putting a bucket over it – the indent in the concrete where it landed was still there when the house was sold!

In 1940, at the height of the bombing, I became an evacuee and I suppose this is when I first became interested in small boats and sailing. I stayed at a smallholding called "The Beeches" at Lisbane, between Comber and Killyleagh and not far from Strangford Lough. This was owned and occupied by the Minnis sisters, five spinster ladies, all of whom would have made splendid country housewives but none of whom ever did marry! When I first went there, there were some quite heavy air raids on Belfast and refugees came out nightly from the city, often on foot, and were accommodated in the barn, if not in the house. Nobody ever asked about their religion or whatever, and all found somewhere to bed down for the night.

I attended Ardmillan Public Elementary School, long since closed and the building now a private house. There were two teachers, a number of local children and quite a few other evacuees, and it was here that my vocabulary was considerably extended by the addition of such words as "stanes" and "sheughs" and my accent became somewhat localised! I remember a favourite activity in class was producing numerous drawings of steam driven traction engines and threshing machines while supposedly learning something else! I had plenty of opportunity to observe these marvellous machines in action and even got to help pitchfork the straw. Newborn calves and kids were another wonder. I also enjoyed splendid times playing in the local fields and woods with my friends, catching sticklebacks and tadpoles in the ponds and streams and trying to fish with a twig, a length of string and a bent pin.

A schoolteacher friend of the Minnis sisters lent me a book to read, *Swallows and Amazons*. At the time I thought the action took place in some faraway country, because of the children's names for various places around the lake. I was really fascinated by the book and after reading this first Arthur Ransome story, I got all the rest in the series as and when they became available. As a result of these books, I grew interested in sailing dinghies and later in larger craft such as the "Goblin" in *We Didn't Mean To Go To Sea*. Due to the war, there was virtually no sailing activity on nearby Strangford Lough and the only yacht club, the recently formed Strangford Lough Yacht Club at Whiterock, was virtually closed down for the duration. In addition none of my family or friends had any interest in boats and certainly had no access to one.

In 1942 I returned to Belfast to the family house in Denorrton Park, off the Holywood Road, and was accepted at Sullivan Upper School in Holywood where I spent the next six years. The "new" school building had only been built and opened at the outbreak of the war and consisted of six classrooms plus a laboratory. There were about 180 pupils and some ten staff including "Jimmy" the caretaker/cleaner/handyman and of course the Headmaster, R.J.(Dick) Grant, whose speciality was Latin. If you didn't like Latin you were a second-class pupil! He was also liberal with the cane for quite minor offences.

My interest in matters maritime continued and, having devoured all the Arthur Ransome books (the last one being *Great Northern*), I avidly read many other "sea-faring" authors, including Percy F. Westerman, who wrote a series of novels about a lad called Alan Carr, following his career from cadet through to captain. The fictitious tramp shipping company was Watmough, Duvant and Co., and their ships were all named "Golden" something, such as "Golden Gain". Other sailing books I enjoyed included those long-distance epics by Joshua Slocum, Alain Gerbault and Conor "Cruise" O'Brien. I visited the local public library at least once a week and sometimes my reading went on late at night by torchlight under the bedcovers.

The war was still going on and like many houses in the area we usually had a serviceman lodger from the nearby Sydenham Airbase or elsewhere. Sunday night was "open night" for service people and there were many visitors from all the services. I was too young to appreciate the Wrens and VAD nurses but one gave me a present of Adlard Coles' *Sailing Days* and another produced a 1938 Blakes' Catalogue for cruisers on the Norfolk Broads. We managed very well without television and all the modern diversions that children seem unable to live without these days but we did have radio and the local BBC station had a children's hour. A Captain Davis had a spot which intrigued me. I think it mainly described his experiences at sea with the locally-based Head Line and he also wrote a regular feature in the Belfast Telegraph. Unbenown to me then, Captain Davis was also a surveyor and examiner of masters and mates with the Board of Trade. Soon I got interested in yacht design, especially the deck and accommodation arrangements. I drew out plans on paper and then transferred them to a full-size layout on the back lawn using a two-foot ruler and firewood sticks!

I think it was towards or at the end of the war that we were able to resume family visits to grandparents and other relations in England, usually for two or three weeks in the summer. Getting the necessary travel documents and indeed official permission to travel at all was quite a business as I remember. We travelled from Belfast to Heysham in ancient ferries that had not been requisitioned and thence by train to stay in Nottingham, Birmingham and Dursley in Gloucestershire, and later even to London to visit Uncle Bert. I loved these journeys especially when I could get a corner seat on a train. Dad was usually seasick on the sea crossing.

At the end of the war I got my first boat, a 12-foot sailing dinghy. I must have stimulated Dad's latent interest in sailing for one day he came home with a little book called *Simple Boat Building* by Geoffrey Prout. He built the boat in a half-empty shed at the Shell Mex & BP oil installation where he was now Assistant Manager, and the materials came from various sources, including timber washed up on the shore at the oil jetties following launches at the Harland & Wolff Shipyard nearby. The jetty foreman, who was a shipwright by trade, was involved in the building work and so was I as far as possible. The design was indeed simple for this was long before the days of fibreglass or even marine plywood. She was basically plank on edge with a flat bottom forward, but cut and pulled into a V section aft. She was partly decked, had a heavy iron centreboard and was gunter rigged, the sails being cut out of some old sails found somewhere. The total cost was in the region of £15! She was named "Titmouse" after Tom's dinghy in Arthur Ransome's *Coot Club* and *Secret Water*. When launched into the Musgrave Channel in Belfast, she floated a bit head down but for the time she was quite a pretty little boat and in her I learned the basics of sailing.

Initially "Titmouse" was moored behind one of the Musgrave Channel oil jetties but Dad had a friend, Jack Weir, who was with Munster Simms, another oil company. Mr. Weir belonged to Holywood Yacht Club and owned "Cloud", one of the 16-foot Holywood Sharpies. Before long "Titmouse" was moved to a chain mooring at Holywood and here I could easily reach her from school on my bicycle. The moorings at Holywood were on the drying

Holywood Bank so the state of the tide determined how you got to your boat: by foot, paddling or launching someone's dinghy. I was not in the least interested in school cricket in the summer and even less in rugby in the winter, more in getting to my boat! In the summer I could easily cycle there from home, and did so at every opportunity. I gained more experience in "Titmouse", sailing as crew in "Cloud" in the local "round the buoys" races, and attending local regattas in Belfast Lough. One day I went unauthorised to Holywood and sailed "Titmouse" to Carrickfergus, four miles across the Lough, and back again single-handed. On the way back I hauled a three-legged stool out of the water, which must have fallen overboard from some passing ship, and carried it home on my bicycle. My reception at home was frosty to say the least but the stool was still at home when the house was sold!

I had various school and other friends keen enough to sail with me. A favourite short trip was to sail out to the Pile Light, which at that time marked the outer end of the Victoria Channel, leading up to Belfast Harbour. The Pile Light was manned and we went out armed with newspapers and fresh vegetables, tied up at the steps and were invited on board by the lighthouse keepers. Nearby was moored the "Lady Dixon", a floating lightship and the pilot station for Belfast at that time.

Dad got more involved in Holywood Yacht Club and late in 1946 bought "Spray", another Holywood Sharpie. He found her at Carrickfergus in poor condition and paid about £25 for her. She spent the winter in a shed at the oil installation and was completely refurbished. The following season Dad and I raced her at Holywood and in some of the regattas around Belfast Lough. We did very well – indeed so well that some of our competitors in the Sharpie class were apparently seen around her at low tide measuring all dimensions! I don't recall that they found anything untoward. "Titmouse", meanwhile, was sold on to someone local but I cannot remember who or where.

My desire to go to sea when I left school continued, though for some reason both my parents thought I should be aiming for university and perhaps a career in architecture. Dad's job at the oil installation meant he was responsible for the unloading of the tankers arriving there and this often involved him going out in the evenings and at weekends. It was a great thrill when I could go with him and sometimes even get on board these vessels. I well remember some of the coasters which came in, such as "San Dario", "Esso Tioga", "Esso Juniata", "Oarsman" and "Rudderman". Most of the deep-sea tankers were either BP, Bowrings or Huntings – I do not recall any Shell tankers! However, Dad brought home the "Shell Magazine" every month and at the back of this was "Fleet News", which I read avidly. There were two Shell deep-sea tanker companies at that time, Anglo-Saxon Petroleum Company and Eagle Oil and Shipping Company, whose activities were worldwide, whereas most other companies were more limited. At Sullivan School a number of boys I knew had already gone to sea and one in particular was Tom Scott, who had been Head Boy. He was serving his time as an apprentice with the Bank Line, which certainly went worldwide, and he sent letters about his voyages to Mr. Frost, our Geography Master, who read them out in class. I found them fascinating and Mr. Frost did say that the best geography lesson was to travel the world!

In 1948 I sat the Northern Ireland Junior Certificate examination and achieved reasonable results. I left school at the end of June and the process of getting me away to sea began. At this time the United Kingdom still had a considerable merchant fleet despite war losses. Shipyards all over the country were busy building vessels to replace those lost. As a stopgap measure many shipping companies had taken on American built ships including the famous "Liberty" ships and "T2" tankers. Almost all deep-sea companies carried apprentices on their ships and so the opportunities were there for almost any lad who wanted to go to sea on deck. I was fascinated with Shell, whose tanker operation was run by the Anglo-Saxon Petroleum Company. Dad knew someone in Shell Mex House in London who knew someone in Anglo-Sax, and in due course I was summoned to their offices at St. Helen's Court in London for an interview and short written examination.

In due course I was accepted, subject to a three-month pre-sea course at a nautical school and a one-month course at the Outward Bound Sea School, both of which Dad had to pay for. (My closest school friend, John Olver, got away to sea as an apprentice with the Head Line of Belfast – and without pre-sea anything!) At that time virtually all nautical colleges were privately run and their function was to cram students with sufficient knowledge to hopefully pass their various statutory examinations. I attended the Belfast Nautical School, one of many establishments around the country. A famous one was Nellist's Nautical College in Newcastle-on-Tyne, apparently run very successfully by two schoolteachers who had never been to sea! Going further back, I have a little book called *Handbook to the Local Marine Board Examinations for the Officers of the British Mercantile Marine*. This was published by a Mrs. Janet Taylor at her "Nautical Academy and Navigation Warehouse", 104 Minories, London, in 1856. She must have been quite a character!

Anyway, the Belfast Nautical School was run by Captain T.J. Boyd of Larne, who had certainly been to sea. He was in fact an excellent teacher who was able to educate the most unlikely students to the standard necessary to pass their statutory examinations. Apart from the Church his main interest was gardening and he was reputed to have very green fingers. I still have a copy of my "satisfactory" certificate issued by Captain Boyd. The school premises consisted of one room in a decrepit office building in Donegal Street, Belfast, and here he catered without assistance for everyone from pre-sea Apprentice to Master Foreign Going. The pre-sea boys had to help him by sweeping the floor and emptying the ashtrays each morning. Apart from weekday attendance there were Saturday morning classes which involved instruction in nautical instruments including use of the sextant, barometer, thermometer and hygrometer.

Many of the mature students at Captain Boyd's school were from the Head Line, Kellys and other local shipping companies which were very much in existence at that time. Diversions from the classroom for mature students included the local "bookies", the Lombard Billiard Hall and the Rosemary Bar, where the barmaid was reputed to be an expert on the "Rules of the Road" or the Collregs, as we call them now. It was not unknown for Captain Boyd to visit these establishments to extract students therefrom.

On 8 January 1949 I started my one-month course at the Outward Bound Sea School at Aberdovey on Cardigan Bay in Wales. This particular establishment was, I think, started during the war for the purpose of giving young people joining the Merchant Navy some basic training in boat handling and survival techniques, which at that time there was every chance they might need. After the war the school continued under the directorship of Dr. Zimmerman who must have been the founder of the Outward Bound Movement which later had other centres, such as the one in the Lake District, catering for young people from all walks of life. However, in my time it was solely for boys about to go to sea, both apprentices and ratings, and since it was sponsored by the Blue Funnel Line and by Shell, many of the trainees were going to sea with those companies. The activities were mainly outdoor and included boatwork, athletics, long walks and hikes and a few days aboard an old French onion boat called the "Garibaldi". Every morning started early with a two-mile run followed by a cold shower, and I was there in January!

I was on the 80th Course and there were some 65 boys in all, divided into six "watches" of about 11 each. I kept a detailed diary on this course and I still have it so all the facts are to hand! I was on the "port" watch and apart from the main activities we had to take our turn at domestic duties such as washing up, swilling out the galley and cleaning out the pigsties. I did not particularly enjoy the athletics but I did enjoy the hiking, for which we were given instruction in map reading and then sent off in groups on increasingly lengthy hikes around the local area. We discovered farmhouses which would provide such delights as beans on toast at a very modest price!

Of course I found the sailing activities interesting and these were based on the wharf at Aberdovey. The school had two open clinker built cutters, one with a standing lug rig and the other with a dipping lug, plus of course plenty of oars. After the "Spray" I found them very heavy and cumbersome. One day I was appointed Quartermaster, which meant I had to stay on the wharf to tend to mooring lines and watch for signals. Both cutters were out and about a mile away up the estuary and both running before the wind and tide when a sudden squall struck. The Dovey estuary can actually be quite treacherous, with drying sandbanks and strong tidal streams. The recall signal was hoisted but both boats were in a very bad position and making no progress to windward. There was an emergency boat of sorts which was sent out, and me with it. Her unseaworthiness made a big impression on me, and she was almost unmanageable when head on to the fairly heavy seas. She was barely able to push herself along let alone tow one of the cutters and after three attempts we gave up and returned to the wharf. The gear in this boat was totally inadequate, the canopy over the engine was loose and appeared about to collapse, while the engine itself frequently conked out. Both cutters beached safely somewhere up the estuary and were recovered later. The "Garibaldi", alongside the wharf, was unable to sail because of the weather and big breaking seas on the bar.

Another activity at the wharf was lifeboat drill and to this end there was an old ship's lifeboat under old-fashioned gooseneck davits. There were competitions to see which watch could prepare the boat, swing it out and lower it to the water in the shortest time. There was, of course, plenty of boy power on hand to man the falls for the recovery operation.

The "Garibaldi" was something else. Each watch was meant to spend a few days in this vessel and my watch was the first to go. Since she was laid up in a mud berth at Pwllheli presumably for repairs, we travelled up the coast to Pwllheli by train to join her. The first two days were spent working on the boat under the direction of the Captain and the Mate. This included antifouling the hull when the tide was out. Captain Purkiss was a retired Blue Funnel Line master and I noted that he was short and stout, wore a cap pulled down over his eyes, and looked to be about 60 years old. I never found out much about the Mate but he was very Welsh and claimed untold knowledge of sailing ships. The "Garibaldi" herself was better than I expected. She was 72 feet long with a beam of 23 feet and a draught of 6 feet 6 inches. She was rigged as a gaff ketch. Down below most of the original hold had been fitted with double berths on either side for the boys, and aft of this were four officers' cabins, plus toilets to port and the offset engine room to starboard. The galley was right up forward!

We sailed or motored from Pwllheli at 0800 on 15 January, 1949, with the help of some locals to get off the beach, and went out into the open sea of Cardigan Bay. I recall having been detailed to help in the galley where a pre-sea Blue Funnel catering rating was attempting to fry sausages for breakfast. He was sick into the frying pan and I recall that we simply cleaned out the pan, wiped off the sausages and went back to work! Who was to know, but in fact all twelve of us boys were soon hanging over the side being sick! This was the only time I ever recall being seasick; indeed, once I had got rid of my breakfast I felt fine and was even able to take a trick at the wheel.

At 1400 we anchored off Abersoch in calm water, where we cleared up down below and prepared a proper hot meal. Later on one of the boats was lowered and four of us rowed the mate ashore to visit friends. On a walk ashore I was interested to look around the outside of the South Carnaervonshire Yacht Club and noticed several nice boats there, including several Dragon Class boats. There had also been quite a few of these at Pwllheli. At 2100 we rowed ashore again to pick up the mate and found him asleep at the top of the steps leading up to the Yacht Club. The four of us had to manhandle him back down the steps, into the boat and back out to the ship! All the boys had to take turns on anchor watch but at 0300 the next morning we hove up and sailed for Aberdovey, presumably to get the tide "right" on the bar. We were alongside the wharf by 0830 and that was the end of my trip in the "Garibaldi"!

All in all I enjoyed Aberdovey but I do recall that, as a result of all the activity, I felt constantly hungry, despite quite good and plentiful food at the school. In our free time we were allowed to walk into town where the local cafes and snack bars did well from our patronage. I noted in my log that on one evening in town, I consumed two bottles of lemonade, one steak and kidney supper, one fish supper, one bag of potato crisps, one cup of tea, four slices of bread and butter and one mince pie!

On 3 February I returned home to await appointment to my first ship. I was now "kitted out" in accordance with the list of requirements sent by Anglo Sax. This involved obtaining extra clothing coupons to buy the uniform and other items. Dad, of course, had to pay for it all – no mean outlay in those days. All that the Company provided was uniform brass buttons and trimmings. These were standard Merchant Navy and not "Shell", as I had expected. Some of the specified items were not necessary, such as a heavy and expensive great coat and white tropical tunics with long trousers; but we did not know that at the time and just went by the list. It even included a mosquito net, which was hard to find and was never used. However I was very pleased with my new uniform and wore it once or twice, certainly when I went back to Sullivan School to see Mr. Frost and some of my old friends.

Before long my first letter of appointment arrived and I was told that I would be joining M.V. "Neocardia" at Falmouth on 19 March, 1949. I'm sure my parents, Mother in particular, were quite distraught at the thought of their 16-year-old only child leaving home for God knows how long. But I certainly looked forward to it! At that time the normal length of a trip with Shell was two years or so; not long before that, four-year trips were quite common. Deep sea tankers traded here, there and everywhere around the world to no fixed pattern and depending on the varying requirements of the petroleum industry. This was particularly so in Shell because of their worldwide operations. Apart from the main fleet they had a Far Eastern fleet based in Singapore which never came near Europe and was manned by British or Dutch officers and Chinese ratings.

On the evening of 17 March, 1949, my parents saw me on board the Heysham ferry with all my kit and that was me away. The following day I travelled by train to Falmouth with changes in London and Truro. I spent the night at a hotel and the next morning reported to the Shell agents, Fox and Co. in Arwenick Street. I had time for a look around the town and then met all the officers and three other apprentices at the Gwendra Hotel for lunch. At 1400 we all went down to the town quay and were taken out to the ship in two boats to where she was lying at anchor in Carrick Roads, about a mile from town. She was on her way from Abadan in the Persian Gulf to Amsterdam with a cargo of motor spirit and kerosine and had only called at Falmouth for a complete crew change. The old crew were still on board so there was some shambles until they left with all their kit.

"Articles" were opened in the dining saloon with the Captain and the local Shipping Master presiding, and here I was signed on as a First Year Apprentice at the princely salary of £6. 5s per month. We sailed for Amsterdam at 2100 hours that evening.

CHAPTER 2: AN APPRENTICESHIP IN SHELL TANKERS – MY FIRST SHIP

The "Neocardia" was one of the Anglo Saxon "N" Class tankers, built during and immediately after the War. These ships were also known as the "Three Twelves" in that they were 12,000 tons deadweight, burned 12 tons of diesel fuel a day and, in moderate conditions, had a speed of 12 knots. Like all deep sea Shell tankers, the "Neocardia" bore the Latin name of a shell and there was a specimen of "Neocardia Angulata" in a glass case in the dining saloon. She carried a crew of 47, which was huge compared with the usual number of crew on a tanker of this size in these days. This crew, apart from the captain and three deck officers, included seven engineers, six petty officers, ten deck hands, eight engine room ratings and eight in the catering department. It was an all "white" crew, unlike that of many ships of the Shell fleet, which had British or Dutch officers and Chinese ratings.

There were four deck apprentices, accommodated in two cabins in the midships accommodation, which I found quite comfortable. (Like most tankers of the time she was a "three island ship" with a raised forecastle, midships bridge and officers accommodation, and crew accommodation in the poop and poop deckhouse. The three "islands" were connected by a raised flying bridge or catwalk – absolutely essential in heavy weather.) I, of course, was the junior or first trip apprentice. There were two second trippers and the senior apprentice, who had a few months to go to "finish his time". He kept very much to himself and spent most of his spare time studying for his Second Mate's Examination, which was probably very sensible. The other two were both "hard cases", or so they thought. They were Scots from the Edinburgh area, and somewhat aggressive and defiant in their attitude to authority. One of them had a whole trunk full of religious books which he only opened once to show the rest of us what a load of rubbish his parents made him take to sea with him! This pair played some tricks on me but this happens to any new apprentice. Anyway, I survived them both; they were removed from the ship after six months.

On our first night at sea after we left Falmouth, and the next day, I was more or less left to myself to find my way around the ship and get to know my shipmates. But after that I was soon introduced to the joys of polishing all the brasswork in and around the Bridge, and scrubbing out the Wheelhouse and Chartroom.

Arriving at Amsterdam I was stationed on the forecastle head with the mate and learned something about mooring operations. As soon as we were alongside I was on deck with the third mate and another apprentice and learned how to measure ullages in the cargo tanks, and to take and record temperatures and specific gravities of the cargo, which in this case was kerosine and motor spirit. While learning something about cargo work while in port I still had to keep all the Bridge brasswork polished! Given a little time off, I was able to draw a "sub" of £1 in Guilders, though I didn't exactly paint the town red when I was allowed ashore in my first foreign port! I did, however, manage to buy souvenirs such as model Dutch clogs and an ashtray, and there was something left over to spend in a cafe!

After two days at Amsterdam we sailed for the Caribbean on 24 March and, once clear of the English Channel, we had several days of quite severe weather with gale force south-west winds and huge seas. Even though the ship was well ballasted, as she crested a wave the propeller came out of the water and the engineers on watch had to constantly adjust the controls to prevent the engine racing. One day the average speed for 24 hours was only three knots, but speed had been reduced anyway to prevent pounding. I now learned the joy of chipping and painting steelwork in a sheltered spot on the poop but there were interesting tasks as well, such as splicing heavy wire ropes and sewing heavy canvas under the guidance of the deck storekeeper. Twelve days out from Amsterdam we were far enough south and west to run out of the bad weather and eventually met the North-East Tradewind. Cleaning of the cargo tanks started and while I was not allowed into the tanks, I was employed on deck hauling up the buckets of scale and dumping them overboard. In due course we noticed weed in the sea and indeed our course took us along the edge of the Sargasso "Sea". The weed appeared in bigger clumps and we apprentices had frequent trips to the poop to haul in the patent log line and clear the weed from the rotator. Once the tank cleaning was finished the mate decided to chip and paint sections of the main deck and this involved all available hands, including me. After each day's work the chipped area was swept and then painted, but not with paint. Shell had a refinery byproduct called PF4 and this was used on the main decks and sometimes also the topsides when we ran out of black paint! It was horrible black gunge similar to road tar and never dried properly, especially in hot weather.

Life was not all hard labour, however, and the deck officers did take some interest in the "academic" progress of the apprentices. We were encouraged to attend on the Bridge at about 0800, weather permitting, when the second and third mates were taking morning sights, and again at "apparent" noon when they fixed the latitude and, after some calculations, established the ship's noon position. We were instructed in or practised the use of the sextant. The second mate also came to visit our quarters quite often for an hour after supper when we would study "Rule of the Road" and similar subjects. Otherwise we spent time playing cards, especially gin rummy, or read any books or magazines that were to hand.

Somewhere in the Atlantic we had received orders by radio to proceed to Baytown, Texas to load for two ports in Cuba, Havana and Santiago, and on 11 April we made landfall at Great Abaco Island in the Bahamas. Thereafter we passed through the Florida Strait against the Gulf Stream current and across the Gulf of Mexico to reach Galveston on 15 April, 22 days out from Amsterdam. From there it was a four-hour passage up the Houston Ship Channel to Baytown, where we loaded two or three grades of "white oil" for Cuba, which took three days, including Easter Sunday. I was intrigued by the port officials and many other shore personnel who nearly all wore high-heeled boots, carried guns and had accents that were difficult to follow!

There was an invitation to attend the local Methodist Church on the Sunday but I was the only one to accept. Luckily, since I was on "daywork", this day was free. The result was that not only did I attend a prolonged Church service but when it was over I was besieged by people who wanted to introduce themselves and take me out for lunch! I enjoyed a Sunday lunch at a restaurant with a variety of food I had never seen at home. After that I was taken on a sightseeing tour and visited the San Jacinto monument and museum, which commemorates the victory of the Texans over the Mexicans in 1836. Nearby was the US Battleship "Texas" which had served in both World Wars but was now laid up and open to the public. This was included in my tour and to crown it all I was taken to the local movie house that evening to see a film called "Tulsa". This was some day and of course I got a lot of flak from my fellow apprentices, who had been on cargo watch most of the day!

The next morning we departed for Havana and arrived there three days later to discharge part of the cargo of motor spirit and kerosine. This was Cuba still under the Batista regime and I had one interesting evening ashore here in company with some of our stewards. The semi open-air bars and cafes with their clientele and numerous "ladies" were fascinating.

I noted that my working time was spent painting the ship's side, which was conveniently adjacent to the quay. As cargo was discharged more of the hull became available for painting. This was a black paint job and while I was on the ground some of the crew were above me on stages, painting the white upperwords. Having discharged part of our cargo, we then sailed round the coast to Santiago de Cuba at the other end of the island. It took nearly four days to complete discharge, due mainly to the primitive shore facilities, and there was plenty of time to go ashore and explore, but no money to spend on anything!

After this we proceeded to Port Arthur, Texas and did the same thing again, loading for Havana and Santiago de Cuba. Port Arthur was a much bigger place than Baytown, with plenty of large stores. By now I had earned enough to draw a $10 sub to spend here and even bought a Baby Brownie camera. However, a lot of my money was invested in ice-creams and sodas at Walgreen's drug store, the like of which I had not seen at home! One afternoon I was sent ashore by the mate on "business" – the business being to find a toy shop and a suitable present for his five-year-old son! I did find a big store with a toy department and was able to report back what I had found. The mate managed to get ashore briefly before the shops closed and came back with a working model telephone set. "Sparks", the radio operator, helped rig this lot up in the alleyway and it got a lot of playing before it went anywhere near the mate's son.

After uneventful second visits to Havana and Santiago we were ordered to Curacao and this was the first of many visits for me over the years, since Curacao was virtually the centre of Shell's operations in this part of the world. When oil was discovered in Lake Maracaibo in Venezuela the problem was getting it out, due to an extensive shallow bar in the entrance. There were three small islands nearby off the coast – Aruba, Curacao and Bonaire – which were Dutch colonies and known as the Netherlands Antilles. Esso built an oil refinery on Aruba and Shell built one on Curacao. They then built fleets of shallow draft tankers, known as "mosquito" boats to ferry the crude oil out to the refineries where there were deep water facilities. Bonaire remained a near barren island with little commercial activity. While the refinery and oil berths at Curacao were built around the *Schottegat* (or inner harbour), the town of Willemstad and other commercial berths were built around St. Anna Bay, which is in fact quite a narrow channel leading in from the sea. Willemstad is a fascinating town built mainly in Dutch colonial style; notable features are the schooner market and Queen Wilhelmina floating bridge across St. Anna Bay. This had to be opened every time a ship arrived or sailed. Even then it was a port of call for passenger liners and now, with the decline of the oil business on the island, it is now very much on the cruise liner circuit.

We spent two days loading various grades of "white" oil and I had time to visit the town. I also found that ship visiting was popular: there were always other Shell tankers in this busy port and visiting them was an interesting diversion, especially among cash-starved apprentices. On this occasion I visited the "Hyalina" which at that time was Shell's "latest and greatest" at 18,000 tons deadweight. I noted that this ship seemed to have a large amount of open deck space and I was shown such modern wonders as the radar installation and the automatic helmsman. A popular place to meet friends was also the Seamen's Club, close to the refinery but, as with everything on Curacao, drink was very expensive. The club was particularly popular with Scandinavian seamen whose ships were inevitably "dry" and they seemed to make up for this when they did get ashore!

We sailed from Curacao on 22 May to "Gibraltar for orders" and on the 24th, we passed through Sonbrero Passage in the Virgin Islands. Later we received orders to discharge at Haifa. This was a fair weather ocean crossing since all available deck hands, including apprentices, were engaged in chipping and painting the decks and superstructure for days on end. We passed Gibraltar on 5 June and reached Haifa on the 14th. Here we spent six days first discharging the cargo and then at anchor while attempts were made to fix a leak in the shell plating forward. Haifa was the main port of the new state of Israel but there was not much sign of the war, except for some ruined buildings away from the centre. Fire regulations were particularly strict and a spark arresting gauze had to be fitted over our funnel, while the galley was closed down and all cooking done in some shack ashore. Everything in the shops were extremely expensive. A haircut cost the equivalent of 6 shillings and even a miserably small ice-cream cost a shilling.

From Haifa we returned back through the Mediterranean and across to Curacao, with a brief call at Gibraltar for bunkers and stores. This was another fair weather passage and once the cargo tank cleaning was finished, the blitz of chipping and painting the superstructures and decks continued.

From Curacao there was a 17-day trip to Rio de Janeiro (my first and only visit to this interesting city), which involved crossing the "Line", which we did on 23 July 1949. There was quite an impressive ceremony on the poop, although Captain Ham and the senior officers took no interest and did not even attend. Two of the firemen played an unlikely Neptune and his wife and other crew played doctor, barber and Neptune's policemen. There were five candidates, two junior engineers, two deck hands and myself. The "punishment" was not as bad as I expected and the third mate produced the necessary certificates. I still have mine.

Earlier during our voyage to Rio, we had two breakdowns at sea involving the main engine and lay drifting for some hours. We spotted a couple of sharks swimming around the ship, and one of these was successfully caught and landed on deck. The rig used was a large meat hook, a long length of quite heavy wire led through a block to a winch on deck and a large lump of meat as bait. Once on deck the shark was a writhing, dangerous creature but the cook managed to get behind it and decapitate it with a meat cleaver. The carcass was thrown overboard but this would not have been the case in some later ships, where we had Chinese crew! Every last part was carefully dissected and the fins were left hanging in the awning spars for weeks to dry out.

Returning to Curacao we called at Point Fortin, Trinidad, to pick up some special cargo required in the refinery, and then backloaded a full cargo of kerosine for Thameshaven on the River Thames, and thence to dry-dock on the River Tyne. We were homeward bound and reached Thameshaven on 10 September. The nearest civilisation to Thameshaven was Stanford Lee Hope, five miles and a taxi ride away, so I didn't bother since we were going to dry-dock. This was my first visit to the Thames. It was then a very busy river with a constant stream of traffic up and down. This included all kinds of liners, colliers, innumerable coastal vessels and not a few Thames sailing barges, still operating under sail! It was fascinating just to stand on deck and watch it all.

Two days later we sailed for the Tyne and berthed at Smith's Dockyard at North Shields. Here we remained for two months, the crew were paid off and of the original crew only Mr. Nicholson (the mate) and I remained. One or two engineers and three apprentices joined during the following days. I was still the Junior Apprentice but I preferred my new mates, one of whom was from Dublin, to those who had left. My time in the dockyard was quite enjoyable, with various jobs on board and errands ashore, plus plenty of time off the ship. I was a frequent patron of the "Comedy" cinema in North Shields, which really was a "flea pit", though there were more up-market cinemas a ferry ride across the river in South Shields. There were two well known establishments in North Shields – the "Jungle", just outside the dock gate, and "Uncle Tom's Cabin" further up the town. At this time I was not a patron of either of them!

With three other apprentices on board the mate let me go home on 12 days' unofficial leave and my parents were pleased to see me in one piece! It was a tiring overnight journey by train and the Stranraer ferry in both directions. Later on I also got a long weekend at home and the return trip was interesting. Due to a severe gale it took the ferry "Princess Maud" 14 hours to get from Larne to Stranraer (instead of the usual 2 hours 15 minutes) and much of this time was at anchor in Loch Ryan. From home I had brought an old wind-up gramophone and a few records to which we added more. Favourites included "Twelfth Street Rag", "Night Riders in the Sky" and "Red Roses for a Blue Lady"!

All the apprentices managed to pick up girlfriends in North Shields and mine was a very attractive young assistant in a photographer's shop where I had gone to get a photograph of myself in uniform at the behest of my mother. This was the only friendship which lasted for any time after we left North Shields; indeed it lasted for a few years! By and large this was a very enjoyable period in my life, and going back to a seagoing routine took getting used to! I had also enjoyed visiting and inspecting other ships in the dockyard, mainly tankers and some dry cargo ships. At that time the Tyne was a very busy river with numerous shipbuilding and repair yards all full to capacity.

Anyway, we sailed on 13 November 1949, out through the Pentland Firth and across the Atlantic again to Punt Cardon, a new oil port near Curacao but on the coast of Venezuela. Returning with a full cargo to Shellhaven, beside Thameshaven, we arrived on Christmas Day. Mr Blight, the manager of the oil installation at Purfleet further up the river, was a friend of my father's and, as it turned out, a friend of our new master, Captain Jamison. As discharge of cargo was deferred until the next morning I was allowed off that afternoon and spent the rest of Christmas Day at home with Mr. Blight and his family, returning to the ship the next morning – a very pleasant interlude. I returned to find that the captain, the mate and their wives were having a very merry Christmas, with the second and third mates looking after cargo operations. My fellow apprentices had also been having a happy time entertaining the chief steward's daughter, who was on board with his wife. The captain's wife remained on board for some months – these were the early days of officers' wives being allowed to go to sea in tankers.

After discharge of part cargo at Shellhaven we had two days at Purfleet discharging the rest before going over to Rotterdam and loading for Gibraltar and Naples. The "Neocardia" was now a "black oil" tanker. As it turned out, we were on our way to the Far East! At Gibraltar we discharged part cargo into one of the bunkering hulks in the bay but there was time to get ashore and it didn't take long to walk around the town and see the immediate sights. At Naples we spent a night at anchor in the bay before berthing, and watches of four men each were arranged, two forward and two aft to watch the mooring ropes. We had been warned that thieves in small boats spent the night waiting for a chance to shin aboard any ship and steal the mooring lines. We four apprentices were on the 0400-0800 watch. When it started to get light there was no sign of any boats. Two of us went to put out the pilot ladder since the berthing pilot was expected shortly and two went to the midships pantry to make tea. While thus engaged there was a shout from the mate on the Bridge and we dashed forward to find two ropes hanging over the side. On heaving them up there was about a quarter the length missing from each and we later found that the thieves used a grappling line to get aboard. The mate was not very pleased and as a result we four were put on "watch and watch" for a month – four hours on watch and four hours off round the clock, and no shore leave. This also enabled the mate to put two more seamen on daywork and thus freed more hands to chip and paint! Those who went ashore reported Naples to be a dirty, rundown town, so I like to think we didn't miss anything!

After Naples we proceeded to Port Said and transited the Suez

Canal, which on this first visit I found fascinating – the "bum boats", "gillie gillie" men (conjurers), dirty postcard-and-booksellers etc. While at Port Said, the cabins, Wheelhouse and any other such space had to be kept locked when unoccupied and all small loose fittings on deck, such as brass fire hose nozzles, were locked away. Clearing the Suez Canal on 22 January, the passage down the Red Sea and round to the Persian (now Arabian) Gulf was uneventful. Being winter the weather in the Gulf was very pleasant, though when we reached Abadan on 4 February it was beginning to get cold. Abadan was at its peak as an oil refinery and major oil terminal and there were some 30 tanker berths on the Iranian side of the Shatt al Arab River. British Petroleum ran this operation, the Shah was still on his throne and I don't think Mossadeq had even been heard of!

Apart from the main liquid cargo we loaded 600 drums of lubricating oil in the dry cargo hold right forward and sailed for Wellington, New Zealand, on 6 February 1950, on what was to be the longest voyage I have ever made! While there were ample bunkers to reach Wellington, there was not ample food and after three weeks at sea things were critical, with no milk or butter and short rations on everything else! The captain eventually radioed London and got permission to call at Freemantle for stores. Here we anchored off the harbour for four hours on 2 March while welcome provisions were lifted on board. I had an aunt living in nearby Perth, whom I had never met, and this was the nearest I ever did get to meeting her!

It was then another 14 days to Wellington and soon we were crossing the Great Australian Bight with some quite big seas and strong winds from the South West. We did have the odd albatross following in our wake to pick up scraps of food. For the whole of the 39-day passage from Abadan, the main activity, apart from rountine watch-keeping, had been chipping and painting, on deck in fine weather and in the accommodation or other sheltered places otherwise. In those days recreational activities on most merchant ships were limited. Some of the officers had shortwave radio sets on which we could usually pick up the BBC Overseas Service or local stations in port or near the coast. There was a small library supplied by the Seafarer's Education Service and always a collection of paperback novels which did the rounds and were traded with other ships in port when the opportunity arose. On this passage we apprentices seemed to play pontoon for a while most evenings and were sometimes joined by an officer. The stakes were cigarettes, which were a very cheap currency for us!

So far as our studies were concerned we did have correspondence courses to follow, supplied by the King Edward VII Nautical College in London, and I think I was reasonably conscientious about this. Annual examinations were provided and marked by the Merchant Navy Training Board, also in London. The second and third mates took some interest in our academic activities but the mate was only interested in our abilities as watch-keepers and dayworkers along with the ratings. The captain, as I remember, took little interest in anything and we thought his wife must have found this long passage particularly boring!

The final part of this passage was across the Tasman Sea where we met some heavy weather and big seas before arriving at Wellington on 16 March 1950. Here we spent three days on an oil berth at Miramar, a suburb and about 20 minutes by tram into the city. The first matter of interest was that no dockers were available to discharge the drums from the forehold, so on the first afternoon we provided our own dockers – we four apprentices, the third mate and the radio operator. Like those in Australia, dockers (or "wharfies", as they were called in New Zealand) were a cossetted breed and highly paid. We each got 4s 8d cash per hour until 1700 and double after that – a useful bonus to spend ashore! Of course there was cargo work and other tasks but still plenty of time to go ashore. Sleep was not important since this could be caught up on when back at sea.

In the nearest grocer's shop many of us bought foodstuffs to take home, such as dried fruit, sugar and cooking fat. It may sound incredible now but there was still rationing at home and these sorts of items were in very short supply. Trips into town meant shopping, at least two cinema visits and splendid meals in cafes. Like Australia, New Zealand at this time had very strict licencing laws and the pubs, which resembled urinals, closed at 6pm. The city virtually became dead at 6pm and the hour after shops and offices closed at 5pm was known as the "Six-o-Clock Swill". The result was a large number of people on the streets in various states of intoxication, trying to get home. I had an interesting tram ride back to Miramar with the inside packed full and many more bodies hanging on the outside! Three of our crew deserted the ship here, apparently in connivance with people ashore, and as far as I knew they got away with it. The galley boy and an ordinary seaman were going to work on a farm 150 miles north of Wellington, while the second cook was joining up with a painting contractor. I recall that after their defection, the chief steward had to do stints in the galley!

From Wellington we proceeded in ballast north to Tarakan on the east coast of Borneo and this included my first passage of the Great Barrier Reef, with a pilot on board between Morton Bay, just north of Brisbane, and Thursday Island in the Torres Strait. The northern part of the reef is particularly impressive and when on the wheel one had to stay well awake to follow the pilot's directions through the intricate channels. Our route took us across the Arafura Sea and through a lot of passages in the East Indian Islands and one morning in drizzly weather I saw my first waterspout, which passed close to the ship. The captain said this was the closest he had ever seen one. (The same phenomenon ashore is a tornado.)

Tarakan was still recovering from the War efforts of the Japanese and the refinery had not long been reopened. Near the oil jetty was a native village and about five miles inland the refinery and Shell staff compound, complete with swimming pool. We visited both places and found that cigarettes were a very good currency here. We loaded a full cargo of light fuel oil for Singapore but before sailing the second mate had to go ashore and drag some of the crew out of a dive in the village – all drunk, of course! They were duly "logged" and fined by the captain. At Singapore we discharged at the Shell islands of Pulo Sambo and Pulo Bukum, with no chance to visit Singapore itself. Both islands, however, had staff clubs with swimming pools, and modest shops. There followed a six-week stint on what was called the "eternal triangle" run between Miri in Sarawak, Pladgoe on Sumatra and Singapore. Miri had oilfields, with offshore loading facilities, Pladgoe had both oilfield and refinery and Singapore had the two Shell oil storage and distribution facilities on Sambo and Bukum. With only about two days at sea between each port, it was quite hard going.

Of the three ports Pladgoe was the biggest problem. While the nearby Shell Club was available only to officers, there was also the native village where the ratings found a plentiful supply of cheap local "hooch" and managed to get well stoned while we were in port. There was nearly always another Shell tanker with "white" crew at one of the other jetties and of course they all got together.

One morning, an hour before sailing, the mate and I had to go round all the crew cabins and after decks to check that all our own crew were on board, then have any "bodies" that were not our crew helped ashore and dumped on the jetty. "White" crew ships in the Far East, and indeed elsewhere, were always a problem when they got at the drink. With Chinese crew there was never any problem.

On our last visit to Miri the main engine had a serious breakdown while we were making fast to the buoys. The chain drive to the camshaft broke and some sprokets were wrecked in the process. After loading cargo we were towed off the berth by a landing craft normally used for carrying stores and equipment and anchored a mile away. Here we remained for eight days while the engineers managed to make some kind of temporary repair but workshop facilities ashore were very limited. Eventually we made it back to Pladgoe and then to Singapore by 29 May, where, after discharge of cargo, we went into Keppel Dockyard on the outskirts of Singapore City for the next seven weeks! Apart from the engine repairs, a lot of other repair and maintenance work was carried out earlier than expected.

This was Singapore not long after the War, when it was still a British colony and long before Lee Kwan Yew came on the scene to turn it into a "squeaky clean" modern island republic! The mate devised a scheme whereby we apprentices were on watch 24 hours a day, but only one at a time, so we had lots of time to spend ashore. There was a private swimming pool near the dockyard which was available to us and not too far away were two Seamen's Missions, Connell House and the Bousted Institute. The first had free films on Tuesdays and Thursdays and the other on Wednesdays, so even when money was short we had somewhere to go for entertainment. The chaplain at Connell House was quite a character and very down-to-earth. He had also served at one time in the Belfast Mission to Seamen, or the "Flying Angel", as this Episcopal organisation is best known. The equivalent Roman Catholic worldwide mission is the Stella Maris but seamen were very ecumenical and went to whichever one offered the most "action". (At that time the Stella Maris often had bar facilities, while the Flying Angel did not!) In some ports the British Sailors' Society had a mission which represented the non-conformist churches and sometimes there was even a Salvation Army Mission. Definitely no alcohol available at either of these! Anyway, at Connell House after the Sunday evening service it was the Chaplain's habit to discard his clericals and head up town

23

with the lads for a night of eating, drinking and other diversions. Racecourse Road and Bougis Street was where the action was but I'm sure this was the first part of town that Lee Kwan Yew cleaned up when he came to power! Singapore was a fascinating place and although I went there many times I have not been back since it became the super-efficient and super-clean city it is now. I think I prefer to remember it as it was and the happy times I had there.

While at Singapore my first year examination papers arrived and the second mate allowed me two weeks for revision. Therefore, apart from watch-keeping and turns ashore, I spent quite a bit of time studying. I duly did the exam papers in the Chartroom, which seemed to be the quietest part of the ship, and despite all the hammering and banging going on nearby, I did quite well and even won a prize, a classic book called *Ship Construction and Calculations*. By today's standards and ship construction methods, this book is ancient history!

Eventually, leaving Keppel Dockyard on 13 July, we loaded two grades of fuel oil, plus about 600 drums of petrol and white spirit at Pulo Sambo and Pulo Bukum and sailed for Hong Kong, a six-day voyage north through the China Sea. At Hong Kong I was intrigued to note that the pilot, a Chinese, came out to the ship in a Sampan. Apparently the crew of this craft were his family. This was in stark contrast to Singapore where the pilots were British and wore immaculate "whites", complete with pith helmet. Each pilot had his own immaculate launch manned by an equally immaculate local crew, and when travelling to or from ships the pilot sat in a cane armchair under an awning on the after deck – real imperial grandeur! Our berth was at an isolated installation on the Kowloon side of the harbour. There was a launch service across to Victoria on Hong Kong Island and I had time for one quick visit.

Not that there wasn't plenty of action on board the ship! Sampans galore came alongside and the ship became something of a floating bazaar. There were innumerable "sew sew" and dhobi women and others who established themselves as helpers in the galley and pantry for a few dollars from the catering crew and any left over food. Last of all there were the "meat boats", of which enough said. The captain and his wife wisely disappeared ashore and spent two nights in a hotel.

It was in Hong Kong that the mate realised his assets in the ARP Locker. Many ships at that time still had an ARP (Air Raid Precautions) locker and ours was a caged area in the Centrecastle. It still had some wartime equipment including a device called a Mackworth fog buoy. When in convoy and in fog, this device was towed astern and produced a jet of water so that a following ship would hopefully see it before running into the ship ahead! Anyway, the ARP Locker was where the mate gathered various junk for trade purposes, such as old mooring ropes and empty oil drums, and in Hong Kong he sold this lot to some junk dealer. With the proceeds the mate bought an almost new motor cycle from someone in the oil installation. This was a 350cc Norton and I was given the job of cleaning and polishing it for him!

From Hong Kong it was back down the China Sea to Miri in Sarawak once again and this was a heavy weather trip with one day spent virtually hove to in heavy seas. This was south west monsoon weather. At Miri we loaded crude oil and headed back north, this time to a refinery near Yokohama, Japan. There was time for a quick visit to Yokohama by train and I noted that there were still signs of heavy bombing. Also, apart from the locals, there seemed to be American servicemen everywhere. The in thing to buy here was Japanese tea sets to take home as presents.

Returning to Miri we made one more trip to Pladjoe and Singapore before loading fuel oil for Aden. As it turned out we were now heading for home, if not directly! On 21 August 1950 my 18th birthday passed without any celebration – my second birthday on board the "Neocardia"! Once clear of Malacca Straits we had heavy weather most of the way across the Indian Ocean in the south-west monsoon and the heavy seas washing across the decks soon made a mess of all our painting efforts over the past months! Average speed was down to 7 or 8 knots.

Aden was still a very busy bunkering port with ships arriving and leaving round the clock. There were no alongside berths and all ships made fast to buoys at Steamer Point some four miles from the town. The "barren rocks of Aden" were well named and it was stinking hot. I noted two emigrant ships which came in, one being the "Somersetshire" of Bibby Line and the other the "Dundalk Bay" of Irish Bay Lines in Belfast, both loaded with passengers on a one-way trip to Australia. I was not ashore on this occasion. From Aden we sailed in ballast to the Arabian Gulf and loaded fuel oil at Kabda Point, about ten miles down the Shatt al Arab River from Abadan. No town and no social facilities here, so we visited other ships in

25

port and exchanged reading material. The cargo was for Port Said so after circumnavigating the Arabian Peninsula we passed through the Suez Canal to reach Port Said on 16 October. Here we spent two days so there was shore leave for those who wanted it. It was an interesting busy place but the constant attention of all manner of hangers-on and opportunists detracted from the pleasure of being ashore.

Well, we were not far from home but were not going there yet! Another voyage back to the Arabian Gulf, via Aden for fresh water, found us at Mena Al Ahmadi, a new oil port in the Sheikdom of Kuwait. A monumental oilfield was discovered here before the War but only developed afterwards and the rest is well-known history! At that time there was just one oil wharf but it was about half a mile long and could accommodate eight tankers at once. It was also very modern and efficient and we loaded a full cargo of crude oil in less than 12 hours, destination Rotterdam!

The passage to Rotterdam was uneventful but of course, it being winter, we met cold and unsettled weather as soon as we transited the Suez Canal and entered the Mediterranean. By this time all hands had the "Channels", a disease seamen get when nearing home after a long time away! At Rotterdam we spent two days discharging cargo and there was time to go ashore for last-minute presents to take home. Dutch chocolates were the favourite purchase here. From Rotterdam we had a slow passage in bad weather back through Dover Strait and down the English Channel to Falmouth where we anchored off late on 2 December, 1950. Here the same procedure took place as on 19 March, 1949, only this time I was leaving the ship instead of joining her! I did not record where the "Neocardia" was bound after that but some years later I saw her in Singapore, laid up and waiting to go to the scrapyard.

So this was my "first trip". Apart from the brief unofficial visits home while in dry dock at North Shields, I had been away for one year, eight months and two weeks, sailed I don't know how many thousands of miles, and certainly visited a few interesting parts of the world. During this time those of my old classmates who had remained at Sullivan Upper School had completed their Senior Certificate and gone on either to university or into the world of work. But not many of them had had the sort of experiences I'd had!

I travelled home by train and Heysham ferry and was allowed two months' leave before being summoned to join my next ship. This leave included Christmas – one of only three I spent at home during 16 years at sea.

CHAPTER 3: TWO MORE SHIPS

My second ship was the turbine electric ship (t.e.s) "Tectarious", one of the numerous "T2" tankers built in the United States during the War. Along with the famous Liberty ships, these and other classes of ship were produced in great numbers all over the USA on a production-line basis and some were built in the most unlikely places. The record for putting one together was apparently four days and the mentality was that if they lasted two trips across the Atlantic they had paid for themselves! After the War many of these ships ended up in the British Merchant Fleet to replace lost ships and Shell acquired a number of them. All, of course, were repainted in Shell colours and given Shell names. The "Tectarious" was originally the "Cahawba" and was built at Mobile, Alabama, in 1944. These ships were about 16,500 tons deadweight, as opposed to the Shell "N" Class, such as the "Neocardia" which were 12,000 tons deadweight. Put simply, they could carry an extra 4,500 tons of cargo.

I joined this ship at Heysham on 10 February, 1951, so I did not have far to travel. On boarding, I found that I had got my first and only rapid promotion from Shell! Of four apprentices, two had less sea time than me and the other was a first tripper, so I became the senior apprentice before I'd barely set foot on board! Our accommodation was a single and quite large cabin at the after end of the midships accommodation. There were two double bunks, one above the other on each side, and our own en-suite bathroom facilities! Apparently this had been gunners' accommodation during the War. All the officers' cabins had en-suite bathrooms, unheard of in British-built ships at that time. However, everything was metal, including all the furniture and until we got used to it, it seemed very clinical.

While deck officers were accommodated amidships the engineers were in the aft accommodation, as was the dining saloon. The galley was "electric everything" rather than the normal oil-fired ranges. The main machinery consisted of two oil-fired watertube boilers providing steam for a turbine-driven generator, which in turn drove an electric propulsion motor. The cargo pumproom was also something different, being right aft between the cargo tanks and the engine room, with four electrically-driven pumps and separate stripping pumps to get out the last drainings from the tanks. Classic British-built tankers had two pumprooms, one on the foredeck between cargo tanks and the same on the after deck, the pumps being steam-driven recriprocating machines.

The master was Captain Maton, a Royal Navy Reserve officer who had served in the Royal Navy during the War. He also had a lot of Royal Navy ideas which did not always fit in with the commercialism of merchant ships and was particularly fond of organising parties and entertaining in port. To this end he was not afraid of incurring the displeasure of the company in London, say when some excuse had to be found for delaying our departure from port because he had a good party going on! He also believed in personally looking after the welfare of the apprentices, which did not always please the mate, but we thought he was just great! Usually one of us had to accompany him when he was going ashore on ship's business and other matters and this would often include a slap-up meal.

For the first seven months our trading was mainly across the Atlantic to Curacao or Venezuelan ports but also ports in the Mediterranean and Western Europe. There were three trips through the Suez Canal to Mena Al Ahmadi and back. Ports worth mentioning included Le Havre, Rouen, Hamburg, Port de Bouc near Marseilles, Tripoli in Lebanon, Ceuta in Spanish Morocco, Spezia in Italy and best of all Piraeus, the port for Athens. It was here that the captain decided the apprentices' knowledge of history required some attention and he simply told the mate that we were having a whole day off and would not be available for cargo watches. We were taken on a guided tour in a company car of all the main historic sites in and around Athens, including the Acropolis and the Parthenon. There was also a splendid meal in a posh restaurant followed by a visit to a cinema, where I think we saw something Shakespearean starring Laurence Olivier and Vivien Leigh.

In June we spent four days in Falmouth, cleaning the cargo tanks before going into dry-dock in Cardiff for nearly a month. A dry-docking period was always welcome on a tanker since it meant no normal watch-keeping and, if in the UK, a chance to visit home. On this occasion I got home for a long weekend and also had time to visit my grandfather who lived near Dursley, Gloucestershire and was easily reachable by bus.

November found us in Curacao once again and we then had four trips between there and the north-east coast of the USA with cargoes of fuel oil. In the winter this was a busy trade and a lot of tankers were involved. We referred to it as "keeping the great American public warm during the winter"! Our first port there was New York, although the discharge berth was at Newark, New Jersey – some distance from Manhattan. Determined to see the "Big Apple", we apprentices rearranged our cargo watch so that two of us one day and two the next could have a whole day off. As usual, sleep was not important! We travelled by train and ended up at Grand Central Station, itself worth a visit. In that one day we got to the top of the Empire State Building, visited the Rockefeller Centre, did some shopping and ended up at the British Apprentices Club on West 22nd Street. This splendid club was started during the War by a charitable lady called Louisa M. Spalding when there were always several British ships and their apprentices in port. It occupied a small suite in the Hotel Chelsea on West 22nd Street, which was otherwise occupied by European immigrants awaiting processing. Here we were made very welcome by the on-duty hostess, were signed up as members, and duly fed and watered. We were able to make fuller use of the Club at a later date but this first visit was necessarily brief.

Our next trip north was also to New York, followed by one to Cornerbrook, Newfoundland, where we discharged at Bowaters' paper mill. Having spent Christmas Day at sea, we arrived at Cornerbook on 31 December to find a real Christmas card scene, complete with deep snow everywhere and even some sea ice in the harbour. It was a small town and on New Year's Eve I think everyone on board had made friends with someone ashore, including plenty of females! The captain had to organise a monumental New Year's party and it was somehow contrived that cargo operations were shut down between midnight and 0600. The large number of people on board certainly included most of the staff from the local hospital!

There had been problems with leaking cargo heating coils and leaking steam and water lines on deck following our Newfoundland trip, and on return to Curacao there was two days of repair work before we loaded another cargo for New York. These problems were nothing compared to what now occurred! Soon after passing through Mona Passage, between Puerto Rico and the Dominican Republic, there was a serious boiler problem due to leaking water tubes and as it turned out both boilers had somehow run short of water and the tubes were badly damaged. One boiler had to be shut down and with the other about to fail we limped along at about 6 knots to Bermuda, where we anchored off St. Georges in Murray's Anchorage. Here we spent five days while temporary repairs were carried out, mostly cutting out and sealing damaged boiler tubes. A launch was available and we apprentices had no less than three trips ashore to look around but we didn't get as far as Hamilton, the capital. One evening we visited the Somers Opera House to see the film "King Solomon's Mines". Incidentally, I noted that the captain went ashore most days to play golf with someone from the Agent's office!

From what I saw, Bermuda was a very picturesque picture postcard sort of place but, although it was a British colony, the American dollar reigned supreme since all the tourists were American. The local population seemed to come in every shade, from pure white to pure black, and there were some very attractive dusky maidens to be seen.

From Bermuda we limped on to New York and after discharge of the cargo at Newark we ended up at the Bethlehem Steel Company's shipyard at Mariner's Harbour on Staten Island. Here we spent three happy weeks while both boilers were completely retubed. I noted that American shipyard workers worked hard and completed a difficult job in much less time that it would have taken in the UK – perhaps they were very well paid, but I was still impressed. There was also a night shift on our job and they worked hard as well!

No doubt this unscheduled docking did nothing for Shell's profits but we apprentices had a great time, sightseeing (we saw "The Greatest Show on Earth" at the Radio City Music Hall, at that time the largest of its type in the world) and making full use of the Apprentices' Club. Most of the regular members of the club were apprentices on ships which were on a regular run to New York. One night I met a schoolfriend from Sullivan Upper School who was an apprentice on the "City of Yokohama", an Ellerman liner. Some nights there was dancing to records, mostly Victor Sylvester and the like, and there seemed to be a good supply of young ladies. It was all very "proper", however, and there was no alcohol allowed on the premises. Some nights we stayed there until early morning and after everyone else had gone home, we watched old movies on the TV. There was always plenty of food and soft drink in the fridge, and we just locked the door behind us when we left. Since the public transport system operated round the clock, we had no problem getting back to the ship.

My impression of the New York Subway at that time was that it was rather grotty and not a patch on the London Underground. Both trains and stations were ancient and dirty and late at night there were certainly some unsavoury looking characters about. However, we were four very fit young men and nobody ever accosted or tackled us!

There was one benefactor of the Apprentices' Club called Duane R. Everson, a middle-aged bachelor who lived with his sister in an apartment in the city. One Sunday he took us on a "conducted tour" of New York, when we visited several churches (one being St. Patrick's Cathedral), General Grant's Tomb, the Rockefeller Centre, Waldorf Astoria Hotel, Central Station and finally a Howard Johnston restaurant for dinner. We had to wear uniform for this occasion and were immediately spotted by the crew on the Staten Island ferry. This resulted in a tour of the ferry and a long discourse from the captain about his experiences at sea.

Our own captain had a happy time during this period and was frequently ashore on ship's business. One day I had to accompany him to the ship's agents in the city to collect cash and mail and this little trip included lunch with agency staff at the Downtown Athletic Club. This was a very swish place and I noted that there was only one floor where women were allowed. King George VI died on 6 February, 1952 and the dance that night at the Apprentices Club was cancelled. His funeral was on 15 February and there was a memorial service in Trinity Church. There was a good contingent from t. e. s. "Tectarious", all in uniform, and all, of course, organised by our Captain Maton!

Before we'd been long in New York, we apprentices had a severe cash flow problem and so did the junior engineers, who were paid little more! The solution to the problem lay on board the ship which, when built, had been fitted with degaussing equipment. Basically this consisted of heavy copper cables arranged all round the hull at deck level; when charged with a current, these cables created a downward magnetic field and supposedly neutralised the field from any magnetic mines below on the sea bed. On deck these cables were under metal covers but in the engine room they were exposed and easy to get at. They were certainly redundant and so those apprentices and junior engineers who were aboard at nights worked away with hacksaws and produced a considerable quantity of scrap copper which was bought for cash by some local merchant. This, incidentally, was before devaluation of the pound and the exchange rate was about $4 to £1, so conversion was easy. A dollar was worth 5 shillings, 50 cents was half a crown and a dime was sixpence.

Now our Captain Maton had some friends on Staten Island, probably from his wartime days. They were an Irish family, the Hickeys, who had four children and one of the girls had her 21st birthday party on 16 February, 1951. And so it happened that apprentices Waters and Knapp attended this party and had a great time. I kept in touch with this family for several years thereafter and visited them when in the New York area.

But this was one of the last delights ashore and we sailed for Tuxpan, Mexico on 19 February to load crude oil for Curacao. Here we backloaded fuel oil and sailed back across the Atlantic to the Mediterranean and a second visit to Piraeus. The last cargo before I left this ship was loaded at Tripoli, in the Lebanon. This in fact was Iraqi crude oil transhipped across the desert by pipeline. We sailed for home and discharged at Heysham, where I had joined the ship. However, as she was yet again going to dry-dock, tank cleaning was necessary and this was carried out during a week at anchor in Bangor Bay with the tank cleaning vessel "Tulipfield" moored alongside. This was the nearest I got to home in any ship I sailed in and it was a novel experience! My parents were able to come out and visit the ship, and my fellow apprentices were given a quick tour of County Down and a visit to my home for a meal.

I was "paid off" just before the ship sailed but I did not record where she went to dry-dock. This was on 21 April and I then had seven weeks' leave before being summoned to join my next ship. Dad still had the Holywood Sharpie "Spray" and I helped him get her ready for the sailing season. I even got in some sailing in her. There were numerous visits to local cinemas, sometimes with female company and, more important, Dad taught me to drive the family car which at that time was a Morris 12. I gave my 5/- for a driving licence, together with two photographs, and that was all there was to it in those days. I was a car driver!

On 11 June, 1952, I joined M.V. "Hyalina" at the Esso oil refinery at Fawley on Southampton Water. This ship had been built at Swan Hunters' yard on the Tyne in 1948 and was John Lamb's answer to the American-built "T2" tanker. John Lamb at that time was the

Chief Marine Engineer Superintendent in Shell and was also responsible for the modification of marine diesel engines for burning heavy residual fuel oil rather than expensive diesel. The "Hyalina", like the "T2s", had steam turbine/electric propulsion but she was 18,000 tons deadweight and at 16 knots had more speed. Bunker consumption at this speed was, however, prodigious and only three of these ships were built. The others were the "Helicina", also in the Shell fleet and a Royal Fleet Auxiliary tanker.

With only about nine months to go to complete my "time" I was again the senior of the four apprentices. Captain Ritchie, a Scotsman from Arbroath, while not in the same league as Captain Maton, believed in the welfare and education of his apprentices. After one trip out to Mena Al Ahmadi and back to the River Thames, we spent five weeks in dry-dock at Falmouth, another pleasant break, especially since it was midsummer. Prior to this I had completed my third year examination and was glad to have that out of the way.

The fleshpots of Falmouth started with the "Chain Locker", which was right outside the dockyard gate. It was really as much a maritime museum as a pub and had lots of artifacts relating to Captain Carlson and the "Flying Enterprise". However, most time ashore seems to have been spent going to the local cinemas and dances at the "Drill Hall". None of us appear to have picked up girlfriends here other than brief encounters at the dance hall! One of the junior engineers was keen on sailing so one day we went to the expense of hiring an 18-ft centreboard boat from the local yacht yard and explored Falmouth Harbour and the adjacent creeks. I also got a week of unofficial leave to go home, a long journey by train to Liverpool and then across to Belfast on the overnight ferry. I recall spending most of this week sailing the "Spray" or driving around in Dad's car.

From Falmouth it was back to Mena Al Ahmadi and a cargo of crude oil for Port de Bouc, near Marseilles. After that there was a cargo to take from Ras Tanura in Saudi Arabia to Sasebo in Japan – an uneventful voyage except for two days of heavy weather in the China Sea while a typhoon crossed ahead of us. At Sasebo I had a good night out with another apprentice and still had money left for some shopping. Japanese tea-sets were still the in thing to take home as presents.

Our next loading port was Umm Said, Qatar, in the Southern part of the Persian Gulf and a newly opened oil terminal. We loaded a full cargo of crude oil at an offshore mooring and all that was to be seen of the shore were barren sand dunes! This particular crude was very rich in hydrogen sulphide and the gas from it, apart from the nauseating smell of rotten eggs, turned most of the white paintwork dirty brown and yellow. This cargo was for Thameshaven and the passage included a full gale in the Bay of Biscay. Between the cargo gas and heavy weather the ship was not very pretty on its arrival on 18 December!

Out next trip was to Tripoli, Lebanon, for a cargo of crude and back to Thameshaven. Christmas Day at sea in the Western Mediterranean was a very low key affair since we had had a change of captain and the new one was ultra puritan. Any partying was very surreptitious and took place behind closed cabin doors!

By now I only had about two months to go to complete my "time" and was looking forward to getting home to sit for my Second Mate's Certificate. I had completed my Third Year Training Board Examination with good results and now put in a lot of spare time doing further study. Apart from the never-ending apprentice's tasks of cleaning, polishing, chipping and painting there was the opportunity of proper bridge watch-keeping under the supervision of an officer, usually the Chief Officer, since this meant he could spend his watch in the Chartroom doing paperwork but was on call if needed. I considered myself reasonably competent in coastal and astral navigation, Rule of the Road and all the other skills and knowledge necessary to become a junior officer!

From Thameshaven it was across the Atlantic to Curacao to load fuel oil for New York, where we arrived on 27 January, 1953, and as it turned out, as on the "Tectarious" we had an extended stay here! Before berthing we had to anchor in an area known as Stapleton Anchorage, off the Staten Island shore, and here we went through the lengthy and rigorous procedures required by the US Customs, Immigration and Port Medical authorities. This was the McCarthy era, when all these authorities were actively looking for "Reds under the bed". The paperwork was prodigious and this included the most detailed crew list imaginable. This document had to be prepared, certified by a US consul, and forwarded under seal from the previous port. The Customs officials went through the ship with a toothcomb and the whole crew had to be mustered for interrogation and examination by Immigration and Medical officers. The questions included "Are you or have you ever been a member of the Communist Party?" – as if anyone who was would have admitted to it! If they thought you looked any way sickly, at the very least you had to drop your pants for a "short arm" inspection!

It was while all this was going on that a passing oil barge crossing our bows misjudged her distance and was carried down on to our bows by the tide, with interesting results. The damage to both vessels was considerable but while we were well stove in forward there was no serious damage to any cargo tanks. The barge, I think, was not loaded and as far as I remember there was no major oil spill in New York Harbour. Anyway, after all the immediate follow-up to this collision we discharged most of our cargo into barges and the rest into a small oil installation at Busheys' Shipyard in Brooklyn. The problem was compounded when all the New York tugboats went on strike and we could not move to Todds' Shipyard, where repairs were to be carried out. In the end we stayed where we were and Todds' men came to us.

The pattern of life for the 14 days we were there was much the same as 12 months before in the "Tectarious". The British Apprentices' Club was a home from home for us apprentices, and some of us paid at least two visits to the Hickeys' house on Staten Island. One visit was for a cocktail party and I noted that we stayed on Manhattans all night and stayed sober. Back on board the ship by 0400 on a Sunday morning! Another highlight was when any crew members, myself included, who had witnessed the collision had to visit a solicitor's office to make statements. We were treated to a splendid meal in a plush restaurant and got useful expenses on top of that!

We left New York on 11 February 1953 and were back in Curacao on the 16th for nine days of tank cleaning and further repairs. After this the ship was ordered to load again for New York, only I didn't go with her. I transferred ashore to the Park Hotel to await transport home. There were quite a few marine staff either coming or going, so I had plenty of company. There was little money available so we spent most of our time at the Shell Club swimming pool during the day and watching whatever free film show we could find in the evening. This soon became frustrating and I was glad when I joined m.v. "Labiosa" which had arrived to load for Dublin and Stanlow, on the Manchester Ship Canal.

The "Labiosa" was one of the Shell "L" Class, similar to the "N's" but only 9,000 tons deadweight and she seemed very small after the "Hyalina". These ships were no greyhounds and averaged about 10 knots in fine weather. This one was fitted to carry bitumen in the centre tanks which had to be kept so hot that fuel oil could be carried in the wing tanks with no extra heating. She had been built on the Tyne in 1948. There were four "supernumeraries", all heading home, and for lack of other accommodation, three of us shared the ship's hospital! Because of the hot bitumen cargo almost immediately underneath, it was stinking hot.

We sailed on 10 March and the passage from Curacao to Dublin took 18 days. March 19th was the fourth anniversary of my joining my first ship and on the 27th I celebrated my last working day as an apprentice by giving my working gear "a passage" – working clothes, boots etc. all went overboard. We arrived in Dublin on Saturday 28 March, where I was "paid off" and travelled home by train the same day.

Including study leave, I now had four months at home but intended to get my "ticket" in less time than that. Because of Easter Holidays I did not sign on at the Marine School until mid-April, when I paid £5 for a six month course. By now Captain Boyd's school in Belfast had been "nationalised" and was part of the Belfast Technical College. It occupied two rooms on the top floor of the city centre building, the others being occupied by the College of Art. Captain Boyd was still there but because he was not sufficiently qualified according to the College requirements, he was only No. 2 and unfortunately the new Principal, who did meet the requirements, was no match for Captain Boyd as a teacher. I got fed up with following the school syllabus, which could easily have gone on for six months, and worked as much as possible on my own syllabus both at school and at home until I was sure I was up to standard. I sat for and passed all the parts of the examination the first week in June and by 8 June, 1953, I was the proud possessor of a Second Mate's Certificate of Competency. The examinations, which were held in the Board of Trade Marine Office in the Custom House, were interrupted for one day on 2 June for Queen Elizabeth's Coronation. At home one of our neighbours had a television set (a rare thing in those days, and something I am, with hindsight, grateful for) and a large crowd gathered to watch the proceedings. In May I had had another boost to my ego when Shell told me I was Apprentice of the Year for 1952 and I had to go to London to receive my prize of a sextant. Since the company at that time had about 300 deck apprentices, I must have done quite well in captains' reports and Training Board Examinations.

My social activities did not suffer in the pursuit of my "ticket" and a favourite haunt of mine was the Scout Hall in Holywood, where there were regular dances. Here I soon met a pleasant girl who worked in a Belfast shipping agency office and she was my companion on many visits to dances and to the cinema. However, she was not interested in sailing and once the sailing season started I got in a lot of sailing at Holywood Yacht Club before I had to go back to sea. Dad still owned the "Spray" and of course I had helped fit her out before she was launched in May. I sailed in other boats as well and did quite well in the local races.

Before the end of my leave I also helped paint the outside of our house – I was, of course, an expert and experienced painter and decorator by now! At the end of June I was summoned to London again, this time for an interview and a medical, after which I signed a two year contract with Shell. I was told that I was lucky to be offered a contract since there were presently some "difficulties" in the Shell fleet, and I would have to sail in an "extra" capacity to begin with.

I returned home to buy a new uniform, for which the company had provided the brass buttons and gold braid – all that they did provide in the way of uniform! I soon discovered that the difficulties lay with the general manager, the very man who had presented me with my sextant! He had been accepting handsome bribes from Greek and other foreign shipowners to take on charter tankers which Shell did not need and it ended up that quite a large number of company-owned tankers had to be laid up, some for several years with the consequent surplus of seagoing officers. A number of these Shell tankers were laid up in Lough Swiley on the North coast of Ireland. I never did hear what became of this general manager but anyway I was duly summoned to join t.e.s. "Thallepus" as Extra Third Officer on 21 July. I didn't have far to go since she was discharging cargo at the Mersey Tanker Moorings off Tranmere. These moorings were connected by pipeline to the Shell refinery at Stanlow.

CHAPTER 4: AN OFFICER AT LAST

As soon as I joined t.e.s. "Thallepus" at Tranmere on 21 July, 1953, and signed on as extra third officer, I found myself on the 0400 to 0800 watch working cargo. Since this was my second "T2" tanker I was familiar with the cargo arrangements and the pipeline layout. Having an extra deck officer on board was a bonus for the mate since he was virtually relieved of keeping a watch.

The mate on this ship was a most peculiar fellow, middle-aged and from somewhere in the west of Wales. His name was Lloyd but he was known throughout the ship as "Trog", and indeed he was something of a hermit, even if he managed to do his job. His standard of dress and general cleanliness left a lot to be desired and his cabin really was a pigsty. He had been with the ship for some time and so had the captain, whose name was W.C. Loughlin. Inevitably, he became known as "Sh**-house" Loughlin, and he too was peculiar in his own way. Like many of his generation, he was fond of the bottle.

I often wondered about some of the senior officers I sailed with in those days. Obviously they had been through the Second World War and perhaps this had affected them, or perhaps it was just the result of long years of service in tankers with long indefinite periods away from home. Some of the masters took very little interest in the running of the ship. They would perhaps appear on the Bridge at noon on a long passage, when the "noon" position was hopefully established, or when making a landfall or entering port. Statutory requirements, such as weekly boat and fire drills, known as "Board of Trade sports", were often just ignored, as was the weekly inspection of the accommodation, provisions and storerooms. Some masters would appear in the dining saloon at lunchtime but otherwise eat in their quarters. Chief engineers were often much the same and rarely ever went into the Engine Room! The fact was that most of the senior mates and senior engineers were experienced, competent and able and the ships ran perfectly well *despite* some of the masters and chief engineers! Mates and second engineers were also hopeful of promotion in due course so they tended to pamper the "boss"! Such would not be the case today, when ships have minimum manning and everyone has to be on the ball, especially masters and chief engineers!

My time in the "Thallepus" started with another trans-Atlantic trip to Mamonal in Columbia, an oil port near Cartagena. Another result of the general manager's over-chartering activities was that most of the company-owned ships were now running at slow speed to save fuel and prolong the time at sea. In our case this meant that one of the two boilers was shut down and we proceeded at a bare 10 knots instead of 14 or more, to reach Mamonal after all of 18 days at sea. I was now keeping the 8-0 to 12-0 watch, the third mate had the 12-0 to 4-0 and the second mate the 4-0 to 8-0. "Trog", the mate, was on daywork which meant he had an easy life except when in port and working cargo. The ship carried four apprentices and I took an interest in their education since this was also good for my own education.. They were encouraged to come on the Bridge for morning sights and again at noon when we fixed the noon position. After supper in the evenings and before I went on watch we had sessions of "Rule of the Road" and other subjects. At that time the "Rules of the Road", or more properly the International Regulations for the Prevention of Collision at Sea, were fairly concise and the phraseology such that the whole lot could be learned off and recited from memory, which is what we did!

I now had to put in 18 months seatime before sitting for my First Mates' Certificate and I had arranged a correspondence course with the Nautical College in Liverpool so that I would be well prepared when the time came.

At Mamonal we loaded crude oil for Curacao, and nearby Aruba for La Spezia in Italy. Two days into this trip was 21 August 1953 – and my 21st birthday, which was just a normal watch-keeping day at sea and certainly no recognition by the captain! The third mate, however, broke open a bottle of Bols gin in my honour!

Out through the Suez Canal then to Umm Said in the Persian Gulf to load crude oil for Thameshaven and after tank cleaning further up the Thames at Purfleet we went to dry-dock in South Shields on the River Tyne. Arriving on 28 October we spent a pleasant month there. I was able to get home for a week and also looked up my girlfriend from my "Neocardia" days in North Shields, with whom I had kept in touch. But although she was very pleasant company, this affair fizzled out shortly afterwards since her only ambition in life was to get married, and at the age of 21 that was not *my* immediate ambition!

Leaving South Shields on 25 November to return to the Caribbean we had several days of very heavy weather in the western approaches with no sun or star sights to fix our position. During my watch on the night of the 30th we unexpectedly sighted the light at Graciosa in the Azores which showed that our dead reckoning was a long way out! Thereafter the weather soon improved and we reached Punta Cardon in Venezuela by 8 December to load fuel oil for Boston. From there we returned to Mamonal for the next cargo, arriving on 25 December after a little incident. We were approaching this port, which is on jungle-lined coast with few landmarks, just as I was about to go on watch at 0800. I was washing and getting dressed in my cabin and looked out of a porthole to see unfamiliar coastline passing by close to. Before I got to the Bridge the engines were stopped and then went astern. When I got there I found that the captain and "Trog" had managed to run the ship aground in some strange creek which was definitely not Mamonal! In all fairness, the entrance to Mamonal is hard to find in the tree lined shore and we had not had a fix for some time due to lack of lighthouses. As it turned out, Mamonal was about 20 miles further along the coast and it was also fortunate that we had clean ballast on board. We simply discharged ballast overboard until the ship came free and then proceeded on our way to reach Mamonal late on Christmas Day. The logbooks were carefully "rigged" so that there was no record of this incident and no-one in London Office was any the wiser.

After another trip north to Boston and one to Fall River, near Providence Rhode Island, we did three trips on the "Lake run". By this time some dredging had been done in the entrance to Lake Maracaibo and larger ships than the shallow draught "mosquito" tankers were able to get into the Lake oil terminals such as Cabimas and San Lorenzo. However, we could only load part cargo to get out again and had to top up at Punta Cardon before returning to Curacao.

On 24 February, 1954, we arrived at Curacao for the last time and spent three days cleaning tanks before loading three grades of oil plus drums of lubrication oil in the dryhold forward, all destined for Sydney, Australia. I looked forward to the trip across the Pacific and as it turned out we sailed right round the world in this ship – the only time I ever did it!

At Curacao Captain W.C. was relieved for long overdue leave. "Trog" had been relieved earlier and the new mate, while something of an "old woman" and an awful worrier, could only be an improvement! The new captain was something else and his reputation was well known throughout the fleet. He was Jimmy Brittain who hailed from Belfast and had served his time in the local Head Line, but he had married a lady on Tyneside and now lived somewhere in that area. He did not smoke or drink, which was a rarity in those days when the vast majority of seafarers indulged in both. He was suspicious of everyone and was wont to go around the accommodation opening cabin doors to see if any drinking was going on, as well as keeping a very careful check on everyone's purchases from the bonded store. He also believed in passing a lot of his paperwork down the line so I found myself lumbered in off-watch time with making up crew lists and helping with his accounts. Yet another attribute of Jimmy's was that when anything went wrong, be it accounts or anything else which was his responsibility, this also got passed down the line and anyone other than himself was to blame! However, since I came from Belfast I sometimes got the impression that he had a soft spot for me in his own peculiar way!

We duly sailed from Curacao and reached Colon two days later to transit the Panama Canal. This was my first time and after the sea-level Suez, surrounded by desert, the Panama was much more interesting with its huge locks and surrounding tropical vegetation. It was operated with typical American efficiency, including the customs and immigration services and all the canal pilots were American. In Gatun Lake we hosed down the whole ship with fresh water, a rare opportunity. It took nine hours to transit the canal and we cleared Balboa on the evening of 4 March for a 23-day passage across the Pacific to Sydney.

On this voyage we soon discovered more of the captain's quirks. It was the practice on any ocean passage for the second and third mates to take the morning sun sights at about 0800 and again at noon, when the sun was on the meridian, to fix the latitude and hence the ship's noon position. Captains rarely took any part in this but our Jimmy was different. He took his own sights every morning and since this ship had me as extra third officer, there were four of us involved, plus any apprentices who were there to learn and practice!

At noon we all stood in a row along the chart table in order of rank and did our final calculations following which Jimmy called each of us for our results. Even in the best conditions there would be slight variations and Jimmy would carefully consider everything before announcing the ship's noon position, which was inevitably the position *he* had calculated! He also believed in keeping apparent time. Anyone knows that as one travels east or west the clocks have to be altered in accordance with longitude and normally this is done an hour at a time so that keeping track of GMT is easy. However, this means that apparent noon, when the sun is exactly north or south of one's position, or even right overhead, can occur anywhere between about 1130 and 1230, and this is when noon sights for latitude are taken. Keeping apparent time it is necessary each noon to estimate the ship's position at noon the next day and then adjust the clocks the number of minutes so that the sun is on the meridian, i.e, exactly north or south, at 1200 ship's time the next day. In our case, on this Pacific crossing, this meant retarding the clocks anywhere between 20 minutes and 30 minutes each day, which was done at about 1900. Since I was now keeping the 0400 to 0800 watch this meant that I had to do the extra time on watch and so did anyone else on this watch. It also played havoc with trying to work out GMT in order to listen to the BBC or any other radio programme! The radio officer, who had to keep his watches according to GMT, became totally confused! (Jimmy was at least meticulous in following statutory requirements and we had weekly lifeboat and fire drills plus Sunday morning "inspections".)

We sighted perhaps two islands going across the Pacific but otherwise it was just empty sea all the way in generally fine weather. There was plenty of chipping and painting and one big job was the flying bridge or "catwalk" connecting forecastle to midships and midships to aft, including the metal walkways. One of these was being dropped on to the main deck when a corner caught one of the apprentices on the thigh and resulted in a very serious wound. Captain Jimmy and the mate did well. They got him onto a table, dosed him with morphine and stitched him up. When he went to hospital in Sydney no further treatment was necessary and he was returned to the ship.

We crossed the dateline on 23 March and so this day was "lost". We arrived in Sydney on 28 March and, with a quick discharge at the Gore Bay Shell installation, only had two days in port. However, everyone got at least one run ashore and I noted that I crossed the Sydney Harbour Bridge four times by train! Sydney struck me as being something of a cross between an English and American city, with shades of Victoriana, especially in the suburbs.

From Sydney we proceeded in ballast via the Great Barrier Reef and the Timor Sea to Miri in Sarawak and there loaded crude oil for Thameshaven. This voyage took exactly one month, including a call at Singapore for bunkers and of course the Suez Canal transit. It was uneventful but I did note that one day at noon, while approaching the Gulf of Aden, the sun was almost directly overhead. All of us on the Bridge, including Jimmy, were looking through our sextants in the wrong direction and missed it when it crossed the meridian! Towards the end of the voyage the chief steward and I got the job of working through Jimmy's accounts of wages, ready for the "pay off" at Thameshaven. He made us work everything out for six different dates, starting with the estimated date of arrival, in case of delays – a tedious task performed in my off-watch time. We had to make a call at Algiers for more bunkers but reached Thameshaven on 11 May and were "paid off" that evening. I arrived home on 13 May.

After just over nine months' service in the "Thallepus" I had two months' leave and since it was summer there was plenty of sailing at Holywood. I sailed in various "Sharpies" in local races and regattas but also in "La Golondrina". This was an 18-ft open boat which my friend John Olver had bought and we spent the first two or three weeks getting it ready for the season. Having been invalided out of the Head Line following a serious accident, John was now serving his time as an accountant and was supposed to be studying hard. However, neither the accountancy nor the studying seemed to be getting much attention, while the boat was. She was fun to sail but needed several crew to act as movable ballast and keep the lee gunwale above water when beating to windward.

My leave was up on 21 July but it was another two months before I was actually back at sea. Because of the number of ships out in the Far East, Shell had to send officers out to Singapore or get them home from there – and this was before flying everywhere was the norm. They used the P&O passenger service to the Far East and this time it was my turn. I embarked on s.s. "Carthage" at Southampton on 23 July, along with some nine other Shell junior officers, and spent an interesting and enjoyable 25 days travelling out to Singapore. The "Carthage" was one of the oldest P&O passenger liners at that time and some features were rather primitive, such as salt water baths and a jug of fresh water to finish off. We travelled in tourist class, which was fine because that was where the action was – the first class section was full of stuffy colonial civil servants and the like! The food was excellent, the drink cheap, the entertainment quite good and in 25 days, there were obviously some interesting liaisons with female passengers. We did the tourist bit at all the ports of call which included the Suez Canal, Aden, Bombay, Colombo and Penang. In Aden the ship had topped up with fresh water and the quality of this water must have accounted for what happened during the next few days. Everyone on board got the "runs" and there was great pressure on the limited toilet facilities. At least everyone joked about it!

On arrival at Singapore we were accommodated in Connell House to await our fate. Another third mate, with whom I had shared a cabin on the way out, was appointed to a small coastal tanker trading locally. Unfortunately she was attacked by pirates somewhere up the Malacca Strait and he was killed in the ensuing melee. I spent over three weeks waiting for m.v. "Neverita" to turn up so that I could join her as third mate. The Shell population at Connell House varied from day to day as officers came and went. When money was plentiful we visited the night spots of Singapore in the evenings and when it wasn't we did the tourist thing and visited museums and such like during the day, Tiger Balm Gardens being particularly interesting.

In due course the "Neverita" turned up, only to go into drydock at Keppel Harbour for three weeks. I was rapidly becoming an old Singapore hand! This was my first ship with Chinese crew but the officers were still all Caucasian, including some engineers from Australia and New Zealand. The crew seemed more mixed than used to be the case. I discovered that while one written language is common to all of China, there are about 27 different spoken dialects so that Chinese from one province cannot speak to those from another. Shell used to employ deck crews from one province, engine room crews from another and catering crews from yet another so that (in theory, anyway!) they would keep apart and not make trouble. There were two galleys on the ship, one European for the officers and catering crew, and the other the crew galley where the deck and engine room ratings each had their own cooks. Compared with a British crew, the Chinese were very rarely any trouble and were always on board and sober at sailing time. They were addicted to gambling, especially Majong, and there was the occasional opium smoker, but they were generally more interested in making and saving money.

A bonus for the officers was that for a very modest fee the stewards or "boys" attended to all the personal laundry. No dhobi and ironing sessions in this ship! Another thing was that the Chinese chief stewards were not allowed to order or organise provisions for the ship; this job was delegated to the third mate who was in fact the victualling officer. He was also responsible for the bonded stores and the sale of cigarettes and drink on board. I soon became adept at checking stock, ordering what was necessary and coping with the company's forms. Working out the cost of feeding the ship, in terms of cost per man per day, was a monthly chore, but the chief steward was very helpful and any perks that came my way from ship's chandlers or wherever, I shared with him!

The standard of food was very good and though there were or course European dishes available (many of the crew had served on Dutch Shell tankers and this was reflected in the menus), I soon developed a taste for Chinese food. The main item for Thursday lunch was always Nasi Goering, an Indonesian dish, and Sunday lunch was always a monumental Rice Taefel – basically curried chicken with a tremendous array of side dishes. One or two junior engineers regarded this as "compost heap", so were offered corned beef and salad as an alternative!

We left the dockyard on 1 October and went over to Pulo Sambo to load a cargo of diesel and fuel oil for Hong Kong. This was an uneventful trip except that after discharge of cargo we spent a day at anchor in Junk Bay, Hong Kong, while a typhoon passed to the South of us. We still met some very heavy weather in the China Sea on the ballast passage to Miri. From there a cargo was delivered to Singapore and here we backloaded a cargo for Mombasa in Kenya and Dar es Salaam in Tanganyika, a 19-day passage across the Indian Ocean. I was now back on an "N" Class ship with a best possible speed of 12 knots. Our Captain Young was a youngish man of about 40 who was quite pleasant and had no particular peculiarities. His wife was also on board since they had no children. The mate was also about 40 and must have been near to promotion since he was particularly well behaved! The chief engineer was a youngish bachelor and, in my opinion, too young for the sedentary life of a chief engineer on a Shell tanker! His name was Kinsella but as he came from Pontefract in Yorkshire, he was known as "Ponte". He used to come to my cabin most evenings bearing beer for an hour of chat or cards before I went on watch at 2000.

I was not impressed by Mombasa and, despite the colonial atmosphere, I thought it was rather a hick town. The chief engineer hired a car for a day and then discovered there was really nowhere to go and that the roads outside town were very poor. At Dar es Salaam the captain allowed us to lower the motor lifeboat and some of us went for a trip around the harbour. We inadvertently landed on an island which was a leper colony but did not see the notice until we were leaving! Most ships' lifeboats rarely if ever got afloat in those days; the attitude of senior officers seemed to be that, since they were safety equipment, they should only be used in emergencies. In fact I think they were more concerned about something going wrong and perhaps losing a boat. My own attitude was that the more the boats were used, the more likely the crew would be able to cope in a real emergency.

From East Africa we headed for the Persian Gulf and loaded crude oil at Mena Al Ahmadi for the UK. It was early December and the weather there was quite cool and pleasant. Also, since it was the North-East Monsoon season on the passage to Suez, the weather off the South East coast of Arabia was generally fine and clear with light winds. We passed quite close along this coast, which is spectacular in places. This would not have been possible in the South-West Monsoon, with strong onshore winds and poor visibility. Except for heavy weather in the Bay of Biscay this was a fine weather passage to our discharge port, which was Eastham on the River Mersey. We spent most of Christmas Day in the Irish Sea. The captain organised a get-together in the Smokeroom, followed by Christmas lunch. Everyone seemed to stay sober, which was just as well since we entered the Mersey that evening and berthed at Eastham just before midnight. In a mere two months I had left home, got to sea in this ship and arrived back home in the UK! We now remained in the Mersey until 12 January, 1955. After discharge at Eastham we backloaded there and at Stanlow Refinery on the Manchester Ship Canal for discharge at Dingle Installation, which is just across the river from Eastham. However, we spent five days anchored out at the Mersey Bar waiting for a berth at Dingle! After that it was back up the canal to a place called Ince Layby where we loaded a cargo of fuel oil for Ceuta on the Moroccan side of the Straits of Gibraltar. There were some good runs ashore on the Mersey to Liverpool, Birkenhead and Ellesmere Port, including visits to cinemas and dance halls, never mind public houses! Discharging and loading were both slow for various reasons and there were numerous delays.

The passage to Ceuta was notable for heavy weather. For a start we could not disembark the Mersey pilot and had to take him to a sheltered spot off Milford Haven where the local pilot boat came out for him. From there it was rocking and rolling all the way, especially across the Bay of Biscay until we turned the corner at Cape St. Vincent and headed for Ceuta. Discharge here was fairly slow and took nearly three days. This included a burst pipeline on the jetty which resulted in fuel oil spraying all over the midships section of the ship and all over the jetty – a lovely mess! Ceuta was quite a clean town visually but had its shady side, with plenty of pimps and touts to pester visitors. I have often wondered why the Spanish are so adamant about regaining Gibraltar when they are equally adamant about hanging onto their own small colony in Morocco!

From Ceuta it was back out to the Far East via the Suez Canal and Fao, Iraq, in the Persian Gulf. Although Singapore was our base port, we loaded cargoes for Japan at various Indonesian oil ports and as usual Miri in Sarawak. Discharge ports included Tokuyama, Shimonoseki, Moji, Kokura and Niigata and at these ports we topped up on provisions, especially fresh vegetables and fruit. As victualling officer, I had to deal with the various ship chandlers and there were usually some little perks including trips ashore at their expense. Some of these places seemed little more than shanty towns with unpaved roads and open sewers but Niigata was quite an impressive city with some big department stores, not unlike Marks & Spencer. It was of course only ten years since the end of the War and some of these places had been heavily bombed.

On one occasion we actually discharged cargo at an Indonesian port rather than load and this was Surabaya on Java, the second largest city in the country. One visit ashore was enough and it was obvious that the whole place had gone downhill since colonial days and an efficient Dutch administration. On one visit to Singapore the Chinese crew were paid off and replaced after a long time on board. The night before, a search of the crew accommodation was organised and as a result several bags of rice, sugar, and other dry stores, plus numerous tins and jars of various foods, were returned to the ship's storerooms. In all fairness we did not confiscate items which the crew had obviously saved to take home from their own rations and as I remember they had all managed to build up a stock of soap cakes. On our arrival, the local customs rummage squad came on board and recovered a considerable quantity of opium from various hidey holes, but no-one was ever charged with smuggling drugs. One activity we did not discourage was the chief steward's dealings with native craft which came alongside in Indonesia, especially in remote anchorages. I always checked the number of tins of this and that which he took from the stores for trade and I was satisfied with the result – usually lots of fresh tropical fruit and, better still, buckets full of fresh king prawns. For spending money ashore everyone traded cigarettes for cash with the locals, a far better deal than the official exchange rate!

On 22 May 1955 we arrived at Miri for the last time and loaded for Rotterdam. The passage home took six weeks, including a call at Singapore for bunkers and stores and another Suez Canal transit. After discharge of cargo we spent another few days at Rotterdam for tank cleaning. There were numerous visits to the excellent nearby Missions to Seamen and one day I organised a special lunch on board for the padre and some of the splendid ladies who helped out there. They really appreciated the Nassi Goreng! I even managed a whole day visit to "E55" in Rotterdam, which was an excellent World Exhibition that would have taken a week to see it all. It was only a 24-hour passage across to the River Tyne where we berthed at Wallsend Slipway on 7 July and the ship duly went into dry-dock. By now I had my time in for my First Mate's Certificate so after a few days I was paid off and went home for leave and study leave, five months in all.

I arrived home to find that we now had a television set! Of course it was black and white and there was only one channel – BBC. However, it was fascinating and became a great time waster!

I signed on at the Belfast Technical College just before they closed down for a month's summer holiday. During this break there was a family trip to the Republic based at Bray, South of Dublin, and one evening I went dancing at the Arcadia Ballroom. The result was that a young man from Lurgan and I ended up in the company of two pleasant girls from Lancashire for the next couple of days but it was all very circumspect! At home there was plenty of sailing activity at Holywood up to the end of the season and my friend John Olver's "La Golondrina" saw most of the action. Carrickfergus Regatta was a "must" but that year it was virtually a flat calm and the racing was a washout. We got close enough to the first mark to throw beer bottles at it before giving up and rowing for the harbour. We had a mixed crew on board and the action ashore was more interesting than the drifting about in Belfast Lough.

At one of the many local dances we attended, I and another first mate candidate from the school met up with two girls who had been in my class at Sullivan Upper School. We subsequently went out as a foursome for a while and the result was that my friend was married soon after. By the time we met up again for our Master's Examination he also had a family!

In September I applied myself seriously to my studies and, the regime at the Belfast college being what it was, I did more useful work on my own at home than I did at school. In mid-November I sat the First Mate's Examination and passed in everything except the Signals. This particular test required a 90% mark to pass and the so-called "block test" in visual morse was a stumbling block for everyone. Not to worry – I had plenty of leave left and a month later I passed the Signals to complete the whole examination. My leave was now nearly up and Shell started making noises about my return to sea. They also advised me that I had been promoted to second mate. First I had to go for a routine medical examination with Dr. Calwell in Belfast, who was the local shipping doctor and had a practice in a not very salubrious terraced house on York Street. He was quite a character and was well known among local seafarers. Dr. Calwell had started a career at sea and had got as far as second mate before deciding to take up medicine, and his second mate's ticket was proudly displayed in his surgery alongside his medical certificates. I well remember him greeting me at the door with a half burnt cigarette hanging from his mouth. On arrival in the surgery he presented me with a chipped and dirty enamel bowl and said "Here son, just pee into this." There were one or two seafarers' haunts nearby, including one known as "Ma Carroll's", and it was reputed that the clientele of these places were among Dr. Calwell's patients. But he had a very good reputation and was still very much interested in the sea since he had a old motor cruiser moored on the River Lagan. In later years, when he retired, his daughter Amy became the local shipping doctor.

I was on my way back to sea by mid-December but once again I was sent out to Singapore on a P&O passenger liner. This was the "Chusan", a much more modern ship than the old "Carthage" and this time I was the only Shell Tankers passenger. We sailed from Tilbury on 16 December and it did not take long to discover that, along with a young rubber planter going out to Malaya, we were the only eligible bachelors in the tourist section. There were one or two single ladies who we figured were going out East, where white single ladies were scarce. It was an interesting trip!

CHAPTER 5: UP THE LADDER – PROMOTION TO SECOND MATE

The passage out to Singapore in the "Chusan" took 23 days and followed the same route as the "Carthage". For a young bachelor it was better than three weeks' extra leave! For the first two days there was some heavy weather, especially in the Bay of Biscay, so that the dining room was nearly empty for some meals and the social life was minimal. By the time we reached Gibraltar things were improving. We spent Christmas Eve and most of Christmas Day in the Suez Canal and by the time we got into the Red Sea and warmer weather the social life had really taken off. Late night there were surreptitious comings and goings down on 'E' deck alleyway and fortunately the masters at arms (ships policeman) seemed to be circumspect in their nightly patrols. Apart from the enjoyment on board there were interesting tours ashore at Aden, Bombay, Colombo and Penang before arriving at Singapore on 8 January, 1956. This time I found myself in the Cosmos Hotel, which I suppose was a bit more upmarket than Connell House, though not for long.

The next morning I reported to the Shell Office to be told that I was joining the "Cerion" for a few days. Now the "Cerion" was one of three dry cargo ships operated by Shell. In outward appearance they looked like tankers but, based at Singapore, they carried numerous petroleum products in drums. They traded to numerous Pacific islands and small ports and anchorages where there were no bulk oil facilities. I would really have enjoyed a year in this ship but unfortunately her days were over and she was laid up at anchor in Singapore Eastern Anchorage, and was up for sale. In the meantime she was used as an accommodation vessel for Chinese crews either waiting to join ships or for repatriation to China, and I was appointed as officer in charge. The second mate I relieved was on his way home.

I spent three weeks on the "Cerion" and life was not unpleasant if somewhat boring at times. I lived in the captain's accommodation where I ate splendid though solitary meals provided by the Chinese chief steward and cook. However, the ship was dead with no power. Lighting was by Tilley lamps and cooking by primus stoves. I managed to provide drinking and sanitary water with the emergency fire pump in the steering flat which was better than the bucket business that had been in use until I joined. I was supposed to put my time in by correcting the extensive chart outfit but this was a lost cause since they were so far out of date and the ship was up for sale anyway. One or two prospective buyers and surveyors did come to call, but in the end I think she was sold for scrap. There was some serious wastage in the hull structure and even a few holes in the decks!

There were two or three other Shell ships laid up in the anchorage and a launch service operated three times a day from Clifford Pier on the waterfront. I soon made friends with the other OICs and we were wont to go ashore together in the evenings when we had funds. Captain English, the Shell superintendent, had an upstairs office in the waterfront Shell Building and a powerful telescope with which to keep an eye on the anchorage. We went ashore to the office most days to order stores and collect cash to pay the crews. However, most of our forays ashore for pleasure were after dark and we returned by sampan long after the official launch service stopped. There were visits to most of the cinemas, sometimes to one of the "Worlds" – giant Chinese funfairs – and we usually ended up on Bougis Street late at night for splendid food cooked and served on the street.

On 28 January I was advised that my services were required as second mate on the "Spondilus", due in Singapore in about two days. Captain English told me to keep an eye out down Singapore Strait and that when I saw a pall of smoke on the horizon I would know the "Spondilus" was on her way! He was quite right too and on 30 January 1956 the ship arrived with her funnel belching smoke to anchor nearby for engine repairs. I handed over the "Cerion" to another in transit second mate and transferred to what must have been the oldest active ship in the Shell fleet at that time. After three days at anchor for repairs we proceeded alongside the passenger ship berths in Keppel Harbour and for some reason loaded fuel oil for nearby Pulo Sambo. What turned up ahead of us on the next berth at Keppel Harbour but the "Chusan" on her return trip from Japan! There seemed to be no problem for visitors and I went on board with some other officers from the "Spondilus" for a drink or two and met up again with some of the round trip passengers still on board I had met on the way out. From Singapore it was a short ballast passage to Miri where we loaded for Niigata, Japan.

The "Spondilus" deserves some description, since it is now

51

nearly fifty years since I spent a very happy twelve months in her. She was built in 1927 at the Wilton shipyard in Holland and so was almost 30 years old, really ancient for any tanker by today's standards, and indeed she would be immediately placed under indefinite "detention" at any port of call under the present "port state control" regime in view of her very many defects! She was 10,700 tons deadweight and was unsuitable for other than straight one grade cargoes since there were leaks between most of the cargo tanks. The main diesel engine was the original Werkspoor and except for one generator the rest of the machinery was of the same vintage. She had a single pumproom with two steam driven reciprocating pumps but there was never enough steam to operate more than one at a time so our maximum discharge rate was about 300 tons per hours, thus ensuring at least two nights in any discharge port. The boiler room was forward of the engine room and the top boiler room doors opened directly on to the main deck close to No.9 cargo tank hatches and ullage plugs. There was something basically wrong with the boiler combustion system since unless it was shut down there was always smoke, soot and even live cinders emanating from the tall funnel and if the wind was from astern this lot would end up on the main deck. Her best speed in favourable conditions was about 12 knots but more usually it was 9 or 10.

She was the only ship I sailed in where the ratings were accommodated in the forecastle, the Chinese deck crew being to starboard and the firemen to port. Deck officers were accommodated midships with the engineers on the upper deck aft and the Chinese catering crew below them on the main deck level. The officers' dining saloon was amidships while the crew messrooms and the galleys were aft. Therefore at mealtimes there was a great deal of movement fore and aft – interesting in heavy weather! There were no outside alleyways aft which was an inconvenience when we visited offshore mooring berths such as at Miri. In this case the heavy and inflexible stern mooring wires which had to be heaved on board could only be led up the port and starboard engineer's alleyways and out on to the main deck. Sometimes a lot of mud and rubbish came up with them. While the officers' cabins were small, they were comfortable, and could perhaps be described as "mellow". The bunks were narrow by today's standards and set high with several deep drawers underneath. Amidships, the captain had an en-suite bathroom, but the rest of us shared a bathroom which opened on to the open deck rather than an inside alleyway.

As with the engine room the bridge was virtually as originally built and the wheelhouse was wooden. There was a standard dry card magnetic compass on the "monkey island" over the wheelhouse and a similar dry card steering compass within. There was an ancient echo sounder and an equally ancient radio direction finder in the Chartoom, neither of which we ever relied on even if we could get them to work. While the steering system was hydraulic and generally reliable, the engine room telegraph was something else. It was an old-fashioned brass monster with clanging bells and was connected to the control station in the engine room by a very long linkage of wires and chains. To transmit an order one had to give the handles a really good swing to activate the bells at the other end, then set them so that the pointer on the dial indicated the required order, say "Full ahead". Hopefully the pointer on the engine room dial would indicate the same order, but not always, and in a critical situation we always telephoned the engine room to make sure they had got the right order! When the linkage broke it often took the engineers forever to find and fix the break. Basically this ship was navigated without the help of any modern navigational aids. When unsure of our position and approaching a poorly or unlit coast or passage at night, or in poor visibility, we frequently slowed down or turned back until conditions improved.

There were one or two officer changes at Singapore and several thereafter but many of us were together for a year or more. Except for the chief engineer we were all young bachelors and sailing for the first time in our respective ranks. Captain Sutherland, from South Shields, though only in his early 30s, had some of the peculiarities of his elder brethren. Emergency drills, inspections of the ship and other statutory requirements were rare events. He normally only appeared in the saloon for one meal a day at lunchtime and otherwise mainly kept to his quarters. He was a serious beer drinker, even if he seldom drank anything stronger. There was always a stack of perhaps two dozen cases of beer against a bulkhead in his bedroom for ready use. As officer in charge of the bonded stores, my instructions were to keep this stack topped up at all times!

The mate, Brimer Dale, from Redcar in Yorkshire, had just passed for his Master's Ticket and been promoted, while the third mate, wee Willie Davidson, was from Buckie in Banffshire where his Dad owned and skippered a fishing boat. He in fact was an uncertificated fourth year apprentice and as soon as he had completed his time he was sent home to sit his Second Mate's Examination. The chief engineer, by contrast, was near retirement age and was on his last ship with Shell. He was very proud of the fact that he had sailed in the "Spondilus" on her maiden voyage as a junior engineer and had sailed in her several times since. I think it was from him that we learned the ship had been somewhere safe in South America during the War years. She would certainly not have lasted long in a wartime situation!

Most of the other engineers were from Australia or New Zealand and they certainly bore the brunt of the work in keeping the ship going. Complete breakdowns and lesser mechanical problems were almost a daily occurrence and they spent little time out of their working clothes! Like the chief engineer, the radio operator was part of the ship. I don't remember how long he had been there when I joined but he was still there when I left a year later and I think remained until she went to the scrapyard some months after that. Like all long-time "sparks" he was definitely "away with it". His cramped cabin was on our alleyway with the equally cramped radio shack right opposite, so he didn't have far to go to get to work! There was a dingo-like dog on board which had been picked up somewhere in Australia and it mostly lived with him. Except for the third mate there were no apprentices and in fact I turned the apprentices' cabin into a darkroom. I had started a developing and printing "business" (black and white only, of course) on the "Neverita" and I was now able to expand the business to offer good quality enlargements as well!

The passage to Niigata took 12 days and, following the engine repairs at Singapore, we only had to stop once for further engine repairs. On 12 February it was Chinese New Year and the catering crew threw a party for the officers in the Sailors' Messroom. This was really good "chow" but most of the dishes we were offered would probably not appear on the menu of the average UK Chinese restaurant. In Japan it was midwinter, with plenty of snow and ice about and several heavy snowfalls while we were there. Discharge of cargo took three days and departure was further delayed by main engine work. Everyone had ample time ashore for whatever pleasures took their fancy and I was able to stock up on photographic materials at modest cost. Our return ballast passage was to Tarakan, Borneo, to load for Singapore and on the way the Mate started a monumental tank cleaning operation. The ship had recently carried some cargoes of what was known as slack wax and the result was that the bottom of the cargo tanks were coated in a thick layer of this stuff. It added unnecessary deadweight to the ship and made proper discharge of subsequent cargoes difficult. The crew worked unwillingly down the tanks, and the mate went down to supervise them. Some hundreds of tons of wax must have been hauled up on deck in buckets and dumped overboard. No law against that in those days!

After loading at Tarakan we spent two days at anchor off the port for engine maintenance and repairs before proceeding to Pulo Sambo at Singapore to discharge. My diary records that on 10 March we had a lifeboat drill and actually turned out the starboard boats, both fore and aft. The boats were original clinker built wooden boats and it took some considerable work to get them even lifted off the chocks. At Singapore, after discharge and reloading for Japan, we spent another two days at anchor for engine repairs.

Our passage back north was uneventful except for stops for engine repairs and this time we had two discharge ports, Kobe and Shimonoseki, with the Japanese Inland Sea between them. I spent a great deal of time plotting the unswept wartime minefields and the courses through them on our charts before we got there. Overcast weather and poor visibility led to some "turnings back" and tentative approaches before we found our way into the Eastern end of the Inland Sea and arrived off Kobe. Here we lay at anchor for two days, first because there was another Shell tanker on the berth and second because when the berth was clear the engine refused to start. Eventually we berthed and discharge of 3,000 tons of cargo took another day. The run through the Inland Sea to Shimonoseki with a Japanese pilot on board was interesting, although we passed the most scenic parts in the dark. We did have to anchor for some time 30 miles short of Shimonoseki and this time it was water in the main engine lub. oil. Eventually we reached port and took another two days to discharge the rest of the cargo. A few of us managed a night ashore and did the rounds of the night spots in nearby Moji.

Returning to Bunyu in ballast we then spent a few weeks trading between this port and Balikpapan with one trip to Surabaya as well. The Shell Club at Balikpapan was the best one I came across at the various oil ports and there were a few good nights ashore on the proceeds of selling cigarettes. In those youthful days I had the stamina to spend a happy evening ashore and then return to the ship by midnight to do my 1200 to 0400 watch – no problem! However it was pleasant to get a longer trip after this when we loaded at Miri for another Japanese port, Shimotsu, about 60 miles South of Kobe but little more than a village. From Shimotsu it was a six-day passage to Hong Kong for dry-docking and the watch-keeping routine went haywire since the mate had to go on daywork, or rather "all work", to supervise the tank cleaning. Lack of water pressure, lack of water temperature and an unwilling crew of "tank divers" made this a difficult protracted task. As usual, all the tank washings and all the oily rubbish brought up from the cargo tanks went straight overboard. The third mate and I worked virtually watch and watch although the old man helped out by doing the occasional 0800 to 1200. Arriving at Hong Kong on 25 May we then spent a very pleasant four weeks at the Taikoo Dockyard on Hong Kong Island, a short tram ride from the city centre.

The first morning I woke up after a welcome full night's sleep I found a young lady offering me tea and toast in my bunk – but that was all she was offering! Most of the Chinese crew were paid off shortly after arrival and the catering department was virtually taken over by a gang of women who were extremely efficient. These ladies were carefully vetted by the dockyard; they came on board early in the morning and all had to be ashore by about 1800. It was all rather novel and enjoyable and we wished we could have taken them to sea with us!

Work progressed on what was really a lost cause and a waste of money. For instance, one evening the engineers pumped up the after-peak fresh water tank ready for testing the next day, only to find in the morning that the tank was empty while the engine room was awash! The cargo tank bulkheads were in a similar condition and no amount of caulking would stop them leaking. Machinery repairs also made little difference since main engine breakdowns and serious shortages of auxiliary power continued after we left Hong Kong! However, the four-week break from watch-keeping was very welcome, as were the almost daily and nightly runs ashore. Unfortunately it was the summer season and the weather was uncomfortably hot and humid. As ever there were frequent visits to cinemas and restaurants and to more exotic places when funds permitted. Shell even laid on a car and driver so that the officers could tour the island and visit the tourist spots. There was a Tiger Balm Garden (though it was not as extensive as the one in Singapore) and the cable railway up the Peak was not as impressive as the one at Penang. There were a number of sub-contractors working on board and they were good for a few nights out, including visits to the floating restaurants at Aberdeen and expensive nightclubs in town. The yard had its own housing complex for European staff and even a Taikoo Club, which we rarely visited. However, just outside the dockyard gate was a more lively establishment called the "Arizona", where we sometimes called in on our way ashore. Our Scottish dockyard manager was intrigued by this place but had never set foot in it. Despite frequent invitations he refused to come with us and I guess was afraid his wife might find out where he had been. We had no such inhibitions!

Leaving Hong Kong on 21 June, 1956, we headed south to Singapore and loaded a cargo for Rangoon in Burma and Chittagong in East Pakistan (now Bangladesh). At both ports the discharge berth was a set of mooring buoys out in the river in strong tides and at Rangoon in particular the arrangements were somewhat interesting. Here both anchors had to be "hung off" and the anchor chains used to secure the ship to the forward buoys. This feat of seamanship was accomplished by the mate, although we nearly lost one anchor in the process. At the after end further lengths of chain had to be hove on board from a barge and used to secure to the buoys astern. This whole business took the best part of a day before we even started discharge of cargo, and the reverse procedure on departure took nearly as long. We were a long way from Rangoon itself and I don't think anyone got ashore. Because it was South-West Monsoon time there was a lot of heavy rain and this did not help on the passage round to Chittagong with low coastlines, few landmarks, and rare sightings of the sun. The berthing arrangement at Chittagong was similar to that at Rangoon but even with a stronger tide only wires were used and there was less excitement. Again we were a long way from town but some of us did get ashore to find that Chittagong was a poor place with even the best hotel little more than a shack – though our Chinese crew did find a lucrative market for empty beer bottles and other such items. Apparently the going rate was one egg for one beer bottle, and they also ended up with a small flock of very scrawny live chickens! These poor creatures roosted in the foredeck winch outside the forecastle for the next few days until they gradually disappeared into the pot.

There followed a two-week passage in the Indian Ocean to

Abadan, where we loaded another cargo for Rangoon and Chittagong, and a two-week passage back. The South-West Monsoon meant some quite heavy weather and not many chances for useful sun or star sights. As it was midsummer, the Persian Gulf was extremely hot, sticky and uncomfortable. The current fourth engineer was an anaemic Englishman nicknamed "Mahogany" (his surname was Wood) who suffered badly in the heat. While we all dosed ourselves with salt tablets in this weather, poor "Mahogany" seemed allergic to them and appeared to be fading fast! "Doctor" Dale, the mate, took control of the situation and the patient spent long hours virtually submerged in a bath full of salt water. He did survive until we reached cooler weather!

"Doctor" Dale dealt with most of the medical problems on board and obviously enjoyed this role. In Hong Kong we had a problem with the dog, which managed to get ashore and roam around creating trouble. It had to be rounded up and put down but before that it managed to bite my leg, resulting in my having to take a course of anti-rabies injections over two weeks – administered, of course, by "Doctor" Dale. Other medical problems included the third engineer with something in his eye, the Chinese carpenter with a piece of wire stuck in his toe and a junior engineer who was just having eyesight problems.

We made the usual stops for engine repairs and I noted that one day we anchored in the middle of the Persian Gulf in 27 fathoms of water for about 12 hours! Back at Rangoon the mooring procedure was the same as the first visit but we did it all in less time! Someone in the shore installation gave me a lift in a truck to visit a local pagoda, which was very interesting – shoes off at the front door and walk around in socked feet. At Chittagong I spent an evening ashore with our "sparks", who found he had some friends working in the installation there. My impression was that there were still many Europeans in East Pakistan, living the good life, and apparently there were about 200 British nationals in and around Chittagong alone.

We actually completed discharge of cargo in good time but there was first a delay in sailing due to the shore organisation being unready to let us go and then a storm warning for the Northern Bay of Bengal which could result in the bar at the river entrance silting up. When we did sail, some 30 hours late, the pilot boat had to go ahead of us to check the depth of water. We returned to the Persian

Gulf in South-West Monsoon weather and loaded a cargo of crude oil at Mina Al Ahmadi for Niigata in Japan, with a stop at Singapore for bunkers and water. A few direct entries from my diaries might be appropriate at this stage, although they are not exactly an advertisement for Shell!

20 Aug 1956. Overcast most of day with strong SW wind and heavy sea. Got "noon" OK between the clouds. Main generator failed at 1600 and only had engine room and navigation lights until 2000

21 Aug. The mate started water rationing today since there was no clean water available at Chittagong. We only have water on tap amidships for about one hour in 24. The sun was almost dead overhead at noon but we got it through the clouds.

22 Aug. Now we are not only on water rationing but power rationing as well. All except the engine room lights are shut off from 0800 until 1600. This lets one of the two old Werkspoor generators have a rest. The main Ruston generator is out of commission yet again.

25 Aug. Stopped for three hours this morning for main engine adjustments. Reports from the engine room vary but we may have full auxiliary power in a day or so.

30 Aug. Some excitement in the 1200 to 0400 this morning when the Ruston generator failed once again and all the lights went out. As we were on electric steering gear we started going round in circles. We were approaching the Quoins, islands in the narrows at the entrance to the Persian Gulf, but fortunately there was no other traffic about at the time! We made it to Mena Al Ahmadi on 2 Sept, loaded in a record six hours and sailed for Niigata.

4 Sept. Turned back for a couple of hours in my watch tonight so as not to reach Jazirat Farur, which is unlit, before daylight. For the volume of traffic in the Gulf the lights are not all they could be. The majority of ships now have radar but of course not us!

10 Sept. Off the Malabar coast of India all day but too far off to

59

see anything of the land.

13 Sept. Stopped for five hours – broken telescopic pipe.

14 Sept. Stopped again today – another telescopic pipe.

18 Sept. Eight hours alongside at Pulo Bukum, Singapore, for bunkers, water and stores. We should have gone to dry-dock!

20 Sept. Stopped for five hours – broken telescopic pipe.

21 Sept. Stopped for 18 hours. Water in the fuel oil but that is only one of many things to be put right. There was a typhoon boiling up to the north of us but in the end it passed clear ahead and well away, although we still got some quite heavy weather.

We reached Niigata on 2 October and it was very pleasant to have three days in a decent port after three months of indifferent ones. After that it was an uneventful trip South to Miri, except for the usual breakdowns, and there we loaded crude oil for Sydney, a 17-day passage, including breakdown time and turnings back as we found our way through the Indonesian islands towards Torres Strait and the pilot for the Great Barrier Reef, which was as interesting as ever. Our Australian pilot was not impressed with the "Spondilus" and her unreliability, especially the necessary stoppages. Also, we had no dedicated pilot cabin and I had to clear out my darkroom so he could sleep there when not on the Bridge. He then found there were bugs in the bunk!

After six delightful days at Gore Bay, Sydney, the passage back up the East Coast of Australia and on through the Indonesian islands was as uneventful as usual, but there was the problem of trying to keep a cargo of heavy fuel oil hot. My diary entry for 14 November, 1956, records that we stopped for engine repairs for four hours and that, though the chief engineer was quite a young man, "he is going very grey and becoming visibly older. Trying to produce enough steam to feed our ancient tank heating coils is another worry for him, despite our being in the tropics".

At this time we were following the goings on in the Suez Canal Zone with some interest, and listened to every possible BBC overseas broadcast. Following the abortive invasion and the aftermath it looked as though the canal would be out of action for many months, with many ships trapped there. The "Spondilus" was certainly not going that way since all our western hemisphere charts had been taken off at Singapore. This reduced the number of charts on board from about 1800 to 800 and greatly reduced my never-ending chore of keeping them up-to-date from the Notices to Mariners.

After Singapore there was a trip to Miri to load for Shimotsu, our second visit there, and then some six weeks trading between, Bunyu, Balikpapan and Surabaya. There were serious problems with both the steam and air whistles on the funnel during this period and the former was removed to the engine room workshop for attention, without much success. One day the air whistle just blew of its own accord for about 15 minutes. The Chinese thought the ship was sinking and rushed to the lifeboats.

After a Christmas Party at Bunyu on 24 December, we sailed for Balikpapan at noon on Christmas Day but once we were clear and in open water the dear old ship conveniently broke down yet again while we had our Christmas lunch. On Boxing Day the motor on the main Ruston generator blew up with a loud bang and we were back to a hand-to-mouth existence with regard to light and power! We celebrated the New Year with a party at Surabaya which went on all night and during this period loading of cargo had to be seriously slowed down for some reason.

11 January, 1957 saw us back at Singapore to load another cargo for Japan, but before departure we spent four days at the Eastern Anchorage for generator and main engine repairs. Our ports in Japan were Kobe and Shimonoseki, with part cargo for each and another passage through the Inland Sea between them. On the passage to get there we met the heaviest weather yet, with gale force winds and heavy seas from the north – real winter monsoon weather. Some days the speed was less than 7 knots and one day both the porthole and the deadlight in one of the firemen's cabins forward were smashed in with resulting flooding and mess before a temporary plug could be fitted. At Kobe we celebrated Chinese New Year, my second on this ship, and there was a fine party in the Seamen's Mess. As usual on such occasions one did not inquire into the contents of some of the dishes on offer. We also had a Lloyd's surveyor on board at Kobe for a Load Line and hopefully a Safety Equipment survey. He was not impressed with the

"Spondilus", refused to do the surveys and went off to report to his superiors. Meanwhile we completed discharge at this port and at Shimonoseki and returned to Miri in ballast. On the way south we got news of some reliefs for leave and these included the mate and myself. We also learned that the ship had to undergo full survey at Singapore before the end of March or she would be refused permission to go any further!

At Miri there was a final event when the pilot managed to get mooring wires and chains tangled around the propeller and we ended up back to front in the offshore loading berth. It took all the next day with divers in attendance to sort out the mess. On 14 February the mate and I, together with the third engineer, said goodbye to the "Spondilus" and transferred to the "Bedford", loading at an adjacent berth to travel to Singapore as supernumeraries. On charter to Shell, this was a modern and well-appointed tanker owned by the Fred Olsen Line of Norway, although under British flag and with an all-British crew. I think the dear old "Spondilus" staggered on for another few months before being scrapped! At Singapore we stayed at Connell House where, because of his rank, the mate had an air-conditioned room. (Likewise on the flight home he travelled first class while I was tourist.) During our four-day stay we managed to acquire Singapore driving licences. This was a clever move, since on arrival home we were able to obtain the "overseas visitor" allowance of petrol coupons, which helped us overcome the petrol rationing due to the Suez crisis.

On 20 February, 1957, we flew home – my first time in an aeroplane. The trip took two full nights and the day in between. The plane was a Super G Constellation of Quantas Airways and fuelling stops were made at Bangkok, Calcutta, Karachi, Bahrain and Istanbul. At each stop we had to disembark and wait in the lounge. Arriving in London early on 22 February, I saw the mate off from Kings Cross, put in a few "tourist" hours, including a visit to Madame Tussauds, and travelled home myself that evening by train and ferry to reach Belfast the next morning for four months' leave.

"Titmouse" at Holywood, 1947

The Holywood Sharpie "Spray", 1948

M.V."Neocardia!", 1949. Note wartime wheelhouse windows

T.E.S. "Tectarius", 1951

T.E.S. "Hyalina", 1952

Noon sights on board T.E.S. "Thallapus", 1954
Shadows indicate the sun the overhead!

"La Golondrina" at Carrickfergus, 1954

T.E.S. "Thallapus", 1954
Heavy weather in the North Atlantic

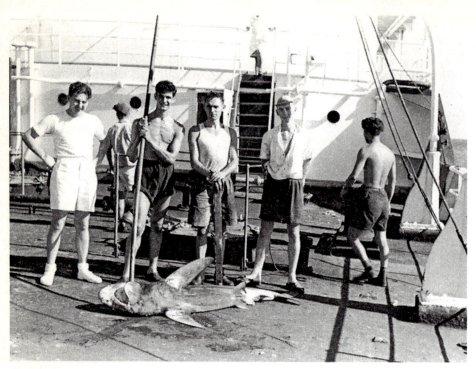

M.V. "Neverita", 1954
Shark Fishing!

M.V. "Neverita", in heavy weather

P & O "Chusan" Tilbury to Singapore, 1956

M.V. "Spondilus" at Rangoon, 1956

M.V. "Spondilus" at Hong Kong, 1956
The author with Wash Amahs and ship's dog!

M.V. "Spondilus", 1956
Quartermaster and bridge boy on watch in the wheelhouse

M.V. "Spondilus", 1956
The dining saloon on Christmas day

S.T.S. "Zenatia", 1958 on the bridge wing

S.T.S. "Asperella", 1960
In the ice at Turku, Finland

S.T.S. "Alan Evelyn", 1961

M.V. "Hamilton", 1963
At anchor in President Roads, Boston

M.V. "Hamilton", 1964
The author and his mother at South Shields

M.V. "Hamilton", 1964
A motley collection of Officers

M.V. "Hamilton", 1965
Heavy weather in the North Atlantic

CHAPTER 6: EXAM SUCCESS, AND OFF TO SEA AGAIN

Back home I enjoyed the usual social activities with my friend John and others, which included work on "La Golondrina". He had also built a plywood outboard runabout called "Nimbus", which was known as "The Yellow Peril" because of its colour. This was launched for the first time in March 1957 and we had some interesting trial trips including one up to Belfast Harbour and up the River Lagan for some way. We were stopped and interviewed by the Harbour Police at one of the bridges since there was some IRA activity at the time and we must have looked suspect! At the end of March I spent a pleasant week at and around Redcar, Yorkshire, where I was best man at "Dr. Dale's" wedding. Later I was godfather at his first daughter's christening and we have kept in touch ever since.

Who should be in Belfast at that time but "Wee Willie" Davidson, who was the first third mate on the "Spondilus". Having passed his Second Mate's Certificate he had left Shell and was now fourth mate on the "Rangititi" of the New Zealand Shipping Company. This passenger/cargo liner was in dry-dock at Harland & Wolff and remained so for several weeks. Willie had a good time in Belfast and later married one of the ship's nursing sisters, but I haven't heard from him since.

On this leave I completely repainted the outside of my parent's house and helped with internal work. Always the willing sailor home from the sea! My social activities included some successful racing in "La Golondrina", as well as various dances with my friends. One night we went to a dance in Bostock House, the nurses' home at the Royal Victoria Hospital, where I met a very attractive young student nurse who became my female companion for the rest of my leave. I became very fond indeed of this young lady but she came from a Presbyterian farming family at Ballynahinch, County Down, and had lived a sheltered life so far. I never did meet any of her family and no doubt they would not have approved of a smoking drinking sailor as a beau for their daughter! Anyway, she was not interested in boats.

Towards the end of May I got my marching orders and on 4 June, 1957, I joined the steam turbine ship "Zenatia" at Cammel Lairds' shipyard in Birkenhead, again as second mate. This was some contrast to the "Spondilus", since she was the latest and greatest in the Shell fleet. She was still fitting out and those officers so far appointed were simply "standing by" and learning all we could about the ship. At 38,500 tons deadweight, the "Zenatia" was one of the largest tankers at that time under the British flag. Her sister ship "Zaphon" was already in service under the command of "Butcher" Shaw, the then Shell Commodore. We had the Vice Commodore, Reg Hanson, who was something of a fiery character, except when his wife was on board! Both were of the "old school" and suspicious of new innovations and anything technical they could not understand. There were lots of stories about these older masters and one about "Butcher" Shaw was that one day, while on leave, he was driving his car through South Shields when a traffic light turned red and he found himself in the middle of the intersection by the time he pulled up. He therefore gave three blasts on his horn and went "full astern" – right into the front of a bus!

The "Zenatia" herself had an outdated "square" appearance little different from much earlier Shell tankers and the "H" Class 18,000-ton ships of the same vintage were just the same. At this time some of the London Greek tanker owners had some very attractive looking ships coming out of shipyards on the River Tees and the big Greek owners such as Onassis, Niarchos and Livanos were building ships that were positively streamlined in appearance! Their standard of accommodation was also way ahead of Shell's. However, the "Zenatia" did have air-conditioned accommodation which, while not all that effective, was welcome in the summer heat of the Persian Gulf. She was fast for a tanker and on full steam the speed was usually around 17 knots. She was also fast in port and it was rare to be more than a day in a loading port and two days in a discharge port. The Bridge was well equipped with the latest radar and radio direction finding equipment and, new to me, a Decca Navigator. Our captain, Captain Hanson, was always suspicious of positions produced using this equipment and of course it was only usable in Western Europe and one or two other isolated areas. The main receiving unit was a large cabinet on the Chartroom bulkhead within which were numerous old-fashioned valves and relays. The display unit on the chart table was the size of a modest television set and of course the dials only gave letters and numbers which then had to be transferred to charts overlaid with the Decca lattice. The latest receivers which appeared shortly before the system was abandoned were the size of a cigar box and gave a direct reading in latitude and longitude. A Sperry autopilot meant that, except when manoeuvring or in close waters, we did not need a helmsman. Another innovation was the Walport Film Service which was then being introduced on British ships. We had a good quality Bell & Howell 16mm film projector, complete with large screen and loudspeaker. A metal case contained three complete programmes including feature films, usually on three reels, and the idea was that you could run a film show about once a week, though in fact a film was usually shown somewhere on board most evenings. At main ports you could exchange your case of films for a different one or you could exchange films with another ship. Nowadays, of course, ships have unlimited television and video facilities but at the time the shipboard films were a great innovation. Another first on this ship was a small built in swimming pool abaft the funnel on the after boat deck. In hot weather it was well used!

Because of her size the ports the "Zenatia" could visit were limited and she was engaged in the crude oil run between Mena Al Ahmadi and Western Europe, the Suez Canal now being back in operation under direct Egyptian administration. Discharge ports were Rotterdam, Le Havre and Port de Bouc, near Marseilles in the South of France. We only once discharged cargo in the UK and this was at Coryton on the River Thames, but one other break was when we crossed the Atlantic to discharge at Portland, Maine, in the USA and then went down to Punta Cardon in Venezuela to load for Rotterdam. In hindsight, this sounds like a very boring and uninteresting existence but at the time it suited me. By now I had decided that I would sit for my Master's Certificate as soon as possible after I got home and then have a go at the Extra Master's Certificate. To this end I spent a lot of my spare time in the "Zenatia" studying and I got outside help with subjects such as mathematics from the Seafarers' Education Service. I also gave a lot of attention to the four apprentices' education which also helped me, although I don't think they fully appreciated my efforts at the time! On our one call in the UK I bought a portable typewriter and a little book called *Teach Yourself Typing*. I made a cardboard mask to cover the keyboard and proceeded to teach myself to touch type reasonably well, something that has been useful to me ever since. The only break from the routine and the watch-keeping came after 12 months on board when the ship returned to Cammell Lairds at Birkenhead for the "guarantee" dry-docking. We were there for three weeks and apart from runs ashore and the relief of no watch-keeping I managed to get home for six days of unofficial leave. In all, I spent 14 months in the "Zenatia", two months longer than I need have done but I wanted to complete the required seatime for my Master's Certificate before I went on leave again.

With regard to time-keeping, Captain Hanson's peculiarity was that the clocks should be advanced or retarded 30 minutes at a time, rather than the more sensible hour. It was one of the second mate's duties to deal with the clocks and this meant that I had twice as many trips around the ship adjusting clocks than was necessary. This was always done after supper and the last clock I attended to was the one on the bulkhead over the captain's desk. In leaning over the desk I could not help but see the glass of whisky he had consumed or not consumed concealed behind a photograph of his wife. Another indicator of the captain's habits came to my notice when I went on watch at midnight at sea. If I went out onto the starboard Bridge wing to have a look around I often heard a window being opened on the deck below me and this would be followed by a bottle being thrown out and landing in the water with a *plop*.

We had the luxury of a fourth mate in this ship, a lumbering lump of a young man known as "Podge" who let his hair grow to rather an excessive length. One day in mid-Atlantic on the way to Portland the captain came on the Bridge at noon while we were fixing the position, and promptly "blew up"! "Podge" was given two days to get a haircut or "bloody well get off the ship". One of the firemen obliged that evening and "Podge" was saved from having to jump overboard. On another occasion we were in the Gulf of Aden trying to fix the noon position in overcast conditions with no sun, but a number of mountain peaks were visible on the Arabian Peninsula. I was well aware that the charted positions of shore features in this area were unreliable but I was doing my best! Our captain arrived on the bridge and did not approve of the result. I was accused of being a "f***ing useless navigator" and was promptly sacked in no uncertain terms!

The third mate was a Scotsman from Coatbridge in Lanarkshire who had been a fireman on a steam locomotive for British Railways before deciding to go to sea. He was known as "Haggis" and he and I got on well together. His hairline was definitely receding and one day he confided to me that this worried him a lot. The result was an order for an expensive course of hair restoration and in due course a large box containing bottles of brightly coloured liquids plus instructions was delivered. The treatment was carried out in the greatest secrecy but although I gave "Haggis" every encouragement, I never noticed any difference!

By and large there were no incidents of note in this ship until my last outward bound voyage to the Persian Gulf in early July 1958. At Port Said we moored to buoys fore and aft while awaiting our turn in a southbound convoy. The canal seemed to be running perfectly well under the new regime but the pilotage was somewhat erratic. In the old days the Suez Canal pilots were a very elite bunch, rather like the Singapore pilots, and they were almost all either French or British. When the "emergency" occurred all of these pilots either left or were sacked and their opinion was that the canal could not operate without them. Well, it did operate and while the authorities appointed as many Egyptian pilots as they could find, any number of willing temporaries of various abilities were taken on. On this occasion we had a Greek who was somewhat excitable. While letting go of the moorings the ship drifted astern until the large after buoy was right under the stern and against the propeller. We were getting uncomfortably close to the ship astern of us and, despite being warned of the situation, the Greek persisted in ringing "Full Ahead". The result was that the buoy was wrecked and a nearby "bumboat" was overturned in the wash, fortunately without any casualties. When we tied up later in the bypass we ascertained that there was considerable damage to the propeller blades. Anyway, we were able to carry on at reduced speed for the remainder of the voyage to Mena Al Ahmadi and brought yet another cargo back to Rotterdam before the ship was dry-docked for repairs. The company received a claim from the Suez Canal Administration for the loss of the buoy and probably one for the loss of the bumboat but I have no idea what the outcome was. On 11 August I left the ship at Rotterdam and went home for a whole year!

I must have been quite determined to get on since I signed on at the Belfast Technical College as soon as I got home and started there on 1 September. I decided to sit for the Master's Examination in October so there was a serious deadline to meet. In my opinion, the scheme of things at the college was sadly lacking, despite Captain Boyd still being there, and I worked out my own timetable, leading towards the second week in October, when the exams took place. I worked at the college during the day and, with suitable breaks (including some sailing), I worked at home for two or three hours most evenings. I found the most difficult part of the Master's Syllabus the compass work and calculations. Anyone of my generation studying for master at that time will remember the difficulty in splitting "B"! There was also the deviascope, a device invented in the 19th century by a Captain Beale and on which candidates had to demonstrate their ability to find and correct the deviation on a ship's magnetic compass. By means of hidden magnets underneath the deck of this thing, sadistic examiners could make the task extremely difficult!

Anyway, I went up for the examination in October and passed all but the signals, which I got a month later and so became a master mariner! I took a two-week break and then started work on Part A of the Extra Master Syllabus. This was the "easy" part with four papers on such subjects as Commercial and Legal Knowledge, Meteorology and Oceanography, Chart Construction and Hydrographic Surveying and Ship Construction. At this time I was the only Extra Master student and the college could not offer any serious tuition but I signed on there anyway, sat in with the masters and mates and worked through a correspondence course provided by the marine college in Liverpool. If for no other reason, I had to be on a full-time educational course after my leave and study leave ran out to qualify for the "dole" and so supplement my modest savings. It also meant there was some discipline to my efforts although I still worked away at home most evenings.

In February of 1959 I got some company when Frank Stolberger, a second mate with the BP Tanker Company, joined me at the college. He was already about halfway through a correspondence course with Sir John Cass College in London, so we were at about the same stage. In addition to our efforts at the college, we made a nuisance of ourselves at the Custom House which, apart from HM Customs, also housed the Mercantile Marine Office, the Marine Survey Office and the Exam Centre. Here we could learn some commercial and legal knowledge at first hand and likewise we learned about the ship construction as currently practised in the Harland & Wolff Shipyard. Once we became known, we found most people very helpful.

My social life during this year ashore followed much the same pattern as on earlier leaves but went on longer. First there was bitter disappointment when my girlfriend from my last leave decided a rough sailor was not for her! However, there followed two other nurses from the same stable (The Royal Victoria Hospital) and then a young neighbour of my friend John who was a medical secretary in the same establishment. Since I was home until mid-August there was plenty of sailing once the season started in various Holywood boats. One evening in June I was racing in "La Golondrina" and John was on the helm. We had four other crew on board – all female, including my girlfriend. Conditions were fresh and a sudden squall heeled us over until the lee gunwale was under water. For some reason the mainsheet could not be freed and the boat simply filled with water and sank under us. The water was about 12 feet deep so we were able to cling to the top of the mast and comfort each other until help arrived. Unfortunately, the first boat on the scene was an unknown motor boat from Carrickfergus, whose owner then went and told the story to the press. The next morning we featured in all the local papers and even in the Daily Mail, and there was something about me saving a girl whose lifejacket failed to inflate – it wasn't an inflatable lifejacket! At low water that night John and I simply walked out to the boat, baled her out and walked her back in to her mooring as the tide rose. I was late getting to the college the next morning and entered the classroom to loud cheers from all hands!

In early July Frank and I spent two days at the Custom House sitting the Part A written examination and a third day for the orals. The orals were the easiest part but there were not many Extra candidates, especially in Belfast – I think we were the first – and I think the examiner just could not think of anything heavy and meaty to ask us! In fact he was in a very affable mood! By the end of July we learned that we had both passed, which was a relief.

It was now time to get back to sea and replenish the coffers before attempting the next part. Frank returned to BP and I returned to Shell, being appointed second mate of the "Asprella" in early August. This was another new ship, fitting out at the Kieler Howaldtswerke shipyard in Kiel, Germany, and I spent two days getting there. Now the "Asprella" was something else. She was, at 18,000 tons deadweight, a "general purpose" tanker, but she was sleek and streamlined with very attractive lines. The accommodation was also a big improvement on my previous ships and every officer had an en-suite bathroom. The air conditioning was rather more effective than that on the "Zenatia" and the bathing pool aft was just as large. She had steam turbine main machinery and was fast, averaging about 15 knots or more at full speed. The navigation equipment was all the latest, including radar and Decca Navigator. We spent a week in some sort of lodging house near the shipyard before we were able to live on board and the fare there was very simple – big platefuls of meat and potatoes plus unlimited "milch".

After successful sea trials the ship was handed over and we sailed in ballast through the Kiel Canal and round to Amsterdam, where we loaded a full cargo of fresh drinking water for Gibraltar. For a brand new ship, this was an ideal first cargo. Anyone who has been to Gibraltar will know that there are extensive corrugated iron catchments on one side of the rock to catch any rain and huge reservoirs inside the rock to store it. However, rain is scarce in the summer and, the Spanish being non co-operative, water had to be imported. Discharge was painfully slow and took four days so there were trips ashore to town and over the border to La Linea. Some of us were given a tour of the rock by the Water Department and were duly impressed by the catchments and the reservoirs inside it.

From Gibraltar we went on out to the Persian Gulf and loaded a cargo of crude oil at Mena Al Ahmadi for discharge at Eastham, on the Mersey, an uneventful six-week round trip. Our Captain Kell was a normal sort of person with no peculiarities and normally very pleasant, but the mate was a born fusser and worrier, and past the age when he should have been promoted. Other than that we seemed to have a reasonable bunch of officers and a quiet British crew. We soon settled down and life became very routine so, other than correcting the chart outfit and other off watch duties, I was able to resume my studies, experiencing most problems with maths and physics. Once again, I turned my attention to the apprentices' education as much for my own benefit as theirs. This was the first ship where we had any of the new-fangled engineer apprentices, but there seemed to be little socialising between them and their deck department counterparts!

Most of my time in the "Asprella" was spent in the western hemisphere but apart from the usual oil ports there were some interesting discharge ports such as Buenos Aires and Montevideo in South America, Freetown, Sierra Leone and Las Palmas in the Canary Islands. On Christmas Day we arrived at Kingston, Jamaica, and here there was no let-up. Mooring up took a long time in pouring rain and we immediately started discharge of cargo. Christmas dinner, such as it was, was a movable feast and I finished mine on the Poop Deck while we were mooring. New Year's Eve at Point Fortin, Trinidad was somewhat better and we even managed to have a party! A welcome break occurred in February 1960 when we returned to Kiel for the "guarantee" dry-docking.

We had two trips up the east coast of the USA, one to Perth Amboy, near New York, where I was able to visit my friends the Hickets from "Tectarious" days, and another, in August 1960, to the Penebscot River in Maine, where we discharged first at Bucksport and then at Brewer, close to Bangor. The "Asprella" was the largest ship ever to navigate the Penobscot and we received lots of attention from the local press and crowds of sightseers who came to have a look. It was not the most up-to-date oil berth at Brewer and I remember that the mooring lines were made fast to trees on the river bank! Some kind local gave the mate and me a tour around the local area which was most interesting. Bangor was somewhat smaller than Bangor, Co. Down, and nearby Belfast was smaller still!

Perhaps the highlight on this ship was our visit to Turku, Finland in early April 1960. We actually loaded the cargo at Bandar Mashur, near Abadan in Iran and it took us almost a month to reach Turku, including passages through the Suez and Kiel Canals. This was the only time I was in the Baltic until I was there in my own boat nearly 40 years later! Some miles to seaward of Uto Light, which is the pilot station for Turku, we encountered unbroken ice and hove to. The ship was not strengthened for navigation in ice and we waited until an icebreaker came out to lead us in. The pilot came out in a motor car rather than a boat and we put over an ordinary ladder rather than the pilot ladder for him to climb aboard. We then followed the icebreaker through the ice and through tortuous channels between islands and rocks until we arrived off Turku. Here we anchored, although it hardly seemed necessary, and the Customs and other officials came out in cars and on motorbikes over the ice! Later there were football games on the ice and some of us went off for long walks! When we did berth discharge took three days and there was time to visit the town with its well-paved roads and modern trams and buses. We found very good shops, bars and restaurants – and very attractive girls!

My only complaint about the "Asprella" was the food, which despite several different cooks and more than one chief steward, was always indifferent. For cold meat dishes there was never anything on offer but salami and such like, never a decent slice of ham or even corned beef. We never had a chicken breast, just legs and wings, and chickens became known as "chicacentipedes"! I think Shell was just having a blitz on the cost of catering but it did nothing for crew morale. Anyway, we arrived at Le Havre on 25 August with a cargo of crude oil from Puerto Miranda in Venezuela and I paid off, having been on the ship for just over a year. I was home by the 27th for another year ashore and hopefully success with the rest of the Extra Master Examination. My friend Frank Stolberger arrived home at virtually the same time and we started work at the College of Technology on 5 September 1960.

CHAPTER 7: DEPARTURE FROM SHELL...

This time round the College of Technology pulled out all the stops to cope with Extra Masters, especially since there were one or two other possible students in the offing. While we had been away at sea for a year the Marine School had relocated to its own dedicated premises, a redundant primary school in Blythe Street, off the famous Sandy Row. This must have been the heyday for the school since it even had a class of pre-sea cadets who had to wear uniform and muster in the yard each morning! There were well enough qualified general staff to cope with our purely nautical subjects and specialist staff from the main college helped us with mathematics, physics and electricity. Captain Boyd, although near retirement, was still there and dealt with ship stability and hydrostatics admirably, although I doubt if he had ever had to cope with this subject to such a high level before! I have met many people since who had no trouble at all with the Extra Examination and more recently such people have obtained BSc or MSc degrees. However, I found it very heavy going, especially the maths and applied maths. The calculus was especially difficult and I never did understand the Binomial Theorem! My friend Frank found it all equally difficult but we persevered despite frequent bouts of depression. Our one break at college was on Friday afternoons when we spent an hour doing the football pools. (We never won more than a few shillings!)

For this year ashore I bought a motor scooter, the first vehicle I owned, mainly for daily travel to and from school, but in Easter 1961 I took it over to England and covered many miles visiting friends and relations. For the serious business of taking out girlfriends I still had the use of the family car, at this time a "Standard 8". My relationship with the medical secretary continued for a while and then fizzled out, after which there was another nurse from the Royal Victoria Hospital. This was another one I became very fond of but she decided to go to sea herself and got a job as a nursing sister on a P&O liner, where she soon got involved with and eventually married some suave junior officer. Having experienced life on two P&O passenger ships myself, I should have known what to expect! Sailing activities at Holywood resumed in the spring but "La Golondrina" was out of commission since John was getting married in June and had more important things to attend to. However, I got to sail an

73

early GP14 called "Titwillow" which was so heavily built that it was incapable of winning anything, despite a competent crew!

In March Frank and I had a "dummy run" at the Part B examination and, inevitably, came down miserably. We made the serious attempt at the next examination session in July and, despite serious misgivings, eventually learned that we had both passed in four of the five subjects and had been referred in Mathematics at 70%. What this meant was that we had to resit this paper within the next twelve months and score 70% to pass, otherwise we would lose the whole examination! We both decided to go back to sea for six months and then spend six months of mathematical misery before attempting the resit. By this time I was seriously considering my future and options if I passed for Extra Master. I decided that I didn't want to spend the rest of my working life going to sea in tankers; my ambition was to command a ship and really earn the title of captain. I contacted Shell to discover that I was No.30 something in seniority on the second mate's list and promotion to mate was unlikely for three or four years at least. As for command, it looked as though I could reach 40 or more before I was anywhere near it, with a long period as first mate before that.

At that time there was a daily shipping paper called the "Liverpool Journal of Commerce" which was available at college and which we scanned avidly. One section listed virtually every British deep-sea shipping company, the ships they operated and their latest movements. There were also advertisements for seagoing staff. It was well known that the smaller companies often could not afford to keep a regular bunch of officers and often they had to make do with the rejects from the larger concerns, or take whatever was available from the Merchant Navy Establishment, or the "Pool", as it was known. I noticed one such company, Stevinson Hardy & Co., that ran three tankers, one of which was actually a Shell-built tanker and on demise or long-term charter to Shell. The other two were owned by the British Oil Shipping Co. and were on time charter (that is, for a limited period) to Shell but managed by Stevinson Hardy. British Oil Shipping was owned by Charles Clore, who was better known for his involvement in the shoe business, notably Saxone and some other chain shoe stores. Its two ships were named "Vivien Louise" after Clore's daughter and "Alan Evelyn" after his son.

I contacted Stevinson Hardy, who were advertising for first and second mates, and was invited to London for an interview, whereupon I was offered the first mate's job on the "Alan Evelyn". I then had to walk round the corner to Shell and ask them to give me early release from my present contract with them. This became almost a tearful occasion when the very persuasive personnel manager pointed out that I was giving up what could be a brilliant career with Shell! I might have had my own doubts but I left anyway and in view of what happened a few years later, I had no reason for any remorse. When the huge decline in the British Flag merchant fleet began the oil companies were not slow to react. The Shell fleet was greatly reduced and what was left was mostly "flagged out" to places like the Isle of Man and the Bahamas. Long-serving and loyal officers were suddenly made redundant or offered very inferior conditions of service under offshore marine manning companies. British ratings and junior officers were replaced by cheap and poorly trained Filipinos.

On 15 August, 1961 I set off for Rotterdam and joined the "Alan Evelyn" there as first mate on the 19th. She had been built in 1957 at the Furness Shipbuilding Yard on the River Tees and was of the attractive design I had admired in a number of London Greek tankers. She was 32,000 tons deadweight and the second largest ship I had ever sailed in. Apart from the "Asprella", the accommodation was far superior to what I had been used to in Shell and the standard of food was very good. I found a mixed bunch of British officers and, a first for me, Indian ratings, nearly all of whom had been aboard for a long time and were overdue for leave. The captain was Arnold Asquith Tully from South Shields, a middle-aged man who, like many a Shell captain, took little interest in what was going on as long as everything was going smoothly! The second mate was a young man who still had to pass his Master's Ticket but the third mate was an old timer who had neither the ability nor the inclination to progress any further. For some reason he was known as the "Professor" and he had frequent shouting matches with the captain, with whom he had sailed on other ships, including some during the War, I think. Anyway, there was some longstanding animosity between them which did not bother me.

After discharge of cargo we sailed for Mena Al Ahmadi to load crude oil for Thameshaven and I was pleased to find that I soon settled into my new duties and responsibilities as mate very easily. The Indian crew were a delight and there was seldom any trouble with them, but unfortunately at Mena Al Ahmadi they went on leave and were replaced by a completely new crew. It took about six heavy lorries to remove the old crew from the ship, together with all the items they had acquired in the past year or so. These included numerous second hand bicycles, sewing machines and other mechanical items, all of great value in their home villages.

In the good old days of the "Raj", to recruit a crew for a ship it was only necessary to appoint a "serang" (or bosun) through some agent ashore. The bosun got his "cut" and then recruited the rest of the crew, mostly his own relatives and friends from his own village, who would of course have to pay him a commission. However, in modern India things were changing and there was now an Indian "pool" and even seamen's unions, although despite the Government's efforts the old caste system and serious religious differences prevailed. I soon discovered that the Serang in our new deck crew was a Hindu, while the rest of them were Muslims. The Serang was therefore virtually a pariah and the crew would have nothing to do with him! When I gave him any orders or instructions about work to be done on deck, he had to pass them on to the Cassab, or Deck Storekeeper, who would then pass them on to the crew! This crew were also devout Muslims who prayed four times a day to Mecca. I well remember on more than one occasion, when we were ready to go to "stations" for sailing, being informed by the serang that the crew were praying and there would be a slight delay!

The catering crew were all Goanese and staunch Roman Catholics with Portuguese names like De Sousa and Fernandes. They had even converted a spare cabin aft into a small chapel. There were two galleys aft, European and Asian and the Deck and Engine Room ratings each had their own cook in the Asian one. The ratings also had quite comfortable accommodation aft, with only two of them to a room and ample toilet facilities, fitted out with the "thunderbox" arrangement required for Indian crews. One thing which this new crew brought with them was urethritis, an inflammation of the urinary system sometimes connected with venereal diseases. Apparently it was endemic in their part of India. As soon as we got back to Thameshaven a large number of the crew requested a visit to the doctor and a bus was needed to take them there and bring them back! They all returned bearing paper bags of medicines and had big smiles on their faces. To my inquiry, the answer was "Sahib" – injection!" Well, since Captain Tully took no interest in medical matters on board it fell to me to deal with this matter. In fact each of these patients was to have a daily injection of penicillin for a period of about ten days and this took some organising. I enlisted the help of the third mate and the daily injection session took place in the ship's hospital after lunch each day. The third mate attended to the sterilizer and maintained a supply of sterile needles and syringes. The crew lined up outside on the deck and came in one at a time to drop their pants and bend over the table. As per the Ship Captain's Medical Guide, intramuscular injections were given in the upper outer quadrant of a buttock where there should be plenty of muscle. However, since some of our crew were rather scrawny, there wasn't even much buttock to aim at, plus the syringes and needles we had were more like something a vet would use! However, there were no complaints and before long I was an expert at the injection business!

In the six months I was in the "Alan Evelyn" we loaded crude oil at Mena Al Ahmadi and Umm Said in the Persian Gulf for discharge at Thameshaven, Rotterdam and Hamburg, and finally made a trip across the Atlantic to Puerto Miranda in Venezuela to load for Thameshaven and Rotterdam. While the captain was never too much in evidence, the chief engineer had to work hard since the second engineer and those below him could perhaps be described as indifferent! However the ship was only four years old and ran smoothly enough with few breakdowns. Her average speed was usually 15 or 16 knots.

The first mate in any ship does not have much spare time but any time I did have was spent studying Mathematics and working through endless practice and old question papers! On the first Sunday morning at sea I asked the captain if he intended to make the statutory inspection of the accommodation and storerooms. He claimed to have a cold and asked me to do it with the chief engineer. The chief claimed to be busy in the engine room and so this left me to do the inspection, together with the Indian purser. When we reached the crew accommodation aft, I felt like the Duke of Edinburgh inspecting a guard of honour! The crew were all lined up in a neat row outside their cabin doors and bowed as we went in followed at a respectful distance by the deck and engine serangs!

Our captain was not great on statutory emergency drills either but I organised lifeboat and fire drills on Saturday mornings at sea and the captain sometimes appeared briefly on the Bridge. At muster stations the Indians again stood in a neat line and recited their boat number and duty perfectly but I had doubts as to just how effective they would be in a real emergency! As with a Chinese crew, we had dedicated helmsmen or quartermasters, known as secunnies, but with the autopilot in use at sea they were mostly engaged in other duties around the Bridge. Below them in rank were the day working sailors, known as kalassies, and lowest of the low were the two topaz, or sweepers, one on deck and the other for the Engine Room. In this ship they shared a cabin but in older ships they would have slept anywhere, usually in a storeroom. They did all the dirty work which no-one else would touch, such as sweeping up the mess when the crew were chipping rust on the decks and only they could clean the toilets and bathrooms.

There were a number of occasions when I really wondered about the Captain's lack of interest in the running of the ship and one of these was while we were transitting the Suez Canal. I was on the Bridge together with an Egyptian pilot and a secunny on the wheel when we ran into a dense sandstorm and the visibility was reduced to near zero. The pilot asked for the captain to come to the Bridge. I got no response from the telephone nor the voice pipe to his bedroom, so I went below to find him fast asleep in bed. Having managed to rouse him, the only response I got was: "What do you need me for?" By this time, if I'd had any doubts about my own potential ability to command a ship, they were disappearing fast!

On 15 February, 1962, we arrived at Rotterdam via Thameshaven to complete discharge of the Puerto Miranda cargo, then proceeded to a tank-cleaning berth before going into dry-dock at the Wilton Shipyard – where the "Spondilus" had been built in 1927! I remained with the ship for another month to see her through the dry-docking and while Captain Tully went home on leave. This was a pleasant time with some good "nights out", courtesy of various contractors, and visits to and from my friends at the Flying Angel Mission in Pernis. On 13 March I left the ship and travelled home to resume a full-time assault on Extra Master Mathematics!

On my arrival home I signed on right away at the Marine College and worked away both there and at home. The main college sent a Maths tutor two or three times a week but even with his help it was still heavy going for me and the Binomial Therom remained a mystery! My friend Frank did not show up until early in May, when I discovered he had suddenly got married during a few days' leave a couple of months earlier! At least I now had company in my efforts.

My social life was limited and the main event most weeks was a visit to Caproni's Ballroom in Bangor on a Saturday night. However, at Easter I took a week off to tour around England on my scooter, visiting friends and relations, and there was some sailing at Holywood Yacht Club once the season started, but my mind was set on the crucial Maths exam, and little else! On Monday 9 July, we duly appeared at the Custom House and sat the exam and immediately afterwards went to see the college Maths tutor, Mr. Black. He went through the question paper with us and thought we had probably reached the critical 70% to pass. Nevertheless, doubts remained in my mind!

I now telephoned Stevinson Hardy to tell them I was available for service, only to be told that the "Alan Evelyn" and the "Vivien Louise" had been taken out of their management and given to Denholms of Glasgow, leaving them only with the "Edward Stevinson", and no job for me at present. What to do? I got hold of the "Liverpool Journal of Commerce", picked out about twelve likely small companies and wrote to them all, offering my services! They all eventually replied and all offered me something, but before that the telephone rang two days later. It was Evan Thomas Radcliffe & Co. of Cardiff: could I join their "Llanishen" as Chief Officer at Tranmere on the Mersey in two days time? I gave the matter an hour's thought and then phoned back to accept.

Radcliffes were a famous old British trampship company who before the War had quite a large fleet of ships. One of their main trades was coal out to the River Plate in Argentina and grain home. I soon found that they now had five ships, including two dry cargo ships, the "Llantrisant" and the "Llanwern". The other three were tankers, two of which were 32,000 ton Shell-built ships on demise charter to Shell. These were the "Llanishen" and the "Llangorse". The third was the "Hamilton", a 20,000 ton products carrier built in Belgium in 1960 and owned, I believe, by a consortium of industrialists in Leeds. The registered owner was the Hamilton Shipping Company of Hamilton, Bermuda, but her port of registry was London. She was on a seven-year time charter to Shell and was managed by Radcliffes. As I discovered when I came to sail in her, she was on a very good charter rate and the owners were doing very nicely out of it!

CHAPTER 8: ... AND QUICKER PROMOTION

Sunday 22 July, 1962, found me joining the "Llanishen" at Tranmere Oil Terminal on the Mersey. I met the engineer superintendent, signed on, and that was all there was to it. I also met the chief officer I was relieving, who was asleep on the floor in his dayroom. Apart from the captain, there was an almost complete change of officers and crew. Captain Kattenburg, a man in his early to mid-50s, was an Estonian, naturalised British with a British wife, and a background of invasion and persecution in Estonia before he found peace in the UK after the war. Occasionally I was able to coax a little bit of history out of him.

My first two days were pretty hectic, getting settled in and discharging the crude oil cargo. We completed discharge at Eastham Oil Dock at the entrance to the Manchester Ship Canal and then sailed for the Persian Gulf. I soon settled in and the shipboard routine was much the same as on any other ship I had sailed in. As chief officer I kept the 0400 to 0800 watch and was also responsible for all cargo work, including the inevitable tank cleaning on ballast passages. On deck maintenance and keeping the deck crew occupied usefully took quite a lot of time. The other officers were generally a pleasant and competent lot and the "Liverpool crowd" (the ratings) who had signed on at Tranmere were average. However the Chief Engineer, who had previously sailed in Orient Line passenger ships, had a serious problem and the second engineer was a hothead, with no sense of tact or diplomacy whatever. This led to trouble later.

On 4 August, just after we had passed through the Suez Canal "sparks" (the radio officer) handed me a message from my parents to say they had received notification from the Board of Trade advising that I had passed the examination. I was now an extra master mariner but really there was no great sense of elation, just relief that four years of effort had finally paid off! I later learned that Frank had also passed. He had simply returned to BP Tankers and was still sailing as second mate, though he eventually got promoted to chief officer and found himself on a ship trading on the New Zealand coast. Here he met some surveyors from the local marine administration and eventually joined them, emigrating to New Zealand with his wife and family. Unfortunately Frank died there at far too early an age and to my knowledge, his wife and family are still there.

However, back to the "Llanishen" and this time in the Persian Gulf we loaded crude oil at Bandar Mashur in Iran, formerly Persia. While this ship was engaged in the crude oil trade, with her modest tonnage we at least got away from the eternal Persian-Gulf-to-Western-Europe trade and this time we loaded for Montreal. The heat at the northern end of the Persian Gulf in mid-August was quite something. Fortunately the air-conditioning worked reasonably well and also we loaded the cargo during the night – about 30,000 tons between midnight and 0900. We then retraced our route back to the Suez Canal, from where it was a 14-day passage back through the Mediterranean and across the North Atlantic to the St. Lawrence. The weather was generally "fair" and I was keen to get the ship looking smart. There was thus more crew overtime than pleased the owners but I got on well with Captain Kattenberg, who did take an interest in the running of the ship. He was meticulous about weekly emergency drills and also about the Sunday inspections of the accommodation and storerooms. He was also meticulous about the Sunday lunchtime "pour out" in his dayroom after these inspections, which I rather enjoyed!

We reached Escomains on the St. Lawrence estuary to pick up a pilot on 4 September 1962, and it was a week later before we dropped the pilot outward bound. This was my first and only visit to the St. Lawrence and the run up the river was very interesting. We passed our sister ship "Llangorse", outward bound for Curacao, before reaching an anchorage close by the Chateau Frontenac at Quebec. Here we had to lighten ship by discharging 2,500 tons of cargo into the local tanker "Eastern Shell." On then to Three Rivers, where we lay at anchor for a whole day waiting for the Eastern Shell to return for another load. Finally arriving at the Montreal refinery, it took two days to discharge the remaining cargo and I even got a couple of runs ashore. One of the shore staff I dealt with brought his wife and two sons down to visit the ship and in return I got a quick conducted car tour of the city. Outward bound for Curacao we anchored for about 12 hours off Three Rivers to fill the ship with fresh water ballast, always in demand on this virtually waterless island.

My main occupation on the seven-day voyage to Curacao, apart from the routine watchkeeping, was tank cleaning, a prolonged job this time with so much fresh water ballast on board. We arrived at the refinery on St. Anna Baai to find the "Llangorse" on a nearby berth and there was much coming and going between the two ships. There had been trouble brewing in the Engine Room for some time and now it came to a head! Our "difficult" second engineer went ashore the first evening and into the nearby Seamen's Club, known to seafarers as the "Madhouse". Here he encountered a number of drunken firemen from both ships and was promptly set upon. Since we were only discharging the fresh water and then going on to Mamonal in Colombia for our next cargo, we were ready for sea at 0300 the next morning but soon found that all our deck and engine ratings were ashore and refused to sail unless the second engineer was removed! Likewise, he refused to sail with the crew so it looked as though we had some sort of mutiny on our hands!

The situation continued throughout the day with all our crew, except the Catering Dept, ashore in the "Madhouse" getting stoned out of their minds. Poor Captain Kattenberg was near demented and of course was in touch with the Shell office ashore and our office in Cardiff. I suppose the crew should have been treated as mutineers but nobody seemed to have much idea of what to do and the important thing was to get the ship to sea. Things were cleared up in the evening when the second engineer agreed to be paid off and flown home. He was replaced by the junior second engineer from the "Llangorse" and we gave them one of our junior engineers in return. We got away to sea early the next morning – with some difficulty, since most of our deck and engine ratings were very drunk and some failed to turn out at all! By the time they were sober we had arrived at Mamonal after a 26-hour passage and here they managed to get hold of cheap booze from the local "bumboats". I later discovered we were missing some tins of paint from the paint store but could not pin it on any one person or persons.

It was a relief to get away for a 13-day passage to Rotterdam where we arrived on 6 October. Many of the ratings paid off there by mutual agreement and were replaced by an assortment of Continentals, who were at least no worse than those we had got rid of. After discharge of cargo we had a day for engine maintenance and I was able to get ashore to visit my friends at the Pernis Mission for Seamen.

There followed a fairly uneventful voyage out to the Persian Gulf where we loaded another crude oil cargo for La Spezia, in Italy. With a slow discharge and two days in port I managed an evening ashore with the second mate. Quite a lot of local booze seemed to find its way on board and many of the ratings were under the weather when we came to sail. However, there was no trouble, which was something! Then it was back out to Mena Al Ahmadi where this time we loaded for Geelong, which is across Port Phillip Bay from Melbourne, in Australia. On instructions from Shell we had been mainly sailing at reduced speed, with one boiler shut down, for some time. Average speed was down to about 10 knots and this made long boring voyages even more boring! However, we were now told to resume full speed but even so, at 15 or 16 knots, it was a three-week passage to Geelong with only 30 hours in port at the end of it! Christmas Day was spent in the Great Australian Bight, without any serious incident and we reached port on 27 December. I managed to get perhaps three hours ashore here!

The ballast passage back to Mena Al Ahmadi took 20 days, where we discharged ballast and loaded a full cargo of crude oil in less than 15 hours! At least we were now homeward bound and were due for dry-docking after discharge of this cargo. Another uneventful passage saw us in Antwerp by 6 February. This place, which I had not visited before, did not impress me. The approach channels from the pilot station at Flushing in Holland were tortuous for a ship of our size, the River Schelde uninteresting, and we had to go through locks to reach the oil berths. I was too busy with preparations for dry-docking to even think of going ashore! As soon as the cargo was out there was a virtual non-stop tank cleaning job which continued until we reached the River Tyne. Here we berthed at North Shields to complete the job and discharge the slops before proceeding up river to Swan Hunters repair berth on 11 February.

After almost seven months of continual watchkeeping, long tedious voyages and no more than a few hours ashore, it was a relief to be able to go ashore in the evenings and then get a full night's sleep. I spent my first evening in the New Dock Inn, Wallsend, just outside the dockyard gate and those of us there could let our hair down. Poor Captain Kattenberg was stuck on board struggling with the accounts ready for paying off the whole crew the next morning. For those of us who remained on the ship through the docking period, the New Dock Inn was usually as far as we got. It had plenty of atmosphere plus music, singing and dancing.

The weather early in 1963 was very severe with heavy snow which lay for weeks, which did not help with work on the outside of the ship, particularly the painting of the hull and decks, but the job got done despite the weather. There were several changes among the officers and Captain Kattenberg went on a well-deserved leave. He was replaced by Captain Rice, a pleasant middle-aged man who was known as "Daddy" Rice. I did manage to get home for four days about halfway through the docking. At Wallsend I had a visit from "Doctor" Dale, who had been mate on the "Spondilus". Family life had made him give up the seagoing life and he was now working as a sales rep. for Michelin Tyres. He later trained as a probation officer and spent the rest of his working life in that profession.

The weather on the Tyne remained bitterly cold and we had trouble with frozen fresh water pipes and lack of heating steam from a shore boiler. However, repair and maintenance work proceeded more or less satisfactorily and on 27 February 1963, we departed Wallsend for where else but dear old Mena Al Ahmadi! Much of my efforts during this passage were spent getting the ship cleaned up after dry-dock. The new captain was quite a chatty soul, but other than that not very sociable. We had regular emergency drills and Sunday morning inspection but there was no "pour out" to follow!

Arriving at Mena on 18 March we were put on a "slow" loading berth so that deballasting and loading took nearly 24 hours. Our cargo was for Thameshaven and when we got there I anticipated going home on leave. The chief officer I had met on the "Llangorse" at Curacao, Mr. Crighton, was presently on leave and was due to relieve me. However, a big surprise came on 23 March while we were off the coast of Oman. Captain Rice handed me a message he had received from Radcliffes, offering me the master's job in the "Hamilton", provided I could join her on the Tyne by 12 April. It took me about five minutes to take this in and accept their offer! I was not going to miss this golden opportunity and the leave could wait! I soon found out the reason for my good luck: Captain Kattenburg, who had been home on leave and was due to join the "Hamilton", had simply collapsed one morning and died of a heart attack. I was very sorry to hear this and while I was keen to get a command, I would not have wished it to be under these circumstances.

We duly reached Thameshaven late on 6 April and started discharge. The next morning various reliefs turned up, including Mr. Crighton to relieve me. That afternoon I travelled up to London by taxi along with the second engineer and third mate who were going on leave. I dispatched my heavy baggage from Kings Cross to

Newcastle and then caught a train from Paddington to Cardiff, where I spent the night at the Merchant Navy Hotel. By 0900 the next morning I reported to Radcliffes' office – Empire House, Mountstewart Square – which was right in the middle of "Tiger Bay" in the docks area. Here I spent the day being brainwashed by two of the directors and the chief accountant but they were all very pleasant and even took me out to lunch at a fancy restaurant. At some stage I managed to slip out to a local naval outfitters and bought a set of four stripes for my uniform jacket, plus a pair of epaulettes, also with four stripes. I never did own a uniform cap with "scrambled egg" on the peak!

By 1730 I was on my way to Newcastle via Liverpool in an eight-seater De Havilland Dove, operated by Dan Air. At Newcastle Airport I was met by a taxi and taken straight to the "Hamilton" at Swan Hunters' Yard, Wallsend, where I boarded the ship at about 2200. When I had sailed from here on 27 February in the "Llanishen", little did I think I would be back six weeks later to take command of a ship! I met Captain Owen Ffoulkes, who was going on leave. He was a real Welsh Welshman, apparently had a fiery temper and was given to frequent tantrums. But with me he was very pleasant!

The next day was very busy as the ship was almost ready to sail with virtually all repair work completed. First it was up to the Custom House in Newcastle with the agent to have my name entered on the ship's register, whereupon I officially became master of m.v. "Hamilton". I felt very pleased and proud of myself! After that it was back to the ship to go through the necessary paperwork involved in the handover, including checking and taking over all the bonded stores. The officers and crew were all on board and at first sight seemed a reasonable bunch. I was particularly lucky with the chief officer, Joe James, who was about my age and a very steady, competent young man. The second mate was also young and reasonably sound but the third mate was one J. Brown, aged about 55, who had been second mate on the "Llanishen" for the first couple of months I was in that ship, and was not totally reliable. The chief engineer was Clarence W. who had also been in the "Llanishen" for a while, and he was a character! He had served as chief engineer with Cunard White Star on the "Queens" and, being RNR, had served on several famous battleships during the War. Having reached retirement age with Cunard, he had no wish to retire and ended up with Radcliffes. Experienced and fully certificated engineers were hard to find for the smaller companies and indeed some quite unsuitable people were often employed simply because they had the necessary certificate of competency. However, Clarence was perfectly sound, despite now being almost 70 years old. He had a wife and apparently lived on an extensive estate in Cumbria but we thought perhaps he had an unhappy home life! He was also a "dirty old man", as I was soon to discover! The second engineer was a young man with a young wife who was sailing with us. She became the subject of the chief's unwelcome attentions before long.

The "Hamilton" had been built in 1960 at the Jos Boel Shipyard, Temise, Belgium, to a Norwegian design, so she was only three years old and, since new, was on a seven-year time charter to Shell. She was almost 20,000 tons deadweight but for trading purposes Shell treated her the same as their own 18,000 ton "H" and "A" class tankers. This meant that it was sometimes a tight fit to get into ports and berths that were an easy fit for the slightly smaller Shell-owned vessels. The "Hamilton" had a 9,000 bhp Sultzer diesel engine which pushed her along at 15 to 16 knots in all but the most severe weather. Unlike the large crude oil carriers, the ports we could visit were much less limited and this made for a more interesting pattern of trade. She was still a "white oil" carrier which meant that we carried various "white" cargoes such as motor gasoline, kerosine, white spirit and diesel oil, usually several grades at once.

The ship's accommodation layout, apart from an extra engineers deck aft, was as originally designed. Thus in the amidships block the captain's accommodation occupied the whole deck immediately below the Bridge and comprised dayroom, bedroom with double bed and en suite bathroom\shower, dining-room, office and pantry. The only other accommodation on this deck was the owner's suite which was also quite comfortably furnished. It was used for pilots, superintendents, and such like when necessary. Had she been Norwegian flag, the elite in the crew, i.e. the captain, chief officer and chief engineer, would have dined in the Captain's Dining Room and all other officers would have dined in the Officers' Messroom in the aft accommodation block, with its adjacent Lounge\Smokeroom. But we followed the British fashion and all officers ate in the messroom aft. The seating order at the table was much the same as in any other ships I had sailed in, with the captain at the head of the table, deck officers in order of rank down one side and engineers down the other. I found that the captain's midships dining-room, immediately adjacent to the office, was a suitable place for dealing with the numerous officials and other shore personnel who came on board immediately after arrival in most ports and required the captain's undivided attention. With a little practice I got it well organised with the necessary paperwork for Customs, Immigration, Port Authority, Ship's Agent, etc. laid out around the table before their arrival.

The second steward in those days of large crews was also the Captain's "tiger" and the first one I had was great! Albert had served in large passenger ships but had come unstuck due to indiscretions. He was, as we used to say at sea, "as queer as a canteen cockroach", and his boyfriend on this ship was one of the rougher firemen. When the shore tribe arrived on board, and found their way up to my quarters, Albert would be standing at the door of the dining room ready to show them to their seats and inquire as to their preference for drinks. He always wore an immaculate white jacket and had an equally immaculate tea towel over his arm. This inevitably got sometimes delicate negotiations off to a good start, especially in South American ports.

Our orders had been to proceed to Rotterdam but just before sailing were changed to Curacao, for which I was thankful, since the 12-day voyage would give me time to settle in and find my feet. We got away after some delay on 11 April, and after fog in the North Sea we had an uneventful passage through Dover Strait, long before the separation zones were established, and down the English Channel. We then had a clear run across to Curacao where we arrived on 23 April 1963. The navigation was in the good old-fashioned way, with daily sights and plottings by the deck officers, with a "Noon Report" to myself. I started off as I meant to continue with the emergency drills on Saturday mornings and full inspection of the ship on Sunday mornings. Following Sunday morning inspections I had a "pour out" for the senior officers, and I never had anyone let me down on these occasions.

We duly made it through Mona Passage, between Puerto Rico and Dominica, to reach Curacao on 23 April. Here we loaded diesel oil and a part refined grade of gasoline for Thameshaven. There was little crew trouble in port and only three "loggings" for failure to turn out on duty when we sailed. However, the local British Consul lumbered me with three "DBS" (Distressed British Seamen) to take back to the UK. As usual, these men had either missed their

87

ship or been paid off sick abroad. The passage back was uneventful but since we were returning to the UK I was faced with closure of the "Articles of Agreement" with the whole crew, and which had only been opened at Wallsend. This involved a full "pay off" and then signing on a whole new crew, whether any of them remained from the current voyage or not. At that time I think the crew and other accounts in the average merchant ship were the captain's biggest headache! All the daily hassle and problems that occurred were one thing, but the accounts were something else!

Radcliffes were still very old-fashioned in some of their methods, especially regarding the accounts. Basically they employed the master and the master then employed the officers and crew, drawing money from the owners as necessary to make the necessary payments. In some ways this was to my advantage especially since the ordering and sale or other disposal of "bonded" stores was entirely my business. It was not to my advantage when a crew member went missing or had to be paid off sick just before sailing from some port and I sometimes had to work out his "pay off" in the middle of the night! Seamen's wages calculations compared to shore employees were extremely complicated – not just income tax, national insurance, pension and Union contributions, but weekly or monthly allotments to family or whoever, leave pay, advances in foreign ports, postage, "bumboat" accounts plus any fines and forfeitures. After a closure of "Articles" such as I was now facing, I had to reconcile my account with the owners and produce a monumental statement known as a portage bill, plus income tax, national insurance and other returns. Hopefully at the end of all this, Radcliffes owed me money and not vice versa. However, first I had to estimate the pay off date and work out some 50 separate accounts of wages for that date. This was always done initially in pencil with good reason. On this occasion I had estimated pay off at Thameshaven on 7 May and worked everything out for that date, but on 2 May we received orders to discharge part cargo at Rotterdam before going to Thameshaven and that meant starting all over again for a later date! Even one day either side of the estimated date can make a big difference to the whole calculation and not just one day's pay. Income tax, national insurance and almost all the components of an account can be affected. Late changes just before arrival in port were a nightmare! The only aid I had was a mechanical adding machine, as modern personal computers had not been invented!

We duly reached Rotterdam on 6 May where we actually spent four days, discharging part of the Curacao cargo and loading three other grades for Thameshaven. This really screwed up the accounts and I virtually had to go back to square one. Radcliffes had sent a young man over from the office to help out but all he would do was check my figures and refused to do any original calculations. Despite all this I managed to get ashore most days. But poor Joe, the mate, was virtually full time on cargo operations and was lucky to get any sleep at all! It was only a six-hour run from the Hook of Holland pilot station across to the Thames pilot station near the Sunk Lightship so I just stayed on the Bridge and gave Joe and the other two mates a chance to grab some sleep.

At Thameshaven we were visited by Radcliffe's engineer superintendent, which was normal, but also by one of the directors, who had obviously come to check that I was coping with the job. The pay off was an extremely busy time for me but all went well and we got the old crew paid off on the morning after arrival and the new crew signed on the same afternoon. After discharge of the cargo, at three different berths, it was back to Rotterdam to clean tanks and load gas oil and aviation gasoline for Hamburg. On the second day there Van Ommerens, the Shell agents, put a car and driver at my disposal and I decided the backlog of accounts work could wait. Together with Clarence, the chief engineer and Mrs. Lennon, the second engineer's wife, I had a splendid all-day tour, visiting the Hague, Scheveningen, Delft, Maduroland and lots of Dutch bulbfields! I noted that Clarence was on his best behaviour all day!

Again on the passage round to Hamburg I stayed on the Bridge virtually the whole way, giving the mates a break for much needed sleep. I would have been there anyway for this overnight passage since we were following the "NEMEDRI" buoyed routes off the coast, the traffic was heavy in both directions and, to help matters, we also had some fog. NEMEDRI stands for North European and Mediterranean Routing Instructions and these buoyed routes were laid out after the War through the cleared areas of the numerous minefields. These routes were so satisfactory in providing "roadways" for ships in areas of heavy traffic that they are still in use today and have even been greatly extended to include the modern day separation zones.

After two weeks of intense activity it was a relief to be sent back out to Curacao in ballast and on this trip I got all up-to-date on paper work and accounts, including the wretched portage bill for the previous voyage. We loaded three grades of cargo on two different berths and then went to nearby Punta Cardon in Venezuela to load two more grades. The destination for this lot was Rotterdam and Thameshaven so I had to start thinking about another pay off! We reached Rotterdam on 16 June, and there now began another period of intense activity, this time lasting for over a month, during which we visited the following ports – Rotterdam, Thameshaven, Shellhaven, Teesport, Saltend, Killingholme, Shellhaven, Jarrow-on-Tyne, Sunderland, Thameshaven, and Rotterdam, in that order. Our discharge ports were all on the north-east coast of England. Joe, the mate, grew exhausted with the continual cargo work in port while I got exhausted with the never-ending changes in the crew and the never-ending paper work and accounts. A deep-sea tanker with a supposedly deep-sea crew working on the home coast is hard going, at least for the captain and chief officer. The passages between ports were too short for any relaxation and I spent most of the time on the Bridge, usually in heavy traffic and often with fog for good measure! There were crew problems every day. At about 0100 one morning, a very drunk seaman came banging on my door, demanding to be paid off immediately. He was so drunk that he fell backwards down a staircase and ended up going ashore again on a stretcher. The next day he made it back to the ship, on crutches, and I duly paid him off!

I managed to get ashore at every port, either on ship's business or pleasure, usually both. Clarence, the chief engineer, was long overdue for leave but no relief could be found for him. He did persuade me to take him ashore with me on numerous occasions and I soon discovered that he knew every low-down dive there was in or near the ports we visited. The Corporation Hotel in Sunderland is one that comes to mind.

In the end the Second Engineer, Mike Lennon, was promoted to chief and the uncertificated third engineer was granted a "dispensation" by a local Board of Trade Engineer Examiner to sail as second. Clarence left us at Thameshaven in mid-July and so did Mrs. Lennon, for which I was thankful. Clarence was now 70 and surely his seagoing career had to be over. A week later in Rotterdam, we had occasion to telephone him at home with some query about engine room records, only to learn that he had not yet arrived home!

One good thing on a time charter ship is that the charter usually allows the ship to take 48 hours out of service for engine maintenance about every three or four months. Towards the end of this intensive coastal trading period we spent 48 hours at anchor off Southend. I think I spent much of this time asleep and the rest tackling the vast backlog of paperwork and accounts! Our last coastal cargo was from Thameshaven to Rotterdam with a cargo called waxy distillate. The ship had now been switched from "clean" oil to "black" oil – crude oil, heavy fuel oil and suchlike.

Leaving Rotterdam on 18 July, we headed back to Curacao in ballast and after a week at sea I was up-to-date with paperwork and accounts while the Mate was up-to-date with tank cleaning! However, we didn't make it to Cuacao, being diverted instead to Port of Spain, Trinidad, for bunkers and then on to nearby Puerto La Cruz in Venezuela. Here we loaded a full cargo of crude oil for the Richmond Oil Co. refinery at Yorktown, Virginia. Here I also cut my teeth on preparing and typing out USA crew lists, which were very complex and the least mistake resulted in all sorts of trouble. These had to be verified by a US consul and sent on ahead of the ship. The local agents were very little help and I spent almost the whole time in port on this task. Fortunately, as I found in most Venezuelan ports, the local Customs and Immigration people were no trouble at all provided they got their initial backhanders of cartons of cigarettes and bottles of booze. After that they would buy any amount of the same at a price which gave me a good profit but was dirt cheap to them. No doubt they made a fortune on resale ashore. They even put in their orders for which brands they would prefer when I came to restocking the bonded stores!

During the passage north to Chesapeake Bay and Yorktown, the second engineer went "down the drain" shortly after sailing. This particular gent had apparently had a nervous breakdown some time earlier but was now supposed to be cured. In the month he had been in the ship he had behaved fairly normally and kept his routine watches but now he just sat in his cabin and stared at the bulkhead. No one could communicate with him and it looked as though he was heading for another breakdown, so I advised the agents at Yorktown that we would certainly need a doctor on arrival and that he might well have to be paid off. After two days and no change we arranged for the junior engineers to sit with him in turn during their off-watch periods. The night before we arrived we were approaching the land in the vicinity of Cape Hatteras with a strong wind, heavy rain and poor visibility. The radar was little help because of the low coastline and there was no Decca coverage here. I was on the Bridge all night until conditions improved with daylight and we finally got a reliable position. I then lay down on the Chartroom settee for a couple of hours as we approached Cape Henry and the Chesapeake Bay pilot station.

Luckily a lookout on the Bridge wing was awake and watching when the second engineer jumped overboard. The unfortunate junior engineer sitting with him had fallen asleep and the second went out through the open ship's side window in his bathroom. Had he jumped during the night, it is most unlikely we would ever have found him, never mind recover him, but he chose to jump in daylight when the visibility was good and the sea now smooth. We immediately released a Bridge wing lifebuoy, executed the classic "Williamson" turn, reduced speed and got more lookouts on vantage points. Meanwhile, the mate and emergency boat crew got the midships motor lifeboat swung out and ready for lowering. First we passed the lifebuoy and then the second engineer, who was on his back in the water and actually waved at us! We were going too fast and had to turn round again, slow down and get the boat away. It took 50 minutes from the shout of "man overboard!" until both man and lifebuoy were picked up. An ambulance and doctor were waiting on berthing at Yorktown and our second engineer – at least alive and conscious – was immediately taken away. I heard later that he spent some time in hospital before being flown home, and I have no idea if he ever went back to sea.

Yorktown is a very historic place where the last battle of the War of Independence took place and General Cornwallis surrendered to the revolutionary forces. There are many historic sites but those of our crew who went ashore only got as far as the nearest place in the village that sold alcohol. I, however, had to visit the agent's office in Newport News, 15 miles away, to attend to ship's business, including the discharge of the second engineer. While there, I told someone who asked that I was on a ship at the Yorktown oil refinery. When asked what I did on the ship, I told him but he simply would not believe me and thought I was joking. I suppose the popular image of a ship's captain must be something like Captain Birdseye. Certainly on the ship I always had to wear my four stripes when meeting shore officials so that they understood who I was! Silly really, since even in sailing ship days there were men younger than me in command of deep-sea ships.

From Yorktown it was a four-day ballast passage back south and this time we loaded fuel oil at Punta Cardon for Bayonne, New Jersey. I have no record of what was done about a replacement second engineer but at Cardon the third mate had to be paid off with some serious ear problem and on the passage north I kept the 0800 to 1200 watch. We had one apprentice on board and he was on watch with me so I could leave the Bridge from time to time. I was pleased to find that I had not forgotten how to take morning and lunchtime sun sights to establish our noon position! Luckily the third mate recovered quickly and was flown up to New York to rejoin us. Bayonne itself is close to New York City and Manhattan and the morning after we arrived the agents, Furness Withy, sent a car to bring me to their office for various ship's business there and at the Custom House. The chief engineer and "sparks", the radio operator, came with me for the ride and afterwards we did a little sightseeing and shopping, including a trip to the top of the Empire State Building, which I had last visited in 1951 as an apprentice in the "Tectarius". I contacted my old friends the Hickeys on Staten Island and they came to visit the ship and took me home for a couple of hours – a brief but pleasant interlude. After discharge of cargo we had a scenic trip up the Hudson River, past Sing Sing Jail, West Point Military Academy and big fleets of laid-up Liberty ships as far as Hyde Park, where we anchored to take on fresh water ballast for Curacao. The next day we were away again and reached Curacao on 25 August, discharged the water and proceeded on to Puerto Miranda on Lake Maracaibo, Venezuela, to load our next cargo. This was a cargo of crude oil for a refinery in Boston.

Reaching Boston on Sunday 1 September we spent a whole day anchored in President Roads because Monday was the Labor Day holiday. It was very rare for tanker operations to be delayed because of a national holiday, even Christmas Day! It was a pity we could not have berthed, cleared the ship inwards and enjoyed getting ashore. As it was, the whole bay was full of yachts and motorboats on both days and they made quite a spectacular sight. Frustrated at all this, I called the coastguard and got their permission to run an "emergency" exercise. Thus we lowered one of the motor lifeboats and about 20 of us went for a scenic cruise around the bay, although since the ship was not cleared inwards by Customs and Immigration, we could not land anywhere. When we did get alongside I had the usual run ashore on ship's business and pleasure. The chief engineer came with me and we had a monumental slap-up meal at a place called "Jimmy's" beside the fish dock. I had some dealings with a "bum-boatman" here and as a result we got a second-hand television set which was immediately set up in the Smokeroom. It worked well in port using a 200 watt lightbulb as an aerial and the engineers spent a lot of time and effort producing bigger and better outside aerials so that it even worked off the coast! On the way back to Curacao we had a diversion into the Delaware River near Philadelphia to take on more fresh water ballast. I got another run ashore here since I had to go with the Agent to visit the Custom House. We had four days at Curacao, since after discharge of the water we loaded bunker fuel at the refinery and then discharged same at Bullen Bay, another terminal a few miles up the coast and at Kleine Wharf, the passenger and cargo ship terminal right in the middle of Willemstad. Our television set was working very well here and many of the local programmes were in English.

From Curacao we proceeded back to Lake Maracaibo and Puerto Miranda, there to load a full cargo of crude oil for Heysham, so we were on the way home and I was looking forward to some leave! The voyage was uneventful but of course I was soon busy with accounts of wages and preparations for a change of command. The second mate had almost enough seatime in to sit for his Master's Certificate and I convinced him that if he helped me it would benefit him when he came to sit the Shipmaster's Business exam paper! We reached Heysham early on 30 September, as I had forecast, but then had nearly two days at anchor in Morecambe Bay due to problems in the refinery ashore. This of course threw the accounts of wages out so there was more reworking to be done. The day we berthed was busy for me with the pay off. Captain Owen Ffoulkes arrived back after six months' leave and signed on the new crew the same afternoon. I was all packed and ready to go and moved into the owner's suite for the night. Next day we were both busy with the change-over, checking documents, bonded stores and lots more. I got all my baggage sent round to the nearby Belfast ferry "Duke of Rothesay" that evening, so all I had to do was walk round to the passenger terminal. We sailed at midnight and I was home for breakfast the next morning! While I was home the "Hamilton" spent much time trading to and in the Baltic, which I would have enjoyed, but I had been away for nearly 15 months and was due for a break.

CHAPTER 9: DRAMA ON LAND, THEN BACK TO THE "HAMILTON"

Having arrived home, I still had a mountain of paperwork and accounts to complete – including the portage bill – before I could relax. My personal bank account was at the Northern Bank, Conns Water, Belfast and still is. The second day home I went down there to lodge a lot of spare cash. The manager at that time was a very chatty gent called Kyle who liked to spend a lot of time out front chatting up the customers in the queue waiting to get to a teller. The result of chatting to him was that I spent the next two days behind the counter with access to adding machines and some nice girls to talk to. The accounts were all completed, the various returns done and the portage bill finished for submission to Radcliffes. I even ended up not owing them any money! With that lot out of the way, it now felt funny to be home for a few months and not have any studying to do! Well, for a start I sold the motor scooter and bought my first car, a four-year-old Sunbeam Rapier, which at that time was described as a "sports saloon". My friend John Olver was at that time chairman of the Belfast Drama Circle and was not one to let a spare pair of hands go to waste. While I certainly had no theatrical ambitions, this organisation was just the thing to occupy me in the winter months. I helped build sets, assisted backstage during productions and put a lot of work into the outfitting of the Circle Theatre, an old mission hall on the New Lodge Road in Belfast, which the drama circle had recently acquired. After a few years this developed into a comfortable little theatre and there were quite a few semi-professional productions which were well attended. Unfortunately it was located in one of the more unstable parts of Belfast and when the "Troubles" really got going in the early 1970s, it was one of the first premises to be burned out. However in 1963 and 64 it was all action and I was part of it. At the end of a production there was always a good party, and of course I ended up having a steady relationship with one of the female members, which lasted throughout this long leave period and then fizzled out.

    I made at least one motoring trip to England to visit friends and relations and to visit Radcliffe's office in Cardiff to discuss various matters. As always, the directors and other staff were all very pleasant. While in this area I motored on out to Pembroke Dock on

Milford Haven to visit the "Hamilton's" adopted school. Many British merchant ships at that time had an adopted school, arranged through the British Ship Adoption Society and, having been contacted by the Society soon after I joined the ship, I had agreed to our adopting St. Mary's Primary School in Pembroke Dock. I was more agreeable to this than Captain Owen Ffoulkes, who would have nothing to do with it! The idea was that there would be correspondence between the schoolchildren and the ship's crew and that this would be good for their education. I had previous experience of this in other ships and in the "Hamilton" it worked quite well. When I received a batch of letters from the children I distributed them to various likely crew members and indeed most of these letters got an answer! I now had no option but to accept an invitation to visit the school and talk to the children. St. Mary's School was Roman Catholic and run by the nuns from the nearby Sacred Heart Convent and the local priest. As a Protestant from Northern Ireland I approached this visit with some trepidation but in fact it couldn't have gone better. I was well looked after and spent two nights in a parishoner's house. Of course I had to appear before the children in my full uniform as otherwise I could have been anybody! I found the nuns to be a jolly lot, most of whom were, needless to say, Irish. The liaison nun, with whom I'd had a lot of correspondence, was Sister Peter Chanel and she turned out to be quite a young woman from the South of Ireland. Obviously well educated, with a sharp mind and an endearing personality, I found her attractive and had she not been a dedicated nun, I would certainly have been interested in further liaison beyond the ship adoption scheme!

Other trips to England included attendance at a radar simulator course at Liverpool Marine College, arranged by Radcliffe's and early in the New Year of 1964 there was a long weekend in London with my drama circle girlfriend, her brother and his fiancee. This included a visit to the London Boat Show which I enjoyed. By February or March I would have been quite happy to go back to sea and I should have been back on the "Hamilton" by April when she was due for another dry-docking, but Shell kept her trading in the Baltic. However there now occurred the annual round of drama festivals in which the Belfast Drama Circle took a full part. I found a role as organiser of transport, hiring vans as necessary and getting sets and props out to the various locations. We appeared at Bangor, Larne, Ballymoney, Newry and even at the unlikely venue of

Carrickmore, County Tyrone. The play on offer was "Fairy Tales of New York" and I remember that for the Catholic audience at Carrickmore the script had to be amended with the deletion of all references to "rubber goods". All these performances were "one night stands" and by the time we got everything dismantled and back to the Circle Theatre, it was sometimes nearly daylight. Having made it to the finals, we appeared at the Grand Opera House in Belfast but I cannot remember how we were placed. Meanwhile at home there was the usual house decoration, inside and out, gardening and other useful activities, but the only sailing I had this year was once in a Scorpion dinghy, a very unstable craft, and once in a single-handed Mark dinghy, which was even more unstable!

At last the "Hamilton" arrived at Brigham & Cowan's ship repair yard in South Shields on 13 May, 1964 and I travelled over to rejoin her on the 18th. I found that there was virtually a full staff of officers on board and best of all Joe James had rejoined as chief officer. Joe had got married while on leave and his wife Joan subsequently sailed with us. Taking over from Captain Owen Ffoulkes was quick and easy this time and he departed the next morning. Until it came to opening "articles" and signing on the new crew, I had an easy time. I spent some good nights ashore at South Shields with Joe, the mate, and our new chief engineer, a young Scotsman called Stan Connel. The second engineer was another young man who had just obtained his First Class Certificate and I was very fortunate to have competent and able senior officers. The second mate, however, was on his way downhill with a drink problem, having made it to chief officer in the Clan Line, and did not last long in the "Hamilton".

By 1 June it was countdown for sailing and after the usual false starts we got away on 3 June, bound for Rotterdam to load two grades of fuel oil for Gibraltar and Casablanca plus 300 drums of bitumen in the forward dry cargo hold. We berthed at Pernis, Rotterdam, at 2000 the next day and once the arrival business was completed the man from Van Ommeren's, the agents, decided that he and I should head up town, to which I did not object. I got a conducted tour of Van Ommeren's fancy new office building but after that it was off to the Casino de Paris and I did not get back on board until 0500! It was an easy trip to Gibraltar except for SW force 8 and big seas in the Bay of Biscay. Discharge at Gibraltar took two days and the first day I sent the mate and his wife ashore sightseeing while I stayed on board. However, that evening the chief engineer and I went ashore and over the border to La Linea to visit a few establishments where the mate would not have taken his wife! The next morning I had a car laid on by the agents and took Mrs. James and our radio operator on a trip up the Rock, where we visited St. Michael's Cave, the apes' den and other tourist attractions.

The following afternoon found us in Casablanca and with only 4,000 tons of cargo left to discharge, it was a quick turnround, though the chief engineer and I had a night in Casablanca. I was told Casablanca was now a very quiet place but it was lively enough for us. We got back to the ship about 0500 and I just went and sat on the Bridge wing until pilot and tugs arrived about an hour later and we sailed for Curacao. Our great circle course took us right through Madeira and the next morning we passed as close as was safe along the south coast so that we got a fine view of the town of Funchal – the nearest I have ever been to Madeira! Shortly we got a change of orders and ended up at Puerto La Cruz to load crude oil for Delaware City. The Venezuelan customs were as amenable as the last time and there was a big trade in bottles of whisky since the bonded store was well stocked and I had all their preferred brands!

Joan, the mate's wife, had worked in the accounts dept, of the South Wales Electricity Board and this fact rang bells in my head. She soon became familiar with ship's accounts and with the preparation of USA crew lists. This was a great help to me and gave her something to do! Delaware City was a city in name only with three bars, two drugstores and a small supermarket! Returning to Punta Cardon we next loaded fuel oil for New York and ended up at an oil terminal on Manhattan. With two full days in port I sent the mate and his wife ashore the first day to do the ship's business and go sightseeing while the second day I spent at the New York World Fair, which was not far from where we were berthed. This exhibition was impressive and while I saw a lot it would have taken a week or more to do it all! The next cargo was crude oil loaded at Punta Cardon and this time we had a longer and more interesting trip through the Panama Canal and up the West Coast to Long Beach, Californias, which is really a suburb of Los Angeles. At Cardon we had taken a few hundred tons of bunkers as usual but this time the chief engineer reckoned we were about eighty tons short of the shore figure and signed the receipt under protest.

The next day at sea was a Saturday and we had an emergency drill. When the fourth engineer went into the forward pumproom to start the emergency fire pump he found it about 10 feet deep in oil – the missing bunkers! There was quite a performance getting this lot to where it should have been and a major clean up job to follow. I may be prejudiced but my experience was that engineers always had more trouble loading a few hundred tons of bunkers slowly that the mates did in loading thousands of tons of cargo at a fast rate. Minor spillages were the norm and major spillages not uncommon! We had a quick 24-hour turnround at Long Beach but there was time for a run ashore to see something of the place. My lasting impression is of all the "nodding donkeys", pumping oil from underground in every location, even in private back yards! This was the only port on the west coast of America, North or South, that I visited while at sea and the Panama Canal transits were two of the only three I ever made. By contrast I was through the Suez Canal 56 times and even the Kiel Canal five times!

Returning through the canal to Punta Cardon we loaded another cargo of fuel oil for New York and this time proceeded up the East River to a berth at Astoria. There then followed about six weeks of what was known as the "Lake run". From New York we went straight to Cabimas, one of the oil ports on Lake Maracaibo to make twelve trips between Lake oil ports and the refinery on Curacao. The passage time in either direction was between 12 and 15 hours and there had to be a stop off Punta Cardon to pick up or disembark a pilot. This was heavy going for everyone, especially those involved in cargo operations. There was just no let up, whatever time of the day or night we arrived or sailed. Ports visited in the Lake included Puerto Miranda, Cabimas and Coloncha, which was up near the head of the Lake. Navigation and pilotage involved transiting fixed routes through the offshore oil rigs and other structures.

After the first six trips, however, the Venezuelan authorities granted me a pilot's licence so that we did not have to stop off Cardon in either direction. One advantage, at least for a select few, was that we got in two rounds of golf a week at the Shell Club course on Curacao! The chief engineer was a keen golfer and the fourth engineer, another young Scotsman, operated off a handicap of two! I had got interested and bought a half set of clubs at Long Beach. Down in the dry cargo hold, forward, we had rigged up some tarpaulins in the form of a net so that we could practise down there and have lessons from the fourth engineer! Now, with twice weekly visits to Curacao, we played some golf ashore. One of the privileges I had was that I only had to phone the agency for a car to come and take us to and from the golf course and we went there at 0600 to play until 0800 before the heat of the day set in, then returned to the ship for breakfast! This nine-hole golf course had some unusual features. The fairways were mostly fairly green as a result of watering but the greens were nothing but smooth bare earth. After a putting session on a green, it then had to be raked smooth again. Natural hazards included cactus bushes and unnatural hazards included oil pipelines!

Apart from the golf practice in the forehold we had a badminton court laid out, having invested in some badminton equipment at Long Beach. This was quite a success. The golfers were also bridge fanatics and the regular four players were myself, the chief engineer, the electrician, who was not a watchkeeper, and the second engineer, who we arranged to have on "daywork" most of the time rather than watchkeeping. At sea we had lengthy sessions either in my dayroom or more often the chief engineer's. For a break we sometimes played Monopoly around my dining-room table and while Joan James had no interest in bridge, she was certainly an expert at Monopoly! This was all good fun, very enjoyable, and filled the evenings at sea between film shows.

At the end of our 12 Lake runs we loaded a crude oil cargo at Punta Cardon and had a two-week passage from there to Buenos Aires, Argentina. The approaches to Buenos Aires in the River Plate are shallow and we soon found ourselves pushing through the mud to reach our first anchorage where the small tanker "Esso Santa Fe" came alongside to relieve us of 3,000 tons of cargo. We then ploughed on through more mud to reach Dok Sud in Buenos Aires on 10 October. Here we spent four days since after discharge of cargo we took another 48 hours maintenance period as per the time charter. By now I was well used to the Venezuelan shore officials and their methods, but the Argentinians were something else! The agent led them on board and presented me with a detailed list of their immediate requirements, for which he would sign and debit to Shell. The list ran to about two cases of whisky and ten cartons of 200 cigarettes! Like the Venezuelans, they were then prepared to pay for anything further I could offer them. I had heard that anything in Argentina which requires official approval can only be achieved after big backhanders have been dispensed, and so it was. I had also heard of ships being delayed indefinitely on a trumped up pretext, simply because the captain would not grease the right palms! Well, my job was to get the ship "turned round" as quickly and efficiently as possible and any delays due to my conscience would not have gone down well with Shell or Radcliffes! There was plenty of time for everyone to have several runs ashore and see the sights but most of the ratings did not get further than a ramshackle shack near the ship which dispensed all manner of local hooch. Most of them were AWOL some or all of the time but at least they were all on board when we sailed and I had them all up for "logging" the first day back at sea. Like many South American cities, Buenos Aires had some beautiful parts but even more seedy, run-down parts. Corruption was rife and probably still is. I often heard it said that Sir Francis Drake or Sir Walter Raleigh should have sorted out the Spanish colonists and we might have ended up with a South America more like Australia or New Zealand!

After this break it was back north to Puerto Miranda and Punta Cardon where we loaded another cargo of crude oil and this time it was home across the Atlantic to discharge at Heysham. The "bridge club" had decided that we should supplement the perfectly good ship's food with something extra and in Buenos Aires I had bought a whole bagful of prime steaks privately from the shipchandler. We already had an electric frying pan which was rigged up in my pantry. One night we produced steak, egg and chips with all the trimmings – the first of several such occasions!

Leaving Cardon on 29 October, 1964, I immediately started work on the accounts towards a pay off on 10 November. Joan James was a great help in the initial calculations and in checking everything as we went along. During the passage we met plenty of heavy weather during the last few days. To help matters the radar broke down and so did the starboard Bridge wing gyro compass repeater. However, when the weather closed in so that we could get no astronomical sights, the Decca Navigator clocked in in due course and we had no problem with our position approaching the south coast of Ireland. We duly located the Fastnet Rock visually and then the Tuskar Rock, from where we headed north up the Irish Sea towards Morecambe Bay. In fact we berthed at Heysham and paid off on 11 November. There was a complete change of ratings and some junior officers but all my key senior officers signed on for another voyage, for which I was thankful. Joan James re-signed as a supernumerary, although it was now obvious that she was pregnant! It was a busy two days in port and I only had time to visit the local dentist to get a troublesome tooth fixed. All too soon we were back at sea and on the way back to Punta Cardon, with more heavy weather for the first few days. With Joan James's help, I got the accounts completed for the last voyage and that was another headache out of the way.

Arriving at Punta Cardon on 26 November, we then spent the next three months trading between Curacao/Lake Maracaibo and ports on the East Coast of the USA, with fuel oil cargoes to keep the Americans warm during the winter, or so we thought! The discharge ports were Providence Rhode Island, Boston and South Weymouth in Massachussets. Groton Conneticut, famous for its submarine base, Baltimore and New York. At Heysham we had signed on two Chinese cooks, both of whom were full British citizens and members of the National Union of Seamen. It was not too difficult to arrange that some Chinese items appeared on the daily menu, which generally went down well, certainly in the Officers' Dining Saloon, and were much to my liking. However, there was some animosity between these two and when the second cook had a go at the chief cook with a meat cleaver he had to be paid off and sent home DBS (Distressed British Seaman)! I wonder what eventually happened to this pair – probably running very successful Chinese restaurants or carry-outs somewhere!

Our bridge and golf activities continued and at Providence, Rhode Island, I invested in a full set of golf clubs. On 14 December we celebrated the Jameses' first wedding anniversary and the Chinese cooks even managed to produce a special cake! On 25 December we arrived back at Punta Cardon from Boston and dropped anchor at 0930. All the berths were occupied and the only information we got from shore was that there was no cargo for us and no orders! I did not object to the catering staff getting drunk later in the day and the only incident was that the two Chinese cooks had another set-to and had to be pulled apart! On Boxing Day we remained at anchor with four other ships ahead of us at anchor waiting to berth. The next day we were told to go to Curacao and on arrival off the harbour entrance we were told to go back to Cardon. We actually berthed there late on 28 December and loaded fuel oil for Groton, Conneticut.

On this trade we were in the tropics for one week out of two, and in the bitter cold of the North East USA winter for the other, with very little in between! There was certainly a change of weather when we crossed the dividing line between the north-east going Gulf Stream and the south-westerly going Labrador Current. Arctic sea smoke was common in this area and quite frequently we met it. It is the result of cold air passing over a warm water surface and can be likened to the steam over a hot bath or swimming pool. We could have virtually nil visibility from the Bridge but if we sent someone up the foremast he could see over the top of it and perhaps the top of the masts of another vessel not far away! Also on the passage north to Groton we experienced some very severe weather for the last three days when the centre a very deep depression passed quite close to the North of us. The result was broken buckled railings on the foredeck and forecastle with one ladder washed away altogether. All the forward spaces, including chain locker, lamp room and the forehold were flooded to some extent and took some time to clear up.

After another trip north, this time to Baltimore, we made what turned out to be our last trip north before returning to the UK, although we didn't know it at the time, and discharged at a remote berth in Jersey City, close to New York. Here we took another overdue 48 hours for engine maintenance and I had plenty of time to visit my friends, the Hickeys, on Staten Island. Here also Mrs. James left us and flew home after visiting a doctor. Her pregnancy was well advanced and she had been experiencing some sickness and pain. Indeed I was getting quite concerned about her condition and had even studied the brief section in the "Ship Captain's Medical Guide" dealing with emergency childbirth! Had we known we were returning home soon she could have stayed, but even so she was safer off the ship and in due course gave birth to a perfectly healthy child.

Returning South to Puerto Miranda we loaded two grades of crude oil for Le Havre and Rouen and after a stop at Cardon for bunkers we were on our way. I now learned that I was to be relieved at Le Havre by a Captain Dixon, who I had not met but had apparently been home on leave since July. Also we learnt that the ship was to proceed to Thameshaven after discharge of cargo. That would mean a complete "pay off" and I would remain on board for that.

On arrival at Le Havre on 26 February I was duly relieved by Captain Dixon, who reminded me of Captain Rice and seemed to be something of a "fuddy duddy", and I became a supernumerary for my last few days on board. There was plenty to do with the change of command and preparing the accounts of wages ready for Thameshaven. The chief steward we had at this time was a competent young man called Mulgrew, from Liverpool, and after the passage up the River Seine to Rouen I invited him to come ashore with me for a drink or two. He went to his cabin to get dressed and seemed to take an interminable time over this so that I eventually went down to see what he was doing. I found him slumped over the WC in his toilet and writhing in agony. Well, I didn't know he had an ulcer and neither, apparently, did he! Anyway, it had burst and poor Mr. Mulgrew was carted off to hospital in an ambulance instead of going ashore for a pleasant evening with me! The next day Captain Dixon and I went to visit him in hospital and paid him off. He eventually recovered and made it home.

Leaving Rouen on 1 March we proceeded back down river, across to the Thames and picked up a pilot off Dungeness. Things now started to go "down the drain" and for a start both the top and bottom bearings of No.3 unit in the main engine gave out and the ship came to a grinding halt! We managed to drop anchor but were right in the middle of the main channel off Ramsgate. This was at 0900 on the 2nd, and by 2200 the engineers had managed to "hang off" the damaged unit. This meant that we could proceed at slow speed on eight cylinders instead of nine and with two tugs in attendance we limped inwards towards Purfleet where the ship would now clean tanks and undergo repairs. Since I was now supernumerary I could spend the night asleep in the owner's suite but I was wakened at an early hour to find that we had managed to bump into a coal boat called the "Cormount" in thick fog off Southend, fortunately with only superficial damage.

There followed a further period at anchor to sort things out but we eventually berthed at Purfleet late on 3 March. The pay off and signing on of new crew took place right away and was all done by midnight. I then attended a farewell party in the chief engineer's quarters, had a few hours sleep, and left the "Hamilton" the following afternoon. I travelled up to London and then to Cardiff for a meeting with Radcliffes the next morning. Then it was back to London in time for the Heysham boat train and I was home for breakfast on the morning of Saturday 6 March.

As it turned out, this was the end of my seagoing career but I was not sure of that yet. Anyway, of more immediate importance I discovered that it was the last night of "A Streetcar Named Desire" at the Circle Theatre, which was followed by a monumental party. On Monday morning I was back behind the counter at the Northern Bank, Connswater, courtesy of the nice Mr. Kyle, the manager, to complete my accounts with Radcliffes. The portage bill and all the other returns were completed over the next two or three days and sent off to Cardiff. It was now coming up to drama festival time and the Circle Theatre was heavily involved, which kept me busy for the next several weeks while I thought about my future career!

CHAPTER 10: THIRTY YEARS A CIVIL SERVANT – THE EARLY DAYS

During my second trip as master of the "Hamilton", I had given some thought to the direction my career was going now that I had reached the grand age of 31. I was very happy with my present situation and even enjoyed the daily hassle and problems. The accounting system was a headache but I had learned to cope with it and not get into any difficulties with Radcliffes. However, having made it to the "top" at sea, I was not sure that I wanted to spend the next 30 or so years in the same situation. Also I think even then the writing was on the wall for the British Merchant Navy, as it was at that time. There was no security of employment in the smaller shipping companies and, as it turned out before long, neither was there in the big companies where one used to be assured of a career for life! Had I stayed with Radcliffes, it was likely I would have been appointed master of the "Llanishen" or "Llangorse" after a few months' leave. As it was, they very kindly left my options open while I decided my future.

With my qualifications and experience there were options and I had already turned down the offer of a lecturer's job at the Belfast Marine School. As it was, soon after I arrived home I applied to the Marine Survey Service for a job. At that time it was part of the Ministry of Transport but to anyone at sea it was simply known as the "Board of Trade", which is what it was when it was first formed in the 1850s. Under various names this organisation has existed since then and is currently known as the Maritime and Coastguard Agency. Basically, it is the government department responsible for merchant shipping and other commercial marine activities, and is comparable to the more recent Civil Aviation Authority, responsible for commercial aviation, or even the division of the Department of the Environment or Transport, responsible for roads and the vehicles thereon.

It seemed to take me forever to get accepted but in due course it happened and Radcliffes kindly released me from my contract with them. I have many happy memories of that company and I enjoyed working for them. After all, they did think enough of me to let me command one of their ships. At that time there were any number of well qualified deck officers available for related shore base jobs,

107

such as marine pilots, harbour masters, company superintendents, marine college lecturers and such like. However, the Marine Survey Service demanded high qualifications and the requirements for Nautical Surveyor and Examiner of Masters and Mates were the Extra Master Certificate and about two years in command of a foreign-going ship. I was concerned that my only experience was in tankers but I need not have worried because with the way the system worked, I soon learned a great deal about all manner of ships, including passenger ships, fishing vessels and almost anything that floated and was mainly operated commercially.

I became a civil servant on 19 July, 1965, and remained so for the next 30 years! The only minus was that, having reached the reasonable salary of about £2,000 p.a. as master at sea, plus perks, my salary now dropped to £1,500 with no free board and lodging and no "duty frees"! I would have been quite happy to start work anywhere but was appointed to the Belfast Office, one of numerous "outport" offices at that time. It was located in the Custom House on Donegal Quay and had been there since it first opened in the 1850s. Here there was still quite a large staff, mainly because the Harland & Wolff Shipyard was still more or less in its heyday. There were two nautical surveyors here, Ted Anderson, the senior, and Ray Newbury, the Examiner of Masters and Mates, who was known to the candidates as "the Newt". There was the boss, who was an engineer with the title "Principal Officer", and several more ex-seagoing engineers, who were titled "Engineer and Ship Surveyors". There were also several of an "inferior" breed called "ship surveyors" who had never been to sea but who, in the terms of their contract, had adequate qualifications and had held a position of responsibility in the shipbuilding industry. There was a considerable back-up staff, including two female "maiden" telephone operators/typists who were more than helpful in my early days but just a bit old for my consideration as other than helpful staff! Finally there were the MSAs or marine survey assistants; there were five of them, and they were the only uniformed staff we had. They were mainly ex-uniformed service ratings fed into a cushy job until their retirement. They had various duties but mostly they just sat around in the entrance to the Custom House, passing the time of day!

There was also an office car, complete with uniformed driver, which was mainly employed in ferrying surveyors to and from the shipyard. This particular gent, Eddie Allen, was enterprising in more ways than one and, with his wife, ran a shop in Groomsport at the southern entrance to Belfast Lough, now nearly a suburb of Bangor. Besides the Marine Survey Office, also in the Custom House, with its own entrance, was the Mercantile Marine Office which again dated from the last century and had basically been established nationwide to ensure some regulation and fair employment for seamen. The "shipping master" had the job of overseeing the signing on or paying off of ship's crews in accordance with the "Articles of Agreement" and even at this time much of the business was conducted in the Mercantile Marine Office rather than aboard the ships. This was certainly the case with the local Head Line ships and local coastwise companies such as Kelly's, who ran a large fleet of colliers. This office had a long high counter which was equally wide, to prevent dissatisfied seamen, sometimes the worse for wear, from getting into close contact with staff on the other side! An interesting feature of this office was a secure strongroom wherein were kept the effects of deceased seamen until legitimately claimed or otherwise disposed of.

Outside the Custom House was Donegal Quay, which was then full of cross-Channel ferries. Closest to Queen's Bridge was the Glasgow cargo boat, the "Lairdscrest" or the "Lairdswood", I think. Then came the Glasgow passenger boat "Royal Ulsterman" or "Royal Scotsman", the Heysham cargo boat "Slieve Bernagh" or "Slieve Broom". The Heysham passenger boat "Duke of Argyll", "Duke of Rothesay" or Duke of Lancaster", the Liverpool passenger boat "Ulster Prince" or Ulster Monarch" and after that the Bristol Channel Steamers, plus the Belfast, Mersey and Manchester cattle boats "Brookmount" or "Mountstewart". However, from our office only the funnels and upperworks were visible above the sheds.

When I first joined Custom House, there was an Indian surveyor in the office, under training, and one morning he asked why all these ships never went to sea! Of course, they all sailed at night and next morning the sister ships were in and tied up long before he got to the office! Across the River Lagan on Queen's quay and in Abercorn Basin there were always Kelly coalboats and I think at that time the Kelly fleet numbered over 20, some of them being quite elderly steam driven jobs. There were still one or two other coalboat owners such as Samuel Stewart and Milligans. Further down the harbour there was nearly always at least one Head Line ship in port. The Head Line then had about 12 owned ships and two or three more on charter. The Harland & Wolff Shipyard, while starting to decline was still very active and all the slipways in the Musgrave Yard had vessels under construction. The huge building dock and the gantry cranes came much later. There were container services of a sort but the ships used were mainly small conventional cargo ships. On deck the containers were often stowed athwartships across the gunwales and sometimes in bad weather badly stowed containers would burst open! I remember one occasion when a whole week's issue of the Radio Times and other magazines bound for Belfast was lost overboard, and another when a load of guttering and drainpipes was lost off the Ards Peninsula. Apparently a lot of fishermen's houses in Portavogie suddenly got new guttering and downpipes!

Numerous coastal ships belonging to various British companies were regular traders to Belfast and other Northern Ireland ports. These included Robertsons and Gardiners of Glasgow, Rowbothams, Coe Metcalfe, Glenlight Shipping, Crescent Shipping, Stephenson Clarke and of course Everards who are one of the few still in business. It has to be remembered that at the time the British Merchant Navy was still at its post-War zenith and, sad to say, in my 30 years in office I saw it decline to what it is today!

Government marine surveyors and examiners must be among the best qualified and trained there are anywhere. Apart from the entry requirements, there follows a two-year training and probationary period. In Belfast I was under the wing of "the Newt" while I learned all about examinations and became especially competent in conducting orals. There followed a few weeks on the Marking Board in London and at the London Examination Centre, until I was finally confirmed as an Examiner of Master and Mates and a Sight Test Examiner. It is interesting that in any of the written papers, candidates had to reach 70 per cent of the total score to pass and it was either pass or fail, with no distinctions either way. Like many other new surveyors, I got one of the clerks on the Marking Board to let me into the archives to locate my own "Extra Master" papers and found that I had scored 73 per cent in my final mathematics paper!

I also had to become competent in statutory survey work and spent several weeks working under both the Engineer Surveyors and Ship Surveyors before spending more time in London in the various Headquarters departments. The marine survey structure could be likened to the medical world, with the outport surveyors being the GPs. The consultants are all in headquarters, with instant experts available on nearly any marine matter. "Makee learn" surveyors like me had to spend a lot of time with each of these experts and become competent in the application of the Loadline Rules, Tonnage Measurement (British, Suez and Panama), Lifesaving and Fire Appliances Rules, Dangerous Good Rules, Crew Accommodation Rules, Passenger Ship Rules and Regulations and much, much more! Of course it was these instant experts who wrote all the Rules and Regulations in the first place!

There were also numerous externally run courses and even after confirmation one is attending various courses throughout one's career. The first courses I attended included Wood Technology at the Forest Products Research Laboratory, Princes Risborough, GRP Technology and GRP Boat Construction at Scott Bader, Wellingborough and at the Watercraft Works, East Molesey on the Thames. One of the best was the Inflatable Life-raft Course, which started off at the RFD Factory, Godalming, progressed to Frankenstien's near Manchester, where they manufactured the fabrics, on then to the Dunlop Life-raft Factory nearby and finally to the Beaufort Life-raft Factory at Birkenhead. The worst were undoubtedly the courses run by the Royal Navy at HMS "Phoenix", Portsmouth. These included Firefighting, Damage Control and NBCD (Nuclear, Ballistic and Chemical Defence). The RN Petty Officers who were in charge had no sympathy for mere civilians and took pleasure in our discomfort. One of the nastier exercises involved a mock-up cross section of a warship, mounted on hydraulic rams. It was riddled with shell holes and in the simulation was sinking fast. We were put into this machine together with a large selection of wooden props, plugs, wedges, other bits of wood and a few hammers. Once we were battened down the water was turned on and we had to try and plug all the holes before the ship sank and we all drowned! There was only very dim emergency lighting and of course the whole thing started to heel over to an alarming angle! It was only when the water was up to our necks that our tormentors relented, turned off the water and opened the hatches! One enjoyable feature of all these courses was to meet surveyors from other offices and compare notes. Also the expenses usually ran to a quite good hotel, with something left over for a few "jars" in the evening.

Back in Belfast I duly became a useful member of the team, "the

Newt" got promoted and was transferred to Middlesbrough, and I settled down to an interesting and enjoyable way of life, if not particularly financially rewarding! At that time there were still plenty of locals coming forward for examination, including the fishermen from Portavogie and Kilkeel. For me the first and second weeks of every month except August were virtually taken up with examination work. It was Second Mates, Mates (Home Trade), Second Hands (limited) and Second Hands (Special) for the first week, then Masters, First Mates, Master (Home Trade) and Skippers (Limited) for the second week. Engineers sat their exams in the same room during the third and fourth weeks of the month. There were 12 ancient desks and chairs, at which I had sat myself on numerous occasions in the past, but usually there were no more than six candidates in a week. On one occasion, however, there were 22 and with imported furniture we got them all in!

There were a number of examiners' clerks over the years but the first one I had was a Mrs. Proctor, the widow of an Orient Line chief engineer. The exam system was surprisingly fast and efficient and candidates could come round on a Monday morning to get their written results. Written papers, with the exception of Chartwork, which was marked locally, were sent to the Marking Board each day on completion and, except for very "heavy" weeks, the results arrived back on the following Monday morning. Mrs. Proctor was a very motherly lady and used to almost melt into tears when telling some hopeful that he had failed! Orals and signals results were known even faster, usually within a few minutes of doing the exam. Apart from this there were usually a few candidates for EDH (Efficient Deck Hand) and CLB (Certificated Life Boatman) on a Friday morning at the local Ratings School. This was situated in the old British Sailors' Society building on Corporation Street and there was an old wooden lifeboat under radial davits in the nearby Clarendon Dock for the practical boat work.

The oral examinations, if there were a lot of candidates, could be quite exhausting for the examiner, never mind the candidates. To adequately cover the syllabus, the average oral examination would last for an hour, more with a slow candidate. Two in the morning and three in the afternoon was enough for one day! Foreign-going Masters obviously got the most intensive treatment and had at least an hour of intensive "Rule of the Road", ship handling, emergency situations and so on, following which they had to spend an hour wrestling with Captain Beale's deviascope, demonstrating their ability to find the deviations on a ship's magnetic compass, in great detail, and then correcting the same. Lord Kelvin, who was the inventor of the "modern" ship's magnetic compass and all its accoutrements, such as soft iron balls, Flinders Bar, and heeling error bucket, had a lot to answer for. A devious examiner could hide deflecting magnets under the deck of this device so that correction became almost impossible and many were the poor candidates who sweated blood in the hour allowed to try and sort it out! Suffice to say that I was long enough in office to see this device dispensed with and the one in the Belfast Examination Centre was donated to the Ulster Folk and Transport Museum! Another item donated to the Museum before I retired some 30 years later was a beautiful 19th Century vernier sextant. Second Mate candidates and indeed even fishermen were required to demonstrate their knowledge of the sextant, and to be able to find and remove the common errors. When up for second mate myself in 1953, I had actually demonstrated my familiarity with this particular item but never at sea had I come across a vermier sextant. We also had a "three circle" micrometer sextant which was more up-to-date and this was the only one I presented to the candidates. The Marine Barometer, slung in gimbals, and with its attached "Gold Slide" for corrections, was another must for virtually all candidates, likewise some hydrometers floating in various salt solutions required attention.

The signals examination, conducted on a Wednesday afternoon on the conclusion of the written papers, was another hurdle many candidates fell apart on. It consisted of receiving visual Morse at a fairly fast rate, likewise semaphore, and then sending the same followed by practical use of the International Code of Signals. Semaphore I had learned in the Boy Scouts and I remember on my first ship we apprentices had practised it, but it was never actually used. Visual Morse, mainly using a high-powered Aldis lamp, was the means of communication with other ships, pilot stations and shore stations until in the last few ships I sailed in when we had the new fangled VHF radio sets. Except for common single and double letter signals the International Code Flags were never used. For instance, flag "G" meant "I require a pilot" and flag "H" meant "I have a pilot on board". The two flags signal "RY", usually flown by a ship on a berth or with another vessel alongside meant "Please pass at slow speed". Well, all the candidates, including the poor fishermen, had to be examined in Morse, semaphore and International Code and the pass mark was 90 per cent! It was a long time before semaphore was dropped and even then the German delegation at IMO (International Maritime Organisation) objected on the grounds that it was the only signalling method which required no equipment. In other words, one could stand up on the upturned hull of a lifeboat in the nude and communicate with one's rescuers by making semaphore signals with one's arms! It is only very much more recently, with the introduction of the GMDSS (Global Maritime Distress and Safety System) using satellite systems, that visual and indeed aural Morse has become redundant. International Code flags are widely used by yacht racing organisations for race management, with totally different flag meanings from those in the international book.

Then there were the sight test examinations. For any young man thinking of going to sea as a deck officer, the first hurdle was to get a sight test certificate, for without this one could only think of some other career, or still go to sea but as an engineer or perhaps radio operator. Examination candidates also had to sit a sight test and it was also required for other purposes, such as shipmasters seeking pilots' certificates for pilotage exemption certificates. The standard required was full normal vision and at that time aids to vision, i.e. glasses or contact lenses, were not allowed. At the office we were open to all comers for sight tests every Monday morning from 0900 until 1200 and at other times by appointment. After paying a fee, a candidate was checked for personal physical features, including height, complexion and colour of eyes. This was done in the Mercantile Marine Office and the candidate was then taken up four flights of hard stone stairs to the attic of the Custom House, where the blacked out Sight Test Room was situated. One older candidate for a Pilot's Certificate remarked to me that we tested his heart before we tested his eyes! The letter test came first and the wall mounted test cards were just the same as might be found in any optician's premises. Having passed the letter test, the candidate then went on to the colour test and this was something else! The colour test machine looked like a Heath Robinson invention or something from outer space. It sat on a tall wooden plinth and was oil fired in that the source of light was a paraffin lantern. The light was allowed to shine through two narrow apertures behind which was a revolving disc containing about 30 glass filters which were either plain glass or various shades of red or green. These lights were reflected in a mirror on the wall a fixed distance from the machine and the idea was that the lights as seen in the mirror represented the navigation lights of a ship on a clear night at their maximum range of visibility. The examiner stood on one side of the machine to operate it and the candidate stood on the other, calling out the colours of the lights as he saw them.

Like a lighthouse lantern, it was essential that this machine and its various parts were kept spotlessly clean and this was the task of one of the marine survey assistants, who was designated to exams. Every Monday morning he would go up to the Sight Test Room, carefully clean all the lenses and the mirror, trim the wick of the lantern and fire it up. There was a whole thick volume of instructions as to procedures and in particular the procedure if a candidate failed or was doubtful. It is a well known fact that about five per cent of the population is colour blind and my experience over the years confirmed this. Failures or doubtful cases were referred to London Headquarters for further assessment. This ancient machine remained in use until about the 1970s, when it was replaced by an electric one and more recently even that has been dispensed with. Colour tests are now done using only the Ishihara Card System. Like other valuable artifacts, the old oil-fired sight test machine in the Belfast Office was donated to the Ulster Folk and Transport Museum.

When not busy with exams, I was employed on general survey work, mainly safety equipment surveys on various vessels and with quite frequent visits to the fishing ports. In later years dedicated fishing vessel surveyors were appointed but at this time any surveyor had to be able to deal with them. I thereby got to know many of the fishing vessel owners/Skippers in Kilkeel, Portavogie, Ardglass and elsewhere. One afternoon in the Custom House I was engaged in oral examinations and one candidate was a Kilkeel fisherman who was up for "Skipper (Limited)". He already had a "Second Hand (Special)" certificate but he now had a larger boat being built and since it was over 50 tons GRT, he now required "Skipper (Limited)". Typical of fishermen, he never thought of obtaining the higher qualification until he actually needed it and, having failed twice, he was now quite desperate. Fortunately, this time he passed and his immediate reaction was to invite me to help him bring the new boat home! I was able to take a few days' leave and went over to Buckie, on the Moray Firth, with him and his crew, where she was ready and waiting at the Jones Buckie Shipyard. The boat was the "Crystal Sea" and we had a very pleasant delivery trip through the Caledonian Canal and thence home to Kilkeel. This was my first of many trips through this canal and at that time many of the locks were still manually operated, with capstans and capstan bars to operate the gates and winch handles to operate the paddles. I subsequently went on a couple of fishing trips in the Irish Sea in this boat and so gained some first hand knowledge of fishing operations, including the gutting and sorting of fish ready for the market! This knowledge could only be useful when conducting the orals in fishermen's examinations.

With my general survey activities, I soon knew many of the masters and senior officers on the cross-Channel ferries, the Head Line and Kellys, to mention but a few, and of course the marine superintendents. Captain Ross and Mr. Stewart of the Head Line, Captain McCallion of Kellys' were early and useful contacts, as was Captain Morrison, who looked after the Belfast Steamship operation, i.e. the Liverpool Boats. I also had many contacts at Harland & Wolff, where I was doing survey work on new constructions and British vessels in for dry-docking and repair. One such was the "Orcoma", for the Pacific Steam Navigation Co., on which I did the tonnage measurement, apart from the safety equipment survey and some other work. Another new ship I was involved in at that time was the Shell tanker "Donax". The triangular shaped mobile oil rig "Sea Quest" for BP was built at this time and occupied three slipways in the Musgrave Yard, delaying the launch of two Bank Line vessels on the outer two slipways. This was clever and innovative work for Harlands but probably not profitable. Then came the "Myrina" for Shell, a 190,000 ton tanker, which involved extending one of the slipways on the shore side, and even with that the after half of the vessel had to be partly launched so that there was room to build on the forward part. This was all clever stuff but again, I doubt if it was profitable! One very useful contact I had in the Yard was Hughie Thompson, who then ran the very extensive Boat Shop. Here they could build beautiful wooden lifeboats but with the arrival of GRP construction the demand for these was falling off. For the Bank Line in particular they could also produce beautiful varnished clinker built sailing dinghies and they had even built the odd yacht over the years, including the whole "Lake" Class of small keelboats for the Royal North of Ireland Yacht Club. A well known small sailing cruiser which they built is "Wee Intombie", based at Carrickfergus and still going strong. Since I was involved in some home boat building at the time this was a useful source of advice and even some bits and pieces which I could not produce myself. The Boat Shop and the associated Joiner's Shop had a wealth of practical talent and sheer craftsmanship at that time. Towards Christmas I noticed that they did a very strong line in producing beautiful dolls' houses, rocking chairs and suchlike, mostly, so I was told, on the night shift.

One particularly enjoyable job was the witnessing of crew emergency drills on the cross-Channel passenger ferries. Regulations require that the crews of Home Trade passenger ships carry out emergency drills once a week and that such drills be witnessed twice a year by Marine Office surveyors. Requirements for foreign-going passenger ships also require the weekly drill and surveyors must witness same before the final departure from a UK port, but I was not involved in any of this until I worked in London. Anyway, on "drill days" in Belfast it meant a walk across the quay at about 1000 in time for morning coffee on whichever vessel was involved, following which we witnessed boat drills and fire drills, which took about two hours. By then it was time for a "pour out" in the first Class bar, followed by lunch in the First Class Dining Saloon. We usually got back across to the Office by about 1500 in time to record any recommendations and suggestions for future drills.

The Atlantic Steam Navigation Company were at that time running an "up market" service between Belfast and Preston, mainly for RoRo freight but also for passengers and their vehicles, where time was not important, and these vessels duly received our attention. However, there was also the Larne to Stranraer service which at that time was operated by the "Caledonian Princess" and a forerunner of the intensive service which would later develop on this 35-mile route. While she had "roll-on/roll-off" facilities and a water-tight stern door, she was still basically a classic cross-Channel ferry with conventional steam turbine propulsion and conventional controls. The earlier vessels on this route had a leisurely routine sailing from Stranraer to Larne in the morning, lying in Larne all day, and sailing back to Stranraer in the evening but the "Cally Princess" was doing two trips a day in each direction, and was backed up by the German registered cargo 'Ro-ro' "Lohengrin" to carry extra cars and freight vehicles. Because of this there was not time in a "turnaround" at Larne to do a full emergency drill and we therefore did part of the drill at Larne and then travelled across to Stranraer to complete the job, or vice versa. The Commodore Master on this route was Captain Joe Unsworth, who was quite a character. He had escaped the "Princess Victoria" disaster simply because he was on leave that day. His performance on the Bridge when berthing or unberthing the ship was nothing less than theatrical, with all the accompaniments of bells, whistles and sirens, unlike later ferries where the captain just stands by a console and everything seems to happen automatically, with no noise at all and no romance! Joe also had a habit, when the ship was in port, of donning a cloth cap and dirty old raincoat to go and mingle with the passengers and hear what they had to say about the service. He often said that his ship only catered for the "quality", and football fans and other rabble should travel on some other ship! He was right in a way, since many of the crew, particularly the stewards, were recruited locally, had never sailed on any other ship, and therefore had no bad habits! With the further development of this route and the involvement of the Seamen's Union, this changed over the years.

When we had nothing else to do we used to got out on "general inspections" and try to find some scruffy-looking foreign ship to inspect for deficiencies. Two of the marine survey assistants were supposed to patrol the Belfast docks each day on the lookout for overloaded or otherwise deficient ships, but I found that their patrols often ended at the "Lifeboat" – a bar just across the road from the Custom House. Immediately round the corner from the "Lifeboat" was another famous establishment known as "Ma Carrol's", favoured, I believe, by Head Line crews. The "Lifeboat" bar is still in existence but the others have long disappeared in the face of redevelopment. Anyway, when we found a likely looking scruffy ship we would go on board and find numerous deficiencies, which were then listed on Form Surveys 70 and handed to the master for attention. In serious cases we had the power to officially detain the ship by instructing HM Customs to refuse clearance. This was long before the present system of Port State Control was introduced, with its computerised records and communications. This enables deficient ships to be hounded and detained wherever they go in Europe and many other parts of the world. We also inspected British ships, especially the smaller ones which did not have to undergo regular surveys for safety equipment. One of the first ships I boarded was on my second day in the office. The "Craigolive" was an old traditional coalboat which was lying on Queen's Quay and about to proceed to the scrapyard. The "Newt" decided we should pay her a visit to see what we could filch off her before she went for scrap! He had a small converted ship's lifeboat, ex. Head Line, and I was building a 20 ft. pocket sailing cruiser. I came away with a traditional lifeboat compass which served well in my new boat!

In about 1967 there were some accidents involving Class V and VI passenger vessels with loss of life, notably the "Prince of Wales" at Barmouth. There are numerous such vessels operating on, say, the River Thames and still a few in Northern Ireland based at local tourist-type ports such as Bangor and Donaghadee. There used to be a large fleet of such boats based at Warrenpoint and they operated across the short stretch of water to O'Meath across Carlingford Lough in the Republic. Their heyday was when there were goods available in the Republic not available in Northern Ireland and when the public houses in the Republic were open on Sundays but not in the North. There was also the "ferry" service between Ballycastle and Rathlin Island, the only inhabited island off the coast of Northern Ireland, which was operated by small open boats devoid of any official certification! Anyway, as a result of the much publicised accident, a number of temporary, summer-only, Grade II surveyors were recruited to watch over these boats and small craft activity generally. Grade II surveyors were mostly retired master mariners who were thus able to supplement their pension and, as we called it, "put some jam on their bread". In Belfast we recruited Captain Tom McGarry who was in his late 50s and this job suited him very well, since in the winter months he had a job as relief coastwise master with the Nigerian National Line. His previous career, including the War years, has been documented elsewhere and makes interesting reading.

At the same time the Boatman's Licence was introduced to ensure that the skippers of these small passenger craft had some official qualifications. The examination for this was purely oral and, wherever possible, practical as well. Initially it was voluntary. In Northern Ireland at that time there were some 28 sea angling clubs and many of these owned boats. Word of the Boatman's Licence got through to them, even though they were not strictly operating commercially nor carrying more than twelve anglers in their boats. I think they discovered that if they had qualified persons in charge of their boats they would get a discount on their insurance premiums. The result was that Boatman's Licence classes sprang up all over the Province and usually they found some retired mariner who was able to give them the necessary instruction in basic "Rule of the Road" and safety matters. A further result was that Captain Mc.Garry and I found ourselves going out to some unlikely venues, usually on winter evenings, to conduct the oral tests. These venues included various "trade" clubs, the back rooms of public houses and even the sitting room in private houses. There was, though, one "up market" class at Newtownards Technical College and this was run by an employee at Short Brothers aircraft factory who had been to sea and held a Second Mate's Certificate. Practical tests had to take place in the summer, when boats were available. More recently the Boatman's Licence has been upgraded to the Boatmaster's Licence, is statutory for commercial vessels, and has three different grades.

CHAPTER 11: LONDON OUTPORT

Early in 1970, I was advised that my services were required in London Outport, which was at least preferable to London Headquarters! However, there was no qualified surveyor able or willing to move to Belfast to take my place, especially since the "Troubles" were starting to warm up again, so in the end the only solution was to induce Captain McGarry to join the office full time, and this he eventually did. At his age it was quite an undertaking, since he had to go to London for training, particularly in examination work, and reach the required high standard. There was a further delay in the summer when there was a seamen's strike or a dockers' strike in England – I forget which it was at that time – and the "Portavogie Navy" swung into action. With all cross-Channel cargo services suspended, normally quiet ports like Donaghadee and Portpatrick became hives of activity! It was soon proved that with careful stowage, the average contents of a 40-foot container, if homogenous (sides of bacon, crates of eggs or mushrooms, for example) could be fitted into and onto the average 70-ft traditional fishing boat. Of course fishing boats do not normally have load lines and are operating illegally when carrying anything other than what they catch. When this sort of situation occurs there is inevitably a lot of dithering in high places and some highly placed civil servants simply try to bury their heads in the sand. To stop this illegal trade would have been political suicide, but how to condone it? This time it was finally agreed that if a boat met all the current statutory requirements for safety equipment and was in reasonable condition, it would be given a simple stability test. If this was satisfactory it would then be issued with a temporary short term loadline exemption certificate. Thus many of us in the Office were out chasing fishing boats, especially in the evenings and at weekends. There were pickets to contend with and on one occasion I remember a container lorry being stopped near Portavogie and broken open. The result was bacon and eggs scattered all over the road!

In late August it was all over and off I went to work in London at the Marine Survey Office in Seething Lane, which was quite close to the Tower of London. Having been over for a pre-visit, I had decided to make my base at Billericay in Essex and initially stayed in the Railway Hotel. It was a one-hour journey to the office, including a 35-minute train ride to Liverpool Street Station, but it was also only a half-hour car trip to Burnham-on-Crouch, where I thought I might get some sailing! Before my transfer expenses ran out I found a maisonette, one of only two in a block, close to the station and the town centre and even with a small patch of garden. With a mortgage, I now became a property owner!

The London Survey District extended from the Wash right around the coast to Bognor Regis and, apart from London and the River Thames, took in numerous other ports including the booming container port of Felixstowe and the busy cross-Channel ferry ports of Harwich, Dover, Folkestone and Newhaven. The office, in Walshingham House, extended over three floors and included the Engineers' Exam Centre. Masters and mates were examined in another building, in Dock Street, about 20 minutes walk away, and while this area has since been "redeveloped", at that time it was still one of the seedier parts of East London. This building was originally a theatre or music hall of some ill repute and extended to three floors with the local Mercantile Marine Office on the ground floor, followed by waiting room, oral examination rooms and senior examiner's office on the first. The main examination hall was on the top floor under the original domed ceiling and could accommodate 60 candidates at a time! Also, because of the large number of candidates coming through, examinations were held during the first four weeks of every month except August. When there was a "fifth" week in the month the examining staff sometimes had a breather and caught up with administrative work.

Almost everything in this building was antique, including the furniture and equipment. The senior examiner's office was a real gem and was huge, with a huge antique desk at one end and a really huge antique boardroom type table in the middle which could seat about thirty people! In one corner was a wooden screen behind which was a Victorian wash stand for the examiners' use, plus antique coat and hat stands. There were some wonderful artefacts around the walls including some splendid old ship models in glass cases and perhaps the best of all was a series of four models of a full rigged sailing ship in some distress. These models clearly showed how to rig a "jury" rudder, using all manner of spars, planks of wood, tackles and lashings, which were probably available in such a ship. Most of the examination equipment, including ship models, deviascope and signalling gear was just the same and of the same vintage as in Belfast.

The Marine Survey Office itself was much bigger in every respect than the Belfast office, with a considerable staff. On the nautical side there were three senior surveyors, five Grade I surveyors and three Grade II surveyors, two of whom were almost permanently employed in conducting Lifeboat and Efficient Deck Hand examinations at the Gravesend Sea School. I found that I was the senior of the Grade I surveyors and was able to get some of the more interesting jobs out in the field. However, the system of working was archaic and really ridiculous. No doubt when the office was established it was somewhere near the right place, when there was much shipping activity nearby. Now, however, the nearby St. Katherine's and London Docks were long since closed and derelict, the West India and Millwall Docks further down the river were going the same way, as were the Surrey Commercial Docks across the river. Further down still the Royal Docks were operating at about half capacity and obviously declining fast. All the action was moving well down river, where Tilbury was expanding fast, especially with the developing container revolution. Felixstowe, in Suffolk, once a tiny port, was expanding rapidly for the same reason.

However, there were still plenty of conventional cargo and passenger/cargo liners. I found myself aboard the ships of many famous shipping companies such as Port Line, Ellermans, Stricks, Ben Line, Glen Line, British India, Blue Star, Royal Mail, New Zealand Shipping and others. The coastal companies such as the General Steam Navigation Co., Crescent Shipping and Everards were very much in evidence, and there was still a considerable fleet of colliers bringing coal to the power stations on the Thames and other South Coast ports. The principal officer in our office, who was a nautical surveyor, and older senior surveyors were very resistant to change, and I think just wanted to coast along quietly to their retirement without any change or upheaval! Thus it was that we surveyors who were doing all the "field" work, except in exceptional circumstances, had to report to the office at 0900 each morning. Of course everyone travelled in by train or other public transport. In my case it was only about an hour's journey in from Billericay but for some others it was much longer. We then sat around in the office for perhaps an hour while the senior "senior" surveyors sorted out and allocated the jobs for the day.

To be sent to Dock Street for a day doing oral exams was not too bad, since after walking over there we would only be about half an hour late for the first candidate. To be sent off to Tilbury to do say a safety equipment or a dangerous goods survey on some cargo liner was something else. Each morning at about 0930 four cars from the Government Car Service Garage at Westminster would arrive outside the office, or as near as they could get parked. The drivers, who were mostly female and wore smart green uniforms, had a rest room where they could hang about until allocated surveyors and journeys. Our seniors regarded this car service as a great privilege and a great status symbol, and would not contemplate any argument for dispensing with it on the grounds of efficiency. The regular cars were immaculate Morris 1800s but when the "House" was not sitting, or ministers were absent, we sometimes got one of their cars, a Daimler at least! Regular drivers knew their way around the areas we visited but strangers had to be navigated by the surveyors. Anyway, with this arrangement it would be 1000 before the show got on the road, usually with two or three other surveyors to be dropped off at other jobs on the way, and also a call at one or more life-raft service stations where rafts being serviced required inspection. By the time we reached Tilbury and I found my way aboard the ship concerned, it would be about 1200 and the captain, superintendent and others I had to deal with would be gathering in the captain's quarters for "nooners". "What would you like to drink?" and "You will of course stay for lunch" was the standard greeting. The car driver was entitled to an hour for lunch and either went off in search of a "loo" and something to eat, hopefully not getting hopelessly lost, or sometimes came aboard the ship and read a book for a couple of hours. I usually managed to get the basic paperwork done before lunch while enjoying the captain's hospitality. Strick Line and British India ships were among my favourites, since with their Indian crews there was always a splendid curry with all the trimmings, among the many courses on offer! After this there was little more than an hour left to do the survey and quite honestly we depended on conscientious superintendents and ship's officers to assure us that everything was as it should be or would be made so!

    The return journey to London had to be started by about 1500, since there were the other surveyors to pick up on the way and the driver had to be back at the garage by 1730. Arriving back in the office, there would perhaps be half an hour of paperwork before rushing out to catch the regular train home! In hindsight the mind boggles, but that is the way it was! Living in Billericay, I could have left home at my usual time in the morning, motored to Tilbury, and been aboard the ship in time for breakfast, never mind lunch. I could have done two or three survey jobs, and done them efficiently, in the area in the one day and still have got home at the usual time. Lloyd's Register, which is more commercially minded, had an office and a full-time surveyor based within Tilbury Docks. Most galling of all was when the Mercantile Marine Office at Tilbury started to contract and there was some excellent spare accommodation available in this already Government owned modern office block. I submitted a report to our seniors, backed by several other surveyors, pointing out the advantages and economics of opening a sub-office in this available accommodation. It was totally rejected out of hand!

Obviously, with the busy ferry ports in the district, there were many visits for the purpose of emergency drills and other work. In this case it was just impossible to go to the Office first and then out to the job. I was ideally placed since from Billericay I could reach say Harwich in an hour and a half by car or Dover in two hours via the Dartford Tunnel. Apart from procedures and operations which were familiar to me I got my introduction to hovercraft at Dover and Ramsgate. I certainly made a few round trips in these craft, sitting on the jump seat behind the pilots and beside the navigator. While still marine craft and manned by Merchant Navy Personnel they were more like aircraft in many ways and there had to be whole set of legislation specially to cover them. Needless to say we had an "instant expert" on hovercraft at London Headquarters. Their trips were advertised as "flights" rather than "sailings". In London we witnessed emergency drills on such foreign-going passenger/cargo ships as the "City of Durban", "Argentina Star" and the new Norwegian-owned Olsen Line ship, "Blenheim", which was under the British flag. We also conducted examinations for Lifeboat Certificates on these ships and on the cross-Channel ferries, which were usually made more interesting by the presence of many female candidates!

Most of the examination work for ratings, however, was done at the seamanship schools. The nearest one was a pleasant walk away from the office in the old St. Katherine's Dock where the London Seamanship School operated and they usually produced 20 or 30 candidates for Certificated Lifeboatman or Efficient Deck Hand Certificates each week. These could be dealt with by two examiners in one day. However down at Gravesend there was the National Sea Training School which had been established to provide pre sea training for virtually all ratings going to sea in the British Merchant Navy as deck or catering ratings. It was a huge, well-equipped and residential establishment and turned out hundreds of junior ratings every year. The official arrangement was that all the trainees sat for the Lifeboat Certificate during their time there and the deck ratings also sat for the Efficient Deck Hand Certificate. If successful they then had to wait until they had gained sufficient time at sea before the certificates could be issued. Really it was like a sausage machine and required two examiners there full-time. The two Grade II surveyors who had been recruited and appointed for this purpose were given a week's break once a month and put on survey duties. They were relieved by Grade I surveyors and I certainly spent quite a number of one-week periods there. The sheer numbers involved made it quite exhausting! Two other establishments were later approved for this scheme and involved my attention. One was the charitable Prince of Wales Sea School at Dover and the other no less than the Cadet Training Ship HMS "Worcester" at Greenhithe on the Thames. Most of my examination work during this period however was simply Masters and Mates Orals and marking of chartwork papers at Dock Street. Here there were many overseas and colonial candidates, unlike Belfast, where they were still 99 per cent locals!

    I had many visits to cargo liners to inspect explosives. In Belfast I suppose we had plenty of explosives imports but never knew of any being exported and this was a new task for me. The "Carriage of Dangerous Goods by Sea Rules" was a whole subject in itself and of course we had a whole team of "instant experts' in the Dangerous Good Section at headquarters. The "Blue Book", later largely replaced by several volumes published by the International Maritime Organisation, was everyone's Bible on this subject. There were detailed drawings and descriptions of how to construct magazines and detailed tables relating to segregation from general cargo. In these general cargo liners the magazines were generally wooden constructions at one end of an upper tween deck and loading took place from a barge out at an explosives anchorage after the rest of the cargo. Large quantities of both military and commercial explosives were shipped to the Far East. Nowadays explosives are mostly loaded into standard steel containers and carried on deck at the forward end of container ships.

While I had been involved in some marine accident work in Belfast, there was more of it here but the procedures and methods were still based in the last century! There was a casualty section in headquarters who were notified of all accidents and decided which of them warranted what was called a "preliminary inquiry" or "PI". They decided which witnesses should be interviewed and then passed this job out to an appointed official. The appointed official was almost always a customs officer, who among other titles held one called "Receiver of Wreck". He then had to summon the witnesses, put them on oath and take down a statements, known as a "depositions". Marine surveyors were required to attend to "assist" the receiver but since he usually had little technical knowledge, if any, of what was involved, the surveyor would usually end up conducting the proceedings themselves. On the basis of these depositions, the casualty section then decided whether to proceed further and if so an appropriate surveyor was given a official "appointment" to conduct the investigation, usually long after the accident or other incident had occurred. It was a ridiculous system but in due course an appropriate surveyor was given an appointment right away and could be on the scene of the accident often soon after it happened. Years later, following the "Herald of Free Enterprise" disaster, the separate Marine Accident Investigation Branch was formed on the lines of the long existing Air Accident Investigation Branch. It is perhaps ironic that marine industry procedures, established in the 19th century, were so outdated that they eventually began to follow air industry procedures, established only in the middle of the 20th!

One of the first inquiries I did in London involved a Belgian passenger ferry which proceeded out through the Eastern Entrance to Dover Harbour at high-speed and ploughed straight through a small bulk carrier lying just outside. Another concerned an Everard coaster, which was leaving Everard's yard at Greenhithe on the Thames. Unfortunately the master failed to look behind him as he started a turn in the river and the vessel was almost cut in half by an Argentinian cargo liner heading upstream. In collision inquiries you take evidence from both parties and then plot everything on the local Admiralty chart. If both are telling the truth, then the accident could not have occurred since each vessel was too far apart to have even touched! Minor bumps and scrapes, collisions with piers, jetties and buoys in and around the Thames area were common and often resulted in no more than a caution.

Apart from accidents we were always on the lookout for breaches of statutory regulations and particularly ships which were overloaded. These were usually reported to us by harbour officials and one such that I dealt with was a Cypriot registered vessel called "Evdelos". She had arrived at Shoreham Harbour, near Brighton and was reported as being seriously overloaded, which she certainly was when I arrived there. I was first of all interested to find that the ship was the ex-"Mountstewart" of the Belfast, Mersey and Manchester Shipping Co, and formerly a cattle carrier. There is a routine procedure for such cases and it takes time to check all the ship's documents, logbooks and other records, and physically inspect the ship, measure draughts and freeboards and check the contents of all tanks and bilges. There then follow calculations to prove she was overloaded and a full report as well. I spent a whole weekend on this task but was rewarded the next week when the master appeared at Steyning Magistrates Court. Steyning is a picturesque small town some miles inland from Brighton and the lay magistrates on the Bench, chaired by an elderly lady, were not familiar with ships and most certainly not with loadlines! Neither were the solicitors appointed to represent the Crown and the master of the ship! We had not got far before the Court had to be adjourned and we all proceeded to Shoreham Harbour and the ship, where everything was explained! The result was that the master was fined £5,000 but this was later considerably reduced on appeal.

Compared with Northern Ireland there was little serious fishing vessel activity in the London District and I never had one fishing candidate for examination while I was there. Most of the boats around the coast were small inshore boats but we did visit some of them when there was time. I well remember a visit to Hastings with another surveyor one day to mount a "blitz" on the local fleet, which were all small boats hauled up on the steep stoney beach. At least they all got lists of the modest safety equipment they were required to carry and we even went to the local shipchandlers to make sure the equipment was available locally. We never did get back to check that the boats were properly equipped – probably not! At peak holiday times we had to go out to back up the summer-only part-time surveyors and marine survey assistants who were checking on passenger-carrying activities, both on small tourist boats and at the main ferry ports. We had to check the number of passengers boarding and disembarking and make sure this did not exceed the number permitted by the Passenger Certificate. This was long before the present day legislation which again follows air industry procedures and requires boarding cards and careful record keeping. I think I visited every passenger boat boarding and landing point on the Thames! Quite often at weekends, if there was a job on a tanker at Thameshaven, I got it since I was only half an hour away by car and it was interesting to go aboard ships of my old company, Shell Tankers.

The winters of 1970/71 and 1971/72 were "winters of discontent" with, if I remember, electricity workers' strikes, postal workers' strikes, binmen's strikes and, of course, miners' strikes. Long power cuts and cold nights were all too frequent in the south-east of England! To add to the misery there were several derailments on the Liverpool Street to Southend railway line, which was the one I used. However, we battled on and, like most London commuters, I learnt to be stoical!

By this time oil pollution at sea and around the coast was quite a hot topic. In about 1966 the tanker "Torry Canyon" had grounded on the Seven Stones Rocks near Land's End and thousands of tons of crude oil had escaped into the sea to be washed up around the coast. This had prompted some action by the government in case another such disaster should occur. It was decided to place strategic stocks of oil dispersant and spraying equipment at all the main ports around the coast and the only problem was who should be responsible for this and its deployment in the event of a future oil spillage. Every government department with any marine connection promptly found good reasons why they could not take on this responsibility but in the end the Marine Survey Service got lumbered with it.

In Belfast we had about 5,000 gallons of dispersant in drums and two sets of spraying equipment which were stored in a shed in Belfast Harbour. In emergency this lot was to be loaded onto two of the local harbour tugs and taken out to the scene of the spillage. We did organise a practice run so that the tug crews knew how to rig and operate the spraying equipment but the first real emergency I was involved in occurred in Dover Strait when the tanker "Panther" ran aground on the Goodwin Sands in March, She was well and truly stuck and while no oil was actually spilled, we had to be prepared in case it was. Various surveyors from the London Office were pulled off other work and sent to Dover for two or three days at a time and I spent the best part of a week there, where we had set up a base in a harbour building. A big tug/tender called the "Calshot" of the Red Funnel Line and a smaller Royal Fleet Auxiliary called the "Felsted" were sent round from Southampton and loaded up with dispersant and spraying equipment. There were, of course, reports of oil spilling from the "Panther" and we had to go out and investigate. I was on the "Calshot", with a colleague on the "Felsted" and after following a search pattern of the area found one or two minor slicks of light oil. These were unlikely to have come from the "Panther" but they were duly sprayed with dispersant for the benefit of the media, who were in evidence! The "Panther", in fact, was loaded with a heavy grade of crude oil on which the dispersant would have had little or no effect and our opinion was that it would be just as effective to p**s on it from a great height! However, in a situation like this, one has to be seen doing something for the benefit of the media and the GBP (Great British Public)! The "Calshot" had ample spare accommodation and I moved on board rather than spend my expenses on a hotel ashore! She had a good cook and we fed well!

Despite the efforts of six tugs in tandem the "Panther" remained stuck fast and the next move was to transfer some of her cargo into small lightning tankers. Despite one day of bad weather, when this effort had to be abandoned, it was eventually achieved and the ship was refloated, without any oil spillage. She then set off for Rotterdam, which was her original destination, at slow speed and our two vessels followed in her wake in case of unknown underwater damage and possible spillage. At the West Hinder Light Vessel we were relieved by two Dutch tugs and turned for home – in thick fog! While the "Calshot" had radar, she did not have a Decca Navigator, but the little "Felsted" had both and she therefore led the way home to Dover in the continuing fog!

In February 1973 I was promoted to senior surveyor and pulled off all my interesting jobs in the field to take charge of the Examination Centre at Dock Street. This was still better than going to headquarters, and I was quite happy to spend a year in this position, which was the norm. This was another "winter of discontent" and among other problems there were railway strikes and work-to-rule to contend with. When this happened I had to spend the night in my office, sleeping on a camp bed, as did the examiner's clerk, to make sure we would be there in the morning. There was as yet no decrease in the number of candidates coming forward and most weeks were busy. While I could call in two other surveyors to help with the oral exams I still had to take as many as I could find time for myself.

By this time there were a number of female deck officers in the pipeline, since some of the larger shipping companies were taking on female cadets. I had one or two appear for second mate and even first mate but the crowning glory was when the first ever British female appeared for master, foreign-going! I cannot remember this lady's name but she was certainly top of the class in her particular group. She even pulled me up after signals examination to point out that I had sent a "J" instead of a "P" in one of the words in the semaphore test! To my knowledge none of these ladies made it to be in command of a ship, though I may be wrong; they mostly followed their female instinct to find the "right man" and start producing the next generation!

Then there were the Yachtmaster candidates. There had always been a Yachtmasters' Certificate but it was in fact the full Master, Foreign-going, Examination, less the Shipmaster's Business paper. It was really aimed at the skippers of large private yachts but apparently was also popular with RNVR personnel during the War, although these examinations were always voluntary rather than statutory. In any event, the exam was totally unsuited to the present-day skipper of a small yacht. Then in about 1966 the whole thing was revised and updated to become two more relevant exams – Yachtmaster Ocean and Yachtmaster Coastal, and they really took off. Before I left Belfast I had examined perhaps a dozen candidates for one or the other, or both, and these were all competent local cruising or racing yachtsmen whom I knew but – fortunately – were not close or personal friends. In London there were many more candidates from London and all over the South-East and we could only deal with them during a "fifth" week when there were no professional candidates. Some of these candidates were high-powered businessmen, eminent barristers and such like and had to be treated with kid gloves! One such claimed he was a close friend of the Prime Minister and kept his yacht on an adjacent marina berth on the Hamble River. When told he had failed, he was not "best pleased" and must have gone off to complain to his friend. Yachtmaster papers were marked locally and not at the Marking Board and shortly afterwards I got a phone call from the Principal Examiner asking for the papers in question to be sent up for checking by the Board. Neither they nor the Principal Examiner could honestly produce a better result than I had, and of course we were all scrupulously honest! I gathered that this affair went on for some time.

To my mind the big disadvantage of the new system was that there was no requirement for "seatime" as there was for the professionals. However, the syllabus stated that a candidate's practical experience and ability would be assessed in the oral examination. Many of the candidates, because of their background, education and obvious application to serious study, turned in beautiful faultless written papers. Some were also totally at home with the "Rule of the Road" and similar subjects, or at least as far as we could assess them in an examination room. One candidate I remember did brilliantly in everything but, when I asked him, he admitted that he had no practical experience of yachts or small boats whatever. He was building a Mirror dinghy in the garage at home and thought the Yachtmaster Certificate might be useful! I did suggest that a practical, basic sailing course might also be useful! Most of the candidates, however, were obviously competent and keen yacht owners, and after they had successfully passed I enjoyed chatting them up!

Because of the popularity of this voluntary Yachtmaster Scheme it was becoming obvious that our examination organisation would very soon be unable to cope with the sheer numbers of candidates, and discussions were already underway with the RYA (Royal Yachting Association) to see if they would be prepared to organise an acceptable voluntary examination system and take the whole thing over from us. At that time I was our "instant expert" on yachting matters simply because I had more practical yachting experience than anyone else in the organisation. I therefore got to sit in with the principal examiner at the various meetings and although I was a personal member of the RYA, I had to wear my official hat on these occasions. The whole scheme, as finally devised, was very complicated to my mind with numerous "grades" and levels of qualification, but over the years since it got started it seems to have settled down and become Nationally and Internationally acceptable. One thing I was pleased to see was the introduction of the requirement for "seatime" and the present day RYA Logbooks are not all that dissimilar to the old-fashioned Seamans's "Discharge Book".

The Grande Finale under the existing scheme, as far as I was concerned, took place during the "fifth" week of April 1973 when we had some 350 Yachtmaster candidates entered for examination at Dock Street. There were two written papers for the Coastal Examination and four for the Ocean. The first took one day, the second two and we got through the whole lot by Thursday, with two or three other examiners from Seething Lane to help with the marking. There was a railway strike this week and I spent two nights sleeping at the office, yet despite the difficulties only one candidate failed to appear! On Friday we had a marathon Signals session, which was just the same as for the Masters and Mates. Candidates paired themselves off for the morse and semaphore reading tests, with the candidate facing the front of the room at a desk to read the light or flags and his mate beside him facing the other way to record what was whispered on the form provided. After the required "block test" and plain language messages had been sent they then reversed places for the same again, but of course different "block tests" and messages. The candidates had been told just to turn up as they were able from 0900 onwards and the result was that the waiting room was full by that time with a queue down the stairs and out onto the street! We just filled the examination hall, ran a session, turned the first lot out and filled up for another one! This went on until well after lunchtime by which time my hands and arms were sore from transmitting morse and semaphore! Marking the papers took three of us the rest of the day! The Oral Examinations, including Signals Orals, started the following week and went on until the end of summer before we got through them all.

In November of that year I was relieved at Dock Street and sent off to Hull Technical College on what was called a "Preliminary Radar Course", which was highly technical and following which I should know enough to not only repair or even rebuild a radar set but deal likewise with a colour television set and similar appliances! It was obvious to me that I was destined for a period on the "Marking Board", but events dictated otherwise! By this time the British Merchant Fleet was starting to go into "free fall" and many traditional Red Ensign ships were being flagged out to dubious Commonwealth and foreign registries for simple economic and business reasons. There had always been a large fleet of British ships under the Hong Kong flag, operating in Eastern waters, where they enjoyed tax advantages and generally a more lenient marine administration than in the UK. The then British Government, which I think had just reverted to Labour after the "winters of discontent", decided to try and bring the Hong Kong marine administration up to UK standards while retaining most of the tax advantages. The aim, of course, was to halt the decline of ships under the Red Ensign. The Hong Kong merchant ship flag was after all just a plain Red Ensign, with no additional badges or other defacements.

To this end a team of three surveyors was dispatched to Hong Kong and the Far East generally for three months to determine what change of legislation would be necessary in Hong Kong and which would satisfy shipowners. The team consisted of an Engineer Surveyor, a Ship Surveyor and a Nautical Surveyor. The Nautical Surveyor was Ted Anderson, who was still the Senior Nautical Surveyor in Belfast and it was not long before the phone rang one day to see if I would be willing to go to Belfast on three months "detached duty" to fill in while he was away. Being pretty well settled in London, I actually had to give this some thought; but since my Dad was still there and so were all my sailing friends, I soon agreed. As it turned out, three months became a year, and then three years, and in the end I spent the remaining 22 years of my service back in the Belfast Office – though I didn't know it would turn out like that at the time!

CHAPTER 12: LATER DAYS

When I arrived for my first day back in the Belfast Office in November 1973, I was almost inclined to take the first plane back to London, and if it had not been for my Dad and many friends being here, I think I would have done so! The "Troubles" were still at their height at this time, and the city centre was dreary and dismal, with many bombed or burnt-out buildings, security barricades, troops and police everywhere. After about 6pm the whole place was virtually dead. There was usually a bombing somewhere each day and numerous false alarms. The Custom House had ample security arrangements but sometime before my arrival a bomb had been planted against an outside wall, resulting in only superficial structural damage but numerous broken windows. The window in my own office was glazed with polythene sheeting.

However, I soon settled in and before long I felt that I had hardly been away for over three years. The staff were virtually the same except that I was now the Senior Nautical Surveyor and had Captain McGarry as my assistant. The pattern of work had changed little if at all in three years but that would change before long. With the now declining British merchant fleet and the decline of British shipbuilding and ship repair work, so the Marine Survey Service also declined. It all happened gradually but by the time I retired in 1995 the combined staff of 25 at the Marine Survey/Mercantile Marine Office had declined to six in what was simply called the Marine Office.

After three months back in Belfast, I was asked to stay for six months and then a year. The fact was that when the "Hong Kong" team returned, Ted Anderson got a promotion and disappeared into London Headquarters. My spell of "detached duty" was then extended to three years, following which I decided to ask for "permanent" transfer to Belfast. The official reply was interesting and basically was that it was not government policy to permanently transfer mainland-based civil servants to Northern Ireland due to the present situation there, and my permanent base was still London. I still had my property in Billericay, which was let out, and I was receiving a "Detached Duty" allowance on top of my salary, so I just let it go on as it was. In fact I was nearly seven years back in Belfast before I was permanently transferred here! Later on, when other local surveyors retired, there was great difficulty in finding replacements for them since there were no qualified locals. The "carrot" to mainland surveyors was to offer a promotion to a Grade I surveyor who had been passed over for promotion, provided he did a three-year stint in Belfast on detached duty! Nevertheless there were occasions when we did not have an Engineer Surveyor or a Ship Surveyor in the office, in which case I had to put on my engineer's "hat" and go off to tackle some engineering or ship construction problem in the shipyard or elsewhere. I simply picked the brains of anyone else on the scene including ship's Chief Engineers, Marine Superintendents, Lloyd's Surveyors or whoever!

By this time all Senior Surveyors had been "upgraded" to Principal Surveyors, which was supposed to make us feel more important, but there was no increase in salary! The Principal Officer in Glasgow, or Chief Surveyor, as this grade was now called, came over for a one-day visit about once a month to check this outpost of his empire. This usually meant that apart from obvious calls in Belfast, such as the Harbour Office and the Shipyard, I transported him around the Province to visit the various smaller ports and generally view the countryside, with lunch out somewhere along the way. The three I had in my time as Surveyor in Charge also came over for such events as the Institute of Marine Engineers Annual Dinner but none of them ever brought their wives over for a visit!

About four years before I was due to retire at the age of 60, I attended a promotion board and could have had the Chief Surveyor's job in Glasgow. However, I was well settled in Belfast with wife and family, and a nice house at Crawfordsburn, Co. Down. This was where I wanted to retire and the only way I would go to Glasgow was on detached duty. The surveyor who took the job moved up from London but when he retired at 60, and wanted to move south again, he had to do so at his own expense and with all the hassle involved. As it was I remained in post until age 63, by which time a local and suitably qualified commercial marine surveyor had been recruited and trained as a Nautical Surveyor. When I left the office the staff, while small, was of high quality, very competent, and all were locals! There was one Nautical and two Engineers, all with university degrees, plus the very experienced Fishing Vessel Surveyor and two girls as back-up staff. The Office was also fully computerised, but that had been a long time in coming!

But back to 1973. The Marine School was by now part of the

Ulster Polytechnic, later part of the University of Ulster at Jordanstown, about six miles outside Belfast. The pattern of examinations was the same and there were still quite a number of mostly local candidates coming forward, though as the years passed the number of white faces decreased and were replaced by mainly brown or black faces! Most of these candidates were Indian, Pakistani and Bangladeshi with a few from West African countries and even the odd Chinaman from Hong Kong. Most of them were also candidates for Master Foreign Going, or Class I as it later became. While most of the countries concerned had a marine administration of some sort and even a marine examination system, these candidates wanted to gain a "proper" British Master's Certificate at the end of the day. British certificates have always been held in high regard worldwide while some others are regarded with less esteem, due to corruption and other shady goings on in the countries concerned. Apparently, due to quirks in the UK system for overseas students, the Ulster Polytechnic was able to offer a better deal for tuition fees and even accommodation than establishments on the mainland, which is why many of them were attracted to Belfast.

Of all these candidates the Bangladeshis were the most remarkable. They had discovered that the Irish Marine College, which was now based in Cork, could offer even lower tuition fees and so a lot of them ended up there. For accommodation they rented a house in Wilton Terrace, Cork, and I noted this address on their application forms for several years. As one group passed the examinations and moved out, another lot moved in! I also heard that only one of a group would actually sign on at the college and attend the course. However, he would make copious notes and collect all the handouts he possibly could, then return to Wilton Terrace where the rest of them worked from the information he had gathered! This was still in the days when there was no mandatory requirement to attend a course before appearing for examination with the Marine Administration. It was also rumoured that these students could survive on a cup full of rice a day! Best of all, when it came to the examinations they did not apply to the Irish Marine Administration but applied to Belfast. They would then travel up by train and spend a few nights at the local Stella Maris Seamen's Club while they sat the examinations. The reason, again, was that they wanted a British Certificate of Competency, with the Royal Coat of Arms on the cover, and not a green Irish one with a Harp on the front! The Irish certificates, I might add, had always been fully recognised by the British Administration.

There were some attempts at bribery by failed students, certainly in the oral examination, until they learnt that our system was not corruptible! At the very least they would break into tears and give me a long tirade about their now ruined career, their impoverished and desperate family at home, and much more, before asking how much money I wanted! On one occasion I had to call in the Police to help remove a failed candidate from the premises! In most cases any candidate could resit whatever part of the examination he had failed as early as a month later, but I suppose in these cases it was extra time and expense they could ill afford! It was also interesting to note from the applications that few of these candidates worked for any of their national shipping lines. They got better wages and conditions sailing under "foreign" flags.

Despite the decline of white faces for Merchant Navy examinations there remained a steady flow of local candidates for the Fishing examinations. In my early years in Belfast I had examined a great many Fishermen candidates and now later on I found that I was examining many of their sons! Most fishing vessels in Northern Ireland are family owned and sons often follow fathers on to the family boat. Apart from the examination room I knew a great many of the local fishing skippers from my activities in the fishing ports. The occasional bag of prawns or other delicacies would be left in my car when out in the ports but in the examination room such offerings were strictly taboo. The examiners are themselves examined from time to time to ensure they remain up to standard and one morning I had the Principal Examiner from London sitting behind me while I conducted a selection of oral examinations. The first candidate was a very bright young Chinaman from Hong Kong up for Master Foreign Going and he passed with no trouble at all. I was off to an impressive start! The second candidate was a fishing skipper's son from Kilkeel, up for Second Hand (Special). He was shown into my office and immediately dumped a large newspaper-wrapped parcel in my desk with the remark "Me Da told me to give you this"! Well, the fish were immediately removed to the general office for distribution to charity, which probably included the general office staff. Whether the Principal Examiner was included in the charity before he returned to London, I never knew!

Some of the last overseas candidates we had were from Mauritius in the Indian Ocean, and all were from the locally based Rodgers Navigation Company. Two of them, one deck officer and one engineer, came over and, having done a course at the local college, appeared for examination; I forget for which grade. Anyway they both passed and returned to Mauritius, following which a whole stream of Mauritians appeared over a few years! There was never any apartheid in Mauritius and the various races must have mixed quite happily since our candidates came in all shades from pure white to pure black. I well remember examining one candidate for Master who was very dark, with Chinese features and a thick French accent. All of them were generally very well prepared for the examinations and were a pleasure to deal with.

At that time we had two delightful girls in the office, one of whom was Martine, the examiner's clerk and the other Evelyn, the typist. Martine received numerous quite romantic cards from many of our successful overseas candidates and indeed several invitations to visit Mauritius! All of these offers were turned down and Martine eventually married a local schoolteacher by whom she produced three candidates of her own!

In the 1980s the whole examination and certification system was completely overhauled and brought up-to-date, including the syllabi, starting with Masters and Mates, Engineers and finally Fishermen. It was quite an upheaval and took some time getting used to. On the deck side, in place of the old Master, first mate and second mate plus Master and Mate (Home Trade), we now had Grades 1 to 5. Grade 1 was Master Mariner but the other four grades also had Command Endorsements which enabled the holder to sail as Master in certain types and sizes of ships and within certain areas. This change also saw the end of "dispensations", of which we had dealt with very many in the Belfast Office and Kelly's coalboat masters were frequent candidates. With the decline in the local bulk coal trade and indeed the import of cheaper Polish coal, their ships were often deployed away from the usual routes within home Trade limits. Sometimes they loaded scrap iron in Belfast for Ports in Northern Spain and brought back grain from French ports in the Bay of Biscay. Because their masters held only Home Trade Master's Certificates they had to apply for a dispensation to enable them to sail outside the Home Trade Limits – River Elbe to Brest, including the British Isles. This involved an eyesight test and a short oral examination, and the resulting certificate was valid for only six months.

The next move after this was to delegate the setting and marking of written papers to outside examination bodies, such as BTEC, and the candidates now sit these papers in the marine colleges, following whatever course they have taken. The signals examinations were also delegated to the colleges, leaving the local surveyor/examiners with only the orals. The signals examinations as I knew them are now totally defunct with the demise of first semaphore and more recently Morse code. We are now in the age of GMDSS (Global Maritime Distress and Safety System) and, naturally, there are courses and examinations to cover this.

In the early 1970s the British shipbuilding and ship repair industry was certainly starting to decline. Harland & Wolff, who had been famous for building numerous large and well known passenger liners, now saw their future in the construction of large tankers and bulk carriers. To this end first the large Belfast Dry Dock and then the huge building dock with its associated huge gantry cranes "Sampson" and "Goliath" were constructed and commissioned while I was in London. I think the first vessels built in the dock were one or two VLCCs (Very large crude carriers) for Esso. When I returned there was a VLCC under construction for World Wide Shipping of Hong Kong and then in 1974 they started on a series of four tankers to the same design but this time for Shell Tankers. These were of the new Shell "L" Class and of about 200,000 tons deadweight. I was involved in all of these vessels and enjoyed working on ships for my old company! My particular involvement was with safety equipment and navigation equipment and I usually went out on the first day of trials, when all the navigation equipment was checked, tested and calibrated.

The practice at this time was to have two trial trips, the first being known as the builder's trial. There could be over 100 people on board for this, on a ship with accommodation for perhaps forty, most being builders' people, plus owners representatives, various technicians from outside contractors and of course Lloyd's and Marine Office surveyors. Additional portable bunks were fitted in all sorts of spaces, and conditions were somewhat cramped, while catering was provided on a more or less continuous basis by a local catering contractor. The appointed Master and Mate would be two Belfast pilots, the Engineers H & W engineer managers and the deck crew H & W riggers. Such a trial could last up to a week. One of my jobs was to ensure that there was sufficient extra safety equipment such as life-rafts and lifejackets to cover all these people and because most of the hundred or so people on board could not be classed as "crew" the ship had to be issued with what was called a Passenger Certificate Exemption. This, of course, also applied to ships built for foreign owners. The second trial, known as the owner's trial, was much more pleasant! By now the ship would have been handed over and have a full complement of the owner's officers and crew, plus only a few shipyard personnel. In the case of the "Lampas", which was the second of the Shell "L" ships, I had got quite friendly with Captain Deane, the Master and his first mate, Mike Cowton. Both were English but both had married local girls at some stage in their career and were resident in Northern Ireland. Thus in November, 1975, while not really necessary from an official point of view, I managed to spend four days at sea on the owner's trial of the "Lampas", which was very enjoyable and indeed instructive. However the Mate was mostly engaged in checking pipelines and decided I should go "tank diving" with him. It is a very long way to the bottom of the cargo tanks of a VLCC and an even longer way to climb back up! Captain Deane was Commodore Master of the Shell Fleet before he retired and Mike Cowton of course got promoted to Master. In retirement both are active members of the Belfast Master Mariner's Club.

For the next few years Harlands continued to turn out large tankers or bulk carriers at the rate of about two a year. I think the two largest ships ever built in the yard were the "Coastal Corpus Christi" and the "Coastal Hercules", both for the American Coastal Corporation but under the Red Ensign. At over 300,000 tons deadweight they took up quite a bit of space in the building dock, which had however been made to build ships of up to 1,000,000 tons, if ever Harlands got an order for such a ship! On completion there were endless arguments between Harlands and the owners before they were accepted and the fact was that since there was no work for them, the owners were using delaying tactics. When they were eventually accepted they only went as far as Loch Striven on the Clyde Estuary to be laid up and I have no idea of what eventually became of them! This was in 1977/78.

Other ships which followed included the "Appleby", "Ravenscraig" and "British Steel" for the British Steel Corporation and two products tankers for Houlder Brothers, the "Hornby Grange" and the "Elstree Grange". In 1979 construction started on four almost identical RoRo ferries for British Rail and these were built in the Musgrave Yard on traditional slipways. They were the last ships to be built there and this yard was subsequently abandoned and eventually dismantled. The first ship was the "Galloway Princess" for the Larne-Stranraer route and in fact this was the first passenger vessel built in the yard since the "Ulster Prince" in about 1968. It seemed as though Harlands' welders had got used to dealing with the very heavy plates used for large tankers and bulk carriers and now had to get used to the much lighter plates for these ferries. A lot of the deck steelwork on the first ship had to be cut out and done again since it was something of a switchback with big humps and hollows! By the time they got to the fourth one everything was got right first time! I enjoyed working on these ships and got on well with the various Masters and officers who came to stand by them. The second and third were the "St. Anselm" and the "St. Christopher" for the Dover-Calais route and the fourth was the "St. David for Holyhead-Dun-Laoghaire route. This one was different in that she had a second Navigating Bridge of, facing aft, at the after end of the Boat Deck and a complete set of "astern" navigation lights. At Holyhead the ferries had to navigate stern first up quite a long narrow channel to reach their berth at the Railway Station.

There were two interesting jobs in 1982 when Harlands refitted the container ship "Atlantic Causeway" and the New Zealand passenger RoRo ferry "Rangatira" on their return from the Falklands conflict. The latter was an early type of RoRo, with very limited headroom on the vehicle deck and had been laid up prior to MoD charter. After the refit she returned to lay-up somewhere and I don't know what eventually became of her. Harlands had also built a number of pontoons which were taken out to the Falklands on a heavy lift ship to form a sort of "Mulberry" harbour at Port Stanley. In the building dock two gas tankers were built for Shell to trade between Borneo and Japan. These were the "Isomeria" and the "Isocardia" and were followed by two medium-sized tankers for BP, the "British Skill" and the "British Success". Next came four "reefer" ships for the Blue Star Line, the first being the "Scottish Star". At only about 15,000 tons deadweight they looked like toy boats in the huge building dock! I think the engines for these ships were the last marine engines built in Harlands' Engine Works before this department was virtually closed down. It is perhaps ironic that when the Koreans first got into shipbuilding in a big way many of the engines for their ships were built at Harland & Wolff and shipped out there for installation. In later years the bulk carriers and tankers built in Belfast had engines which had been made in Korea and shipped here for installation!

In the late 1980s and early 1990s the yard took on three jobs which were innovative, complicated and did nothing to help the balance sheet. For some time now the yard had been wholly government-owned and was only surviving with massive cash injections. The container ship "Contender Bezant", owned by Sea Containers, had been in the Falklands and had proved her worth as a helicopter base ship. The result was that the MoD kept her and Harlands converted her into an aircraft training ship or ATS. It was a long and protracted business and took about five years to complete, at some monumental cost. She remained a merchant ship as part of the Royal Fleet Auxiliary and so of course our Office was heavily involved. A more unlikely merchant ship I have yet to see since she was nothing less than an aircraft carrier!

Trying to apply merchant ship rules and regulations to this ship was a five-year headache but at the end of the day she departed as RFA "Argus" and was even registered in Belfast! I did hear that the MoD were very pleased with what they got and she was also the largest ship in the MoD fleet, naval or merchant! The next "clever" and costly job was the SWOPS (Single well oil production ship) for BP, and was named "Suillean". This was another very complex vessel and in outward appearance looked like a tanker with an oil rig amidships. She was designed to extract oil from small North Sea oil fields which did not justify the construction of a permanent rig over them and apparently was successful in this role. She had a complicated propulsion system of numerous thrusters, all computer controlled, which also enabled her to remain stationary in one spot over an oil well while she coupled up and extracted oil into her own cargo tanks. Then there was the RFA "Fort Victoria" for the MoD, which again because of the many complexities was a long time in building. She was basically half tanker and half dry cargo ship and was intended to carry all manner of naval stores, including ammunition, plus various grades of aviation and marine fuel. Once again there were difficulties in trying to apply the merchant ship rules and regulations while at the same time trying to satisfy the MoD requirements, and once again I believe there was a massive cost overrun. A sister ship, "Fort George", was built at Swan Hunters' Yard on the

Tyne.

By this time I was "Surveyor in Charge" at the Belfast Office and one of the few perks was an invitation for myself and my wife to the naming ceremony of all Harland's ships and to the luncheon which followed. My wife certainly enjoyed these occasions, though the naming of a ship already afloat is not as spectacular as a good old-fashioned launch from a slipway! In the case of "Fort Victoria" the sponsor was from the Royal Family – "Fergie" no less – and the security was very tight. A fleet of coaches was laid on to take the guests from the Shipyard to Belfast Harbour Office, where the luncheon was held. The route was cleared, lined with policemen and the convoy had an escort of police on motorbikes. I have never travelled so fast through the centre of Belfast before or since!

At about this time Harland & Wolff were finally privatised and taken over by the Norwegian shipowner Fred Olsen, but they were still struggling and the workforce continued to decline. The adjacent Shorts' Aircraft Factory was also privatised and sold the Canadian group Bombardier, but they have gone from strength to strength! Harlands, in conjunction with the Japanese Shipyard Kawasaki, introduced Japanese methods into the yard and they also produced a standard design of bulk carrier/tanker. Five or six such tankers were built for Fred Olsen but all were under flags of convenience and our Office had little input except for the sea trials equipment. One such bulk carrier was built for the China Navigation Company and named "Erridale". She was registered in Hong Kong and we were involved in this one. I noted that Harlands were really trying to cut back on costs and the officers and crew accommodation in particular was Spartan compared with what they used to turn out. Even so, the owners were apparently not particularly happy with what they got for what she cost. At the time of my retirement in 1995 the yard was still struggling on but it was a shadow of what it had been in its heyday.

On the fishing vessel scene things remained much as they had been until the mid-70s. So far as the local fleet was concerned the statutory requirements were covered mainly by sections in the Merchant Shipping Lifesaving and Fire Appliances Regulations. There was still no requirement for regular surveys or certification and we just dealt with them as best we could. However, a number of serious fishing vessel casualties, in particular the loss of the "Gaul" with all hands, changed all that. As ever it took a serious casualty and all the attendant publicity to bring about a change in the law. In this case the result was the Fishing Vessel (Safety Provisions) Regulations 1975. These applied to all British fishing vessels of 12 metres or more in length and at the time we had some 200 such vessels in Northern Ireland. There was a phase in period, the oldest boats being dealt with first, and when the whole scheme was implemented these boats had to have a very detailed survey every four years for the issue of a United Kingdom Fishing Vessel Certificate. There was also an intermediate survey at two years. All of us in the Office tackled this monumental task but it was obviously too much for the existing staff and before long dedicated Fishing Vessel Surveyors were recruited throughout the UK. In Belfast we got an engineer from Harland & Wolff, who soon settled in and proved to be excellent at the job. As usual, when new regulations follow a disaster, there was a great deal of "overkill". Applying them to a new vessel under construction was easy but existing vessels and particularly the old ones were another matter. Along with their certificate they would end up with a long list of exemptions from the parts of the rules they simply could not meet. Producing the paperwork could take more time than the actual survey! Over the following years I did not notice any reduction in the number of accidents involving local fishing vessels. The level of collisions, groundings and sinkings continued at about the same level as before the new regulations! Also a whole new breed of fishing vessel started to appear on the scene, which had a length of, say, 11.99 metres, so as to fall outside the regulations. Some appeared to be almost as beamy as they were long and, with their high superstructures, looked almost unstable!

In 1992 the powers that be decided we should start regular inspections of vessels under 12 metres, which still had to meet basic safety requirements but were not subject to survey. Since the Fishing Vessel Surveyor was fully occupied with the larger vessels the rest of us took on this task when we had time. In fact it made a nice day out in good weather to go off round the coast chasing up small fishing boats! Not only around the coast. On Lough Neagh, the largest freshwater lake in the British Isles, there were some 200 small commercial fishing boats, most with high power outboard engines, but we could only scratch the surface in this area. Lough Neagh also has some high quality fresh water sand, much in demand by the construction industry, and there were about 20 sand dredgers which we had always known about but had never had time to visit. Most of these were old motor barges and most were seriously deficient in even basic safety matters. Some of these did now receive attention but not always with the willing co-operation of the owners! One of our surveyors was almost attacked by fierce dogs as he attempted to board one of them.

In the early 1990s we got involved in "Klondykers". These are East European, mostly Russian, large factory fishing vessels which appeared in British waters. While not allowed to fish here, they would anchor somewhere close to a major fishing port and buy fish directly from the local fishing boats. Lerwick in Shetland and Ullapool on the West Coast of Scotland attracted quite a fleet of them. Most of these vessels were in a very sorry state due to lack of money for maintenance or repairs and some of the crews were not much better. When some of them dragged anchor, ran aground or otherwise posed a threat to the coastline, there was of course publicity and something had to be done! One of them ended up a total wreck on the west coast of the small island of Gigha in the Sound of Jura. It was decided that they should all be inspected and major defects put right but there were difficulties since they were out at anchor and not in port. Also, when serious defects were listed and given to the Master or Agent, there was usually no money available to do anything about it! Because there were so many of these vessels, local surveyors in the outports concerned could not cope and inspection teams were formed, drawing surveyors from all over the country. Our youngest and most agile surveyors in Belfast did two or three stints in Lerwick or Ullapool as part of a team. It was not an enviable job in the middle of winter!

I became involved when two of these vessels, both Latvian, arrived in Belfast for urgent engine repairs and having inspected them found that there was much more than engines requiring essential repair. They were of course placed under "detention" until at least they were very basically safe to go to sea! Well of course Harlands and anyone else involved wanted money "up front" before they would do anything and at the end of the day I think an advance was arranged on the estimated value of the fish cargo they would take home. The crews seemed to be totally demoralised and incapable of doing even those repairs they could have done themselves. Probably they had not been paid for months and they certainly survived on very poor food. I think the local seamen's missions took care of these poor souls while they were in Belfast! The best I can say is that these two ships left Belfast in a better state than when they arrived. The main machinery worked, they could drop and recover the anchors and if they started to sink, the lifeboats could be launched and the inflatable life-rafts were usable!

There was a quite considerable decline in the number of local fishing vessels before I retired, due to over-fishing. There were various decommissioning schemes and the vessels which managed to get a decommissioning grant had to be rendered totally unusable for further fishing. There were a few spectacular bonfires on the beach at Portavogie! I think the West coast of Scotland ports were the worst hit, since I have observed that once bustling fishing ports there are now almost dead.

CHAPTER 13: MARINE POLLUTION AND OTHER ACCIDENTS AT SEA

I suppose oil and chemical pollution at sea and on the coastline is hardly a subject to inspire much general interest unless one is personally involved or suffers as a result of a spillage! However, the Marine Survey offices remained directly responsible for clean-up operations at sea for some time and so I had to take an interest. Facilities in the ports for dealing with spillages were gradually improved but remained somewhat primitive. In 1975 I attended a ten-day oil pollution course in the south of England. It was interesting and included visits to oil refineries and tanker terminals, and even some practical exercises at sea and on the beach. In 1977 we ran a two-day exercise from the Belfast Office in conjunction with HM Coastguard, they being primarily concerned with search and rescue operations. The worst scenario we could think of was a serious collision between a very large tanker, loaded with crude oil and heading south from Shetland down the North Channel, and one of the Larne-Stranraer ferries, with 1,200 passengers on board! It was called Exercise Osprey and while the "assets" included RNLI lifeboats, a helicopter and two Belfast-based dispersant tugs, most of it was a paper and communications exercise. We were satisfied with the result of the exercise but the real thing didn't bear thinking about!

But real-life accidents happened. In 1978, the loaded Greek tanker "Eleni V" broke in half in the North Sea and the forward half, full of crude oil, drifted about for several days not far from Great Yarmouth. I was summoned to Great Yarmouth to "help out" for a week but all we could do was keep an eye on the wreck and have a fleet of dispersant tugs on stand-by in case of oil spillage. If I remember rightly the two halves were eventually towed to Rotterdam to remove the oil without any serious incident.

Also in 1978, we had an interesting operation at Rathlin Island off the north coast of Northern Ireland. During the First World War the battleship HMS "Drake" sank in Church Bay, Rathlin Island. I think she was torpedoed. Just after the Second World War the Fleetwood trawler "Ella Hewitt" went into Church Bay to shelter from a gale of wind, hit the wreck of the "Drake" and sank on top of her. A wreck buoy was placed on the site. Many years later the inhabitants of Rathlin Island, and particularly the boatmen, started complaining of oil coming ashore on their beaches and fouling the boats in their tiny harbour. Officialdom took little notice until their MP started making noises. Now the MP for North Antrim, which includes Rathlin Island, was and at the time of writing still is, the Reverend Doctor Ian Kyle Paisley, otherwise known locally as "the Big Man". The 100-strong population of the island was about 97 per cent Roman Catholic, but apparently they thought a lot of "the Big Man" because he got things done for them! Also, while he apparently considered them to be lost souls, they were his constituents and he was going to look after them! The result was that the problem had to be dealt with and the best way to do that was to blow up the wreckage and then either recover or disperse whatever oil came to the surface. Unlike an emergency this was a carefully planned operation and involved our Office, the local Department of the Environment and the Royal Navy. The planning started months before it happened and it was amazing the number of people and organisations who had to have their input. The RSPB sent me a lengthy missive telling me exactly how to go about the job and we could not possibly do it before September, when the bird population on Rathlin would be at its lowest. Warren Spring Laboratory, the government "pollution" laboratory in England, sent an expert over to come up with a plan of operation but his input was rather tentative. The local DoE came to meetings but their engineer assigned to the task had little input and was less than helpful.

We did do the job in September and were blessed with fine weather for it. I had assembled a fleet of vessels for the operation – two dispersant spraying tugs, two smaller tugs to deploy floating booms to contain oil and a self propelled barge to carry out the booms and mechanical devices, called skimmers, which were supposed to remove oil from the sea surface. All these vessels were based in Belfast and there was also a fine 50ft research vessel called "Farset", owned by the DoE and used for water sampling and testing. I decided the "Farset" would make a fine "command" ship and virtually commandeered her. She was only lying in Belfast doing nothing at the time; I knew the Skipper and he agreed to take her up to Ballycastle. When the DoE found out they protested vehemently, but since they were supposed to be co-operating the protest fell on deaf ears and they could hardly recall her!

Our Principal Officer was in a state of trepidation about the whole affair but I was enjoying it! We had quite a generous budget and it was like organising a yacht club regatta with expense no object! By 20 September the whole fleet was assembled off Ballycastle or in Church Bay Rathlin. HMS "Laymoor", a Naval boom defence vessel, had arrived earlier from the Clyde with a team of Navy divers to survey the wrecks and make their own plans for blowing them up. When I arrived most of her crew were ashore playing football with the Rathlin Islanders. Missing from the scene were the Warren Springs expert, who said he was unable to attend, and the DoE engineer, who had arranged to be away on holiday!

The next morning the weather remained fine and at about 1100 we all stood well clear, including the press, while the charges were ignited. The result was quite spectacular, something like several depth charges going off. Once the divers had given the all clear we closed in to find quite a lot of oil had come to the surface. We surrounded this with booms before it could spread too far and the skimmers were put to work. Unfortunately a lot of granulated cork insulation was mixed in with the oil and the skimmers soon choked up. We then very gently towed the booms towards the beach and anchored them there, still containing the oil. Any that escaped or still came up from the wrecks was dealt with by the dispersant tugs and it was now up to the DoE to deal with what was at the beach. Despite all the planning meetings they had made no preparations for this and in fact all they had done was arm a few locals in their employ with buckets and shovels. The weather was now set to deteriorate and the fleet dispersed that evening before being caught out. This was a very long time before there were sheltered harbours at Ballycastle and Rathlin Island!

The next day there was a severe south-west gale, the booms broke loose and there was oil all over the place in Church Bay. The bad weather continued for some time so that the small piers at Ballycastle and Rathlin were untenable and even the regular small ferries could not operate. The DoE were reduced to ferrying out equipment and dispersant to the island by RAF helicopters, which I heard cost £400 per hour! After some time and effort the mess was cleaned up. A week or two later HMS "Laymoor" came back and did a second blow up just to be sure. We had a dispersant tug standing by just in case, but no more oil came up and to my knowledge there has been none since.

In October 1978 a loaded tanker called the "Christos Betas" was heading up the Irish Sea, bound for the oil refinery at Belfast, when she somehow managed to run aground on the Smalls Rocks off Anglesey. I don't think there was much spillage but our Liverpool office had to deal with it and the ship never did make it to Belfast! Also at about this time the tanker "Amoco Cadiz" came to grief in the English Channel with massive oil pollution, especially on the French coast. Our "powers that be" now decided that there should be a full-time organisation devoted to marine pollution and so the Marine Pollution Control Unit, or MPCU, was set up. A retired Royal Navy Rear Admiral was appointed to head and organise this organisation, and this he most certainly did. Unlike the heads of the Marine Survey Service, he must have had good contacts in government for expense was no object in the first instance! He got together a headquarters team which included the most experienced scientist from Warren Spring Laboratory and then set about appointing dedicated Oil Pollution Officers in all the Marine Survey offices. This was ridiculous, since once they had been trained and produced the local instructions and contacts list, there was nothing for them to do except in case of an emergency.

 The Marine Survey offices were not consulted and I soon found that the person to be appointed to the Belfast Office was someone well known to us and I would not have wanted him near the office in any capacity. I managed to convince the MPCU that this appointment was totally unnecessary and it was never made! Before long the MPCU decided that aerial spraying of dispersant would be far more efficient than using non-dedicated tug boats and so the Admiral began to build up his own air force. It started off with one or two old Tri Islanders, which could carry one ton of dispersant, but soon there were some old Dakotas or DC3s which could carry three tons. These aircraft were based at airfields in the South of England, Scotland and, I think, Wales. They had full-time pilots on stand-by and I did hear that these mostly started small businesses on the airfields to keep them occupied, such as servicing or restoring old motor cars! In later years the MPCU was more or less integrated with the Coastguard. Those of the Oil Pollution Officers, who were sufficiently qualified and experienced, were employed as surveyors and others became Coastguard Officers. The latest addition to the "airforce" I heard of was a dedicated spotter and command plane with all the latest infra red and other detection equipment.

 One of the most interesting parts of a surveyor's work was the investigation of marine accidents, but following the "Herald of Free Enterprise" disaster in 1987, most of this work fell to the newly formed Marine Accident Investigation Branch (MAIB). While the investigators were all experienced surveyors and examiners from the main body of the Marine Survey Service, they operated independently and reported directly to the secretary of State for Transport. The idea was that surveyors should not be in the position of both surveying and certifying vessels and then perhaps investigating the same vessels when something went wrong. This was yet another case where marine procedures followed those already applying in the civil aviation industry. The Air Accident Investigation Branch, or AAIB, was already long established. The following selection of accidents which I personally investigated may be of interest. Most of them were the basis for an article in the Belfast Master Mariner's magazine "The Seamews".

A small and well found German bulk carrier was on passage from the River Mersey to the Clyde and, having rounded the Chicken Rock, south of the Isle of Man, course was set towards the North Channel. The Master himself was on watch and at about this time the radar failed. However, it was a reasonably clear night and, the helm being on auto pilot, he set out to try and find the fault in the radar. After an indeterminate time he looked out and saw a white Gp. Fl 2 light fine on the port bow, which from the chart he identified as Killantringan near Portpatrick on the Scottish coast. He therefore altered course to port so as to pass it well to starboard and resumed work on the radar. Not long after this the vessel came to a grinding halt as she ran onto a beach, but as the tide was rising she managed to back off after a while. The Master just did not seem to understand where he was or what had happened and again he set a course to pass the light well to starboard. This time she ran aground among the rocks in the middle of Knockinelder Bay, south of Cloughy on the County Down coast, and stayed aground. One of the Corys' Belfast tugs came round the next morning to pull her off and tow her to Belfast, which is where I came on the scene. I think the poor man had become too involved in his radar problem to keep track of where he was. Anyway, he had mistaken the South Rock Lightship off the County Down coast for Killantringan Lighthouse. Both lights have the same characteristic – Gp. Fl 2 – and, although not far apart, they are on opposite sides of the Channel. It was after this incident that the colour of the South Rock light was changed from white to red!

Another well found vessel, this one Dutch and about 1,600 grt, was on passage from the Clyde to Belfast and rounded Black Head about half a mile off on a fine clear night to set course for Belfast. The radar was either faulty, not in use or not being looked at. In addition, the only local chart on board was the small scale "North Channel to the Firth of Lorne" and this was out-of-date. The Master saw the bright lights of Belfast ahead of him but what he did not realise was that some of these lights were on the power station jetty at Clochan Point, which extends about three-quarters of a mile from the shore and is set on pilings. This was not shown on his chart. As the vessel went under the jetty the foremast came down first, followed by a couple of derricks. Then the top of the wheelhouse was taken off together with the signal mast and all communications aerials, but the vessel stopped before the funnel reached the deck of the jetty. Unfortunately the tide was rising and as the vessel rose with it there was considerable damage to the jetty. Also, with all main radios down, the crew had to fire off distress rockets to attract attention. A small tug came out from nearby Carrickfergus but could do nothing and the following morning one of Corys' tugs came down to tow her stern first up to Belfast.

Another case involving shore lights occurred off Carrickfergus. A certain gentleman was in the habit of going over to Bangor alone in his fast motorboat to spend some time in a local hostelry before "driving" back to Carrickfergus. On his last return trip, late at night, we could only assume that because of the bright lights of Carrickfergus ahead of him, he did not notice the lights of a low freeboard cargo vessel anchored off the harbour. Apparently the impact was spectacular with bits of fibreglass boat ending up all over the deck. The Donaghadee lifeboat recovered the body from the water the next morning, and at the inquest the medical evidence suggested that the driver may have been ejected from the cockpit and hit his head on the side of the ship.

One fine clear night and just to seaward of No.1 Buoy in Belfast Lough, a Norwegian-owned tanker of about 30,000 tons deadweight and loaded with molasses was inward bound, and about to pick up a Belfast pilot. Outward bound in ballast was a similar size bulk carrier, also Norwegian owned, in ballast, and she had just dropped her pilot. Both of these ships were under flags of convenience and both had full Filipino crews. There was apparently no communication between them and obviously one of them misunderstood the intended manoeuvres of the other. The tanker ploughed into the side of the bulk carrier amidships, with quite interesting results. The tanker's bulbous bow was completely stove in and the bow above badly damaged while the other's topsides were split open from waterline to deck. The bulk carrier was carrying bunker fuel in topside saddle tanks and so, apart from the investigation, there was an oil pollution clean-up job as well. In fact one of our local tugs managed to disperse the spillage before it reached the shore and meanwhile both vessels made it into Belfast Harbour. I never did find out exactly how this collision occurred. In cases like this you take statements from both parties and then plot everything on the large scale chart. If both are telling the truth then the collision could not have occurred since they were too far apart to have even touched!

One calm foggy night in Belfast Lough a container ship was outward bound in the Victoria Channel on her regular run between Belfast and Heysham. Inward bound was one of the more modern local colliers, fully laden, and both of these vessels had pilots on board. Both had all the latest navigational equipment, including, of course, radar. They met end on as it turned out, despite trying to pass "port to port", but at least they were only proceeding slowly. I remember that I was either in the Yacht Club on the seafront at Cultra or in a friend's house nearby when we all heard an almighty crash and the tearing of metal out in the Channel! Next morning, I went down the harbour to have a look at these two ships and start the investigation. Despite their slow speed at the time of impact they both had seriously re-shaped bows. After all the questioning I could only conclude that despite trying to pass "port to port" they were also worried about getting too far to starboard and grounding at the side of the Channel or hitting one of the marker beacons.

The Glenlight Shipping Co. of Glasgow ran what were in effect the last of the Clyde "puffers" and they were frequent visitors to this part of the world. In fact much of Harland & Wolff's steel came across in these little ships. Para Handy and the "Vital Spark" will be remembered from the film and TV series and believe me, Para Handy lived! He was not just fiction!

One vessel was on passage from the Clyde to Belfast in thick fog and managed to drive straight on to the Maidens' Rocks, off Larne. The four-man crew simply climbed over the bow on to the rocks, whereupon the poor boat just slid backwards and sank. There was still a lighthouse keeper on the Maidens at that time and he simply telephoned ashore for a boat to come out and get them. Another was on passage from, I think, the Bristol Channel to a port on the River Shannon on the west coast of Ireland, in winter. In my opinion such a small vulnerable ship should not have been sent on such an exposed voyage in winter. In any event, they met seriously bad weather and were simply overwhelmed somewhere south-east of Cork. Fortunately the crew escaped into a life-raft, having broadcast their estimated position. Unfortunately this was 50 or 60 miles out. The rescue services were looking for them in one area while the Cork to Swansea passenger ferry just happened to come across them and picked them up!

Another vessel went into Kilroot salt jetty on the north side of Belfast Lough and loaded a cargo of salt for Poole, Dorset. The wind was fresh southerly with a jumpy sea, and when she left the jetty she suddenly took on a serious list. Something was obviously wrong, so the Skipper took her over to the lee shore at Bangor and beached her alongside the Central Pier. The cargo of salt was off-loaded onto the pier with her own crane and grab. This was an older vessel, constructed with "open" floors and a wooden ceiling. We got the ceiling lifted at the after end of the hold in way of the sounding pipes to find a considerable depth of water. Because of the open construction there was a large free surface of water and this was the cause of the list. The crew claimed to have frequently sounded the hold bilge, but because the bottoms of the sounding pipes were totally choked up with coal dust they were getting a dry reading every time! This saga went on for over a week and made the headlines in the local paper. The locals all came to see the boat and the poor distressed crew, some of them even donating money for food that was mainly invested in the pub across the road! It was coming up to Christmas and I remember going aboard on a Sunday morning to see how things were progressing. The crew were sitting around the cabin table with a 40-ounce bottle of whisky in front of them – the last thing they needed – plus a huge turkey, both apparently won in a raffle at the pub the night before. I suspect the raffle may have been rigged in their favour! The whisky was no doubt easily disposed of but the turkey was far too big to fit into the small yacht type cooker they had. They took it back to the pub and had it cooked there. One very sad outcome of this saga was that one night the engineer left the pub before the rest of the crew to return to the boat, and his body was fished out of the harbour the next morning.

The US Air Force was extending the runway at their base at Machrahanish, near Campbeltown at the south end of the Kintyre Peninsula, and Scott's of Toombridge on Lough Neagh got the contract to supply the sand. It was transported from Belfast to Campbeltown in Glenlight vessels and one very wet day two of them arrived in York Dock to load. The deadweight of each vessel was 200 tons and 400 tons of sand was already on the quayside. A mobile crane loaded the first vessel until she reached her "marks" and the vessel then departed. The mobile crane then loaded the second vessel with the remainder of the sand and it was about 1600 when I got a call from a berthing master to please come and have a look. There was no crew on board and the vessel's decks were awash, with the loadline well under the water. We found the crew in the nearest pub and of course the crane had to be brought back to off-load the excess cargo. Well, the first vessel had loaded to her marks but the very wet weather meant there was well over 200 tons of sand loaded into the second one!

A small Danish gas tanker was bound for Larne, where there used to be a small liquid gas installation. Having suffered engine failure in the approaches to Larne, with a strong onshore wind, she managed to end up aground on the top of a spring high water close to the back garden of a house on the seaward side of the coast road. At low water she was high and dry and one could walk out to her, but for high water access the coastguard rigged up the old-fashioned Breeches Buoy arrangement, the only time I have ever seen this equipment used for real! Road tankers were brought to the scene and the gas cargo carefully transferred to them, the coast road being closed in this area during the operation and the unfortunate occupants of the house being evacuated. Even when lightened two Belfast tugs could not pull her off the rocks and a large Naval salvage tug was summoned from the Clyde. This time she did come off with much grinding and scraping of steel on rock. When I saw her in dry-dock in Belfast the bottom was not a pretty sight, but she was patched up and went off elsewhere, either for permanent repair or scrapping.

Another vessel that came to grief in this area was one of the Irish Lights Commissioners' tenders and this was surprising since these vessels are well used to manoeuvring close to rocks! This particular vessel was out at the Maiden's Lighthouse when she managed to get too close to the rocks, with a strong tide setting her on. As a result she did herself a serious injury and started to flood. A local tug came out and towed her to nearby Brown's Bay where she was beached on sand for temporary repairs. She subsequently spent a long time in dry-dock in Belfast for permanent repairs. The most embarrassing thing about this incident was that the actual Commissioners of Irish Lights were on board as part of their annual inspection! Then there was a commercial survey vessel which in fact was a redundant Trinity House pilot vessel. She had been working somewhere on the Scottish coast and ended up at Oban before heading back south. Leaving Oban, she headed down the relatively narrow Kerrera Sound in the middle of which are the underwater Ferrymans' Rocks. These are well marked by buoys with a clear channel on either side but whoever was on the bridge cannot have looked at the chart and got totally confused by the various buoys. Anyway she proceeded right down the middle, duly encountered the rocks and fortunately made it to Belfast for dry-docking under her own power!

One winter day when there was a strong north-easterly gale, one of the Larne-Stranraer ferries sailed from Larne on a routine passage to Stranraer. Only a mile or two out of Larne, it suffered a total "blackout" due to a switchboard fire, which meant they had lost all main engine and auxiliary power. The vessel began drifting towards the rocky shore of Islandmagee, just south of Larne, but fortunately when both anchors were dropped they held. She was still in a perilous position close to a dangerous lee shore and the Master, in consultation with the Belfast coastguard, decided to evacuate the passengers. The only way to do this was by helicopter and I think two were involved, both from RAF Aldergrove. There were only about 200 passengers to evacuate but even so, the operation, which landed them in a car park in Larne, took several hours and one wonders how long a full complement of 1,200 passengers would have taken! Since the helicopters could not land on the vessel the passengers had to be winched up one at a time and this must have been a traumatic experience for them. The anchors continued to hold and when the weather moderated somewhat the ship was towed to Belfast for repairs, and our investigation into the cause of the "blackout" and the effectiveness of the emergency procedures began. This involved our Principal Engineer Surveyor

157

and myself.

Most of the accidents which occurred locally involved fishing vessels, and probably still do. Common causes of collisions and groundings were someone simply falling asleep at the wheel or the Skipper leaving the wheelhouse to go on deck and help the crew deal with the catch. Accidents involving fishing gear were quite common and unfortunately some were fatal. Mysterious sinkings were also not uncommon: "The boat was feeling sluggish so I went below and found water in the engine room and cabin. I couldn't find where it was coming from. We tried pumping but the pumps choked up. I called Willie John on the boat fishing nearest to us and he came over. We all got off on to Willie John's boat before our own boat sank" – end of story! There were also the boats that managed to catch a submarine, with sometimes dangerous results. If nothing else they lost their nets. A typical fishing boat accident involved a large steel trawler which was returning to Kilkeel from fishing somewhere up north. All the crew, except for the man on watch, were asleep down below and he had fallen asleep in the comfortable chair at the control position in the wheelhouse, with the helm on autopilot. He did not even wake up when they hit a small wooden fishing boat off Portavogie on the County Down coast and cut it in half. Fortunately this small boat, while not required to carry a life-raft, did in fact have one and so the four-man crew survived to tell the tale!

Two small fishing boats left Portrush on the North Antrim coast one morning in thick fog and proceeded in line ahead towards some fishing ground to the north. After about half an hour the one ahead decided the fog was too thick to continue and told the one behind on the radio that he was turning back. He immediately executed a U-turn and the result was a beautiful end-on collision! The one that was least damaged managed to tow the other one back to Portrush.

Another typical collision involved two Portavogie boats, one of which was approaching Portavogie with a full catch of prawns. The Skipper put the helm on auto and went on deck to help top and tail the prawns. The second vessel was just leaving Portavogie Harbour, so it had the right of way, and when the other vessel failed to alter course, it was too late to take evasive action. Again the result was a quite splendid collision!

It is not only fishermen who fall asleep at the wheel. There was a small container vessel, German-owned and with a mainly German crew but registered in Cyprus, trading on a daily basis between

Belfast and Garston on the River Mersey. One night she sailed from Belfast and once clear of the Channel the Master put the helm on auto. When off the Copeland Islands he should have altered course to the south towards the Chicken Rock, off the Isle of Man. The remains of this vessel can still be seen on the rocks close to Killantringan Lighthouse over on the Scottish coast.

A very sad case took me to the island of Islay, since the Glasgow office were too busy to deal with it. This involved a 40-ft catamaran with powerful twin engines which was based in the inhospitable Loch Gruinart and was used for lobster fishing. Lobsters, of course, live in rocky places and the Skipper/owner had discovered a prolific source of them in an area to the west of Islay, known locally as the Irish Ground. In anything but very settled weather this is a very dangerous place for small boats and even the admiralty chart is inscribed "Heavy overfalls in unsettled weather". Well one day the owner, who was not in his first youth, stayed at home and his most experienced crew member took the boat out with three other crew on board. She was heavily laden with lobster pots and because the weather was certainly unsettled they were advised not to go anywhere near the Irish Ground. Yet all the indications were that this is just where they did head for and neither the boat nor the crew were ever heard from or seen again. The owner did admit that the boat had no life-raft nor indeed any safety equipment, since he was so confident in the integrity of the boat that he didn't think he needed it. A sister boat, which I did inspect, was similarly devoid of safety equipment. I had two trips to Islay, one for the investigation, which, with no boat and no crew, could only be speculative, and the second for the Death Inquiry, in lieu of an inquest.

On a lighter note, we had always had problems with certain Portavogie fishing vessels towards the end of May when they were wont to go over to Peel on the Isle of Man, carrying passengers for which they had no safety equipment and motor cycles which counted as cargo and which they were not allowed to carry. This of course was the time of the Isle of Man TT Motor Cycle Races. While we could not spend precious time trying to catch them leaving, usually late at night, the Isle of Man Harbour Authority often met them on arrival and immediately informed us. Because of the "Troubles" they were always suspicious of unlicensed boats arriving from Ireland with passengers and cargo. Despite one or two successful prosecutions at Newtownards Petty Sessions, this trade persisted and one year a privately-owned fishing vessel converted into a yacht got in on the act. This boat sailed at night from Strangford Lough with about twelve passengers and eight expensive motorbikes on board. They got no further than the seaward end of Strangford Narrows where they hit the Patrick Rock and the vessel sank. There was a large life-raft on board and there was no loss of life but I don't think the sinking did the motorbikes a lot of good! They were subsequently salvaged by a team of divers, but the boat was a write-off.

While working in London I had one or two interesting cases. One concerned an Everard coaster, which was leaving Everard's Yard at Greenhithe on the Thames. Unfortunately the Master failed to look behind him as he started a turn in the river and the vessel was almost cut in half by an Argentinian cargo liner heading upstream. She managed to beach near the river bank and after some temporary plating was welded on she made it back into the yard for repairs. Another was in Dover, where a Belgian car ferry proceeded out through the breakwaters at high-speed and straight through a small bulk carrier lying just outside. It was always said in Dover that the Belgian captains were real speed merchants and even wore their caps back to front! Then there was the tanker barge which was proceeding with the flood tide up the Thames to an up-river oil terminal. Unfortunately the tide had risen a bit more than was expected and she didn't quite make it under one of the bridges without taking off the top of the wheelhouse.

Not many yacht casualties are investigated by the Marine Offices but when there is loss of life and bodies are not found then they are normally involved because of the need for a Death Inquiry. One unusual case was the loss of an ex-Prime Minister's racing yacht while on a delivery trip from Burnham on Crouch to the Solent and with only a delivery crew on board. They encountered some very severe weather and big seas in the English Channel and when the boat "fell off the top of a wave" she stove in the gunwale and, before long, sank. While she had a life-raft and all but one of the crew escaped into it, it turned over several times in the big seas and another man was lost before they were driven on to the beach at Brighton. The Conservatives had just lost an election and Labour was back in office after a long absence. The then Secretary of State for Transport personally ordered the inquiry. I was back in Belfast but at that time I was heavily involved in offshore yacht racing and was the Department's "instant expert" on yachting matters! This had to be a very thorough and comprehensive investigation and I spent many days in the south of England interviewing survivors, witnesses and boat-builders and inspecting bits of wreckage and equipment wherever they turned up. Producing the detailed report also took some time. Eventually the bodies of the lost crewmen were found and recovered so I attended an Inquest rather than a Death Inquiry.

One unfortunate yacht accident occurred nearer home off the County Down coast. There had been an "Old Gaffers" rally in Strangford Lough and one of the boats was an old and well-known Galway Hooker. The morning after the rally the weather was very unsettled with a strong westerly wind, forecast to go north-west. However, the owner of this hooker was anxious to get back to his base at Carrickfergus and he sailed anyway, with his female partner on board. At about 1100, Liverpool coastguards picked up a faint "Mayday" on the radio and that was the last that was heard of this boat and her crew. Working from the time she was known to have left Portaferry, we estimated that she would probably have been somewhere just North of Portavogie at 1100. We then contacted every fishing boat known to have been in the area at the time and even found one that had sighted her some time before 1100, when all seemed to be well, although she was hard on the wind. We also established that a sudden line squally had passed over the area at about 1100 and concluded that the casualty had probably suffered a "knock down".

Talking to as many people who had recently sailed in this boat as possible, I was able to learn a lot about her. She had been built in the last century and had been little altered since then. There was a huge open cockpit and a small cabin forward of that. There were no watertight bulkheads and the bilges were completely open from one end to the other. There was also a considerable quantity of stone in the bilges by way of internal ballast. We could only conclude that if she had suffered a knock down and dipping the gunwale under the water she would have filled up and sunk very quickly. The body of the female crew was found the next day but the body of the owner was never found and we could only assume that he was at the radio in the cabin as the boat was sinking and got trapped there. It was also clear that the boat was sadly deficient in any sort of safety equipment. There was certainly no life-raft and it was doubtful whether there were any lifebuoys or lifejackets. In this case I attended a Departmental Death Inquiry and a Coroner's Inquest all on the same day.

CHAPTER 14: DECLINE AND CHANGE

In the general field, apart from the gradual decline of activities at the Harland & Wolff Shipyard, and the changing pattern of the examinations, perhaps the biggest change was in the decline in the number of British registered ships visiting Belfast and other ports. Trade and other business continued to increase but there were now some "funny" flags flying on the sterns of ships! The flag of Antigua and Barbuda was a common one. Many of the remaining British ships "flagged out" to the Isle of Man, the Bahamas, Gibraltar or the Cayman Islands. The local Head Line fleet disappeared over a period of about ten years, the ships being sold for further trading under foreign flags. The last ship to go was the "Inishownen Head", which had been converted to a cellular container ship but was no longer competitive. She was sold to Canadian interests and left Belfast for the last time as the "Sun Hermine" with the hull painted a sickly green colour and the upperworks yellow, in place of the Head Lines smart black hull and white upperworks! The Kelly coal boat fleet was finally reduced to four modern ships which were absorbed into the parent company, Stephenson Clarke. They were repainted, renamed, and re-registered in the Isle of Man but sometimes reappeared in Northern Ireland in their new guise.

While our statutory survey work declined as a result, our general inspection work increased and in 1982 the Paris Memorandum of Understanding was introduced. This initially involved 14 European nations (and later more) in a co-operative effort to deal with sub-standard ships. A headquarters and data base was established at St. Malo in France to which we had to send daily reports on any ships we had inspected, including defects found and any action taken. This information was then available to the surveyors anywhere in the organisation. Initially the system was slow and cumbersome but with full computerisation and the Internet it later became very efficient. Our surveyors would pick likely ships for inspection from the daily lists supplied by harbour authorities and then check their history with St. Malo before going on board. Detention of ships for serious defects became more frequent and as the system became proven it was adopted in other parts of the world. It is generally known as "Port State Control".

One quite steady job we had for some time was the moisture

testing of outward bound cargoes of anthracite slack. When coal is handled in bulk, both on board ship and ashore, there always accrues a considerable quantity of slack, which is coal dust and fine grains of coal. I can remember in Belfast when this slack was sold as such for "banking up" domestic fires or converted into coal briquettes which were sold around the houses by men with horses and carts! However, anthracite slack in particular could be burned in certain power stations, mainly in the south of England and on the continent and cargoes of this material were exported from most coal receiving ports. Here the main ports were Belfast, Larne and Warrenpoint. I think it was in the 1970s when a small British ship called the "Lovat" had loaded such a cargo at a South Wales port in very wet weather. The cargo was so wet that it was almost liquid by all accounts, and soon after she sailed the cargo shifted. As a result the ship capsized completely and, if I remember correctly, all or most of the crew were lost.

Anyway, shipowners and others engaged in this trade were advised to have all cargoes checked for moisture content and to this end all the marine offices were issued with a "Speedy" moisture-testing kit. The basic unit in this kit resembled a large cocktail shaker with a dial on the end. Measured amounts of slack and carbide were put into this and then well shaken, like a James Bond cocktail! The magic number was 19% and any reading below this was basically safe. However, it was well known that if a pile of slack was unsafe you could tell just by looking at it. I don't recall ever having to turn a cargo down. We used to check samples from the main stockpile, wherever that was, from the pile on the quay and also from what had been loaded in the ship's hold. We would also give the ship concerned a good general inspection while we were at it.

Another steady job we had in the later years was regular visits to the RFD Life-raft Factory at Dunmerry, near Lisburn. This factory was turning out some 90 inflatable life-rafts of various types and sizes each week and while the British Marine Administration did not require individual inspection of each raft, certain foreign ones did, particularly France, Italy and Spain. We did this work on their behalf and the paperwork involved was quite something. I think a French raft required no less than 30 signatures! We also gave the whole factory a thorough quality inspection about twice a year, which could take up to two days. When the RFD Headquarters were transferred from England to Dunmurry, we became involved in the testing of prototype rafts and marine escape systems, which was very interesting. Drop tests were carried out at Carrickfergus Marina where a large mobile crane dropped the rafts from a great height into the water. Hot tests were carried out at a nearby Shorts/Bombardier factory where they had an autoclave or oven large enough to take the largest rafts and cold tests at a meat storage plant out in the country where they had cold stores large enough and cold enough to meet requirements. Overload tests were held in the swimming pool at the University of Ulster, where there were plenty of students willing to overload a raft for a very modest fee! Other tests were carried out at sea and there were often practical tests on board the local cross-Channel ferries in which the crew were involved.

There were very big changes on the cross-Channel ferry scene with the rapid development of container and RoRo services, but our survey and other work on these vessels increased especially after 1987 when the "Herald of Free Enterprise" disaster occurred. Perhaps the first change on the traditional scene was the closing of the Burns & Lairds Lines Belfast-Glasgow passenger service. The two "Royal" ships were replaced by the RoRo/Passenger ferry "Lion", which operated a daylight service for some time between Belfast and Ardrossan, before it also was axed. The three British Rail Belfast-Heysham "Dukes" paid a visit to Harland & Wolff, where stern doors were fitted and one complete deck of cabins gutted to make way for cars. Since they could not carry heavy commercial traffic this arrangement was short-lived and the Heysham passenger service was closed for many years, although freight-only services prospered. Passenger services only resumed in the late 1990s when Seacat started a Heysham service.

The two latest Belfast-Liverpool ferries, "Ulster Prince" and "Ulster Queen", had been built in the late 1960s and had a car deck, plus headroom at the after end for two coaches, but again there was no space for heavy commercial vehicles. P&O withdrew the service in due course as uneconomical, but shortly afterwards the Irish Continental Line formed a subsidiary called Belfast Car Ferries and put one of their redundant ships on the run. She was renamed "St. Colum I" and operated from Liverpool to Belfast by day and back to Liverpool by night, which was not convenient for many people. While she had limited vehicle accommodation, she operated for several years before withdrawal. Finally a Norwegian company and some of the big Northern Ireland transport concerns formed Norse Irish Ferries and chartered two big RoRo ferries. One was an ex-Canadian train ferry, now registered in the Netherlands Antilles, and the other a big cargo RoRo, owned by the Swedish Stena Line. These were renamed "Norse Lagan" and "Norse Mersey". Both had the capacity to carry about 100 large commercial vehicles and the limited passenger accommodation was virtually restricted to lorry drivers. This new service was a success and the ships have since been replaced by two new purpose-built ferries with the same cargo capacity but more passenger accommodation. The service was advertised and became popular with the general public, many of whom are probably unaware that these ships are Italian registered, with Italian officers and Portuguese or Cape Verde Island ratings. The catering and cabin crew are, however, recruited locally and these are the only crew members the average passenger will meet! These new ships were called "Lagan Viking" and "Mersey Viking".

With the introduction of the "Caledonian Princess" in the early 1960s, the British Rail Larne-Stranraer service was saved and thereafter proceeded to expand. There followed the "Antrim Princess" and "Ailsa Princess", plus a number of cargo-only ferries, and then the "Darnia". The 1980 "Galloway Princess" provided large cargo and large passenger capacity. On privatisation of the British Rail fleet the service was operated first by Sea Containers under the name of Sealink, and more recently by the Swedish Stena Line. The Atlantic Steam Navigation Co., who had operated a high-class passenger and RoRo service between Belfast and Preston, transferred their operations to Larne-Cairnryan and so competed directly with the Larne-Stranraer route. Atlantic Steam was subsequently taken over by Townsend Thoresen and this concern was in turn taken over by P&O, who also operate a cargo RoRo service between Larne and Fleetwood.

There were numerous vessels involved in all these routes over the years and all received our attention as and when necessary, not least for the statutory witnessing of emergency drills. In about 1990 the first high-speed catamaran appeared on the local scene and this was the "Seacat Scotland", operated between Belfast and Stranraer by Sea Containers. One of a series built in Australia, this vessel reached Belfast under her own power and a sister ship had already broken the record for an Atlantic crossing by a passenger vessel.

Not to be outdone, P&O introduced an Italian-built high-speed ferry on the Larne-Cairnryan route but she had rather cramped accommodation and was also not very reliable, so was later replaced by something better. It was only after I retired in 1995 that Stena Line introduced their much larger high-speed ships (HSS), with one soon operating between Belfast and Stranraer. I have never yet been on board one of these vessels and cannot comment on them! Sea containers, who now had several Seacats, gave up the service to Stranraer and operated instead to Troon on the Firth of Clyde. They also operated to Heysham, the first passenger service to that port since the old British Rail "Dukes" were withdrawn, and a seasonal service to the Isle of Man.

I well remember one evening in March 1987 when I was at home and was actually having a shower. My wife was watching the TV news and came running into the bathroom to tell me there had been a terrible accident on a passenger ferry. As soon as I saw the news myself I wondered what the outcome of this disaster would be. The "Herald of Free Enterprise" had sailed from Zeebrugge for Dover with the bow doors open and had shipped enough water on to the expansive main vehicle deck to cause her to capsize. In fact she ended up on her side on an underwater sand bank and there had been considerable loss of life.

Well, within about the next two days Marine Office surveyors had checked every RoRo ferry using British ports. We carefully inspected the operation of all bow and stern doors and any side doors as well but more important we checked the system of reporting the closing and securing of such doors to the Bridge. This was only a start and there was a tremendous amount of what was called "HOFE Follow Up". Headquarters turned out countless directives which were followed by numerous new Statutory Instruments over the next two or three years. Surveyors spent more time than ever before on these ferries! Some of the measures introduced included indicator red and green lights on the bridge for each door and television surveillance of the doors and vehicle decks in general. A positive reporting system from the vehicle decks to the bridge became mandatory. Passenger boarding cards and careful recording of passenger numbers also became mandatory with sealed records kept ashore for official inspection. Safety announcements on the public address system immediately before sailing were introduced and once again we were following what was already airline practice. The stability of every ferry had to be calculated after loading and prior to sailing, and to this end all freight vehicles had to be weighed immediately before embarkation. This necessitated the installation of sophisticated weighbridges in the loading area. Some of these were automatic and provided a detailed printout including photographs of the vehicle in question and which clearly showed the registration and other identifying marks. I used to test them by driving my car on and collecting a printout! Another innovation was the provision of emergency equipment lockers in strategic locations on deck. Among other items these contained sledge hammers, crowbars and tripods, complete with tackles and a lifting harness. In the event of a vessel being on her side, these could be used to smash in side windows and pull out survivors.

We were still dealing with "HOFE Follow Up" when the "Marchioness" disaster occurred in 1989. This Class V passenger vessel was on a night-time dinner cruise on the Thames when she was run down and sunk by a dredger called the "Bowbelle". Again, there was considerable loss of life and the repercussions were similar to those following the "Herald of Free Enterprise". The safety requirements for passenger vessels which only operated close to the coast or in sheltered waters had not been basically updated since the last century but now there was a virtual blitz on them! In place of the old "buoyant apparatus" and lifebuoys as the only flotation equipment, they now had to carry inflatable life-rafts to carry all on board. The manufactures produced a novel type of raft to meet this requirement called an "open reversible life-raft". For the first time lifejackets had to be carried for all on board but because of stowage problems, aircraft type inflatable lifejackets were permitted. Proper passenger number counting and recording was instituted and there were other measures as well. For some of the smaller operators the cost of all this was just too much unless they got a grant and some of them simply went out of business.

Another result was that somewhere well up the line of authority, it was decided we should have local safety committees all over the country, headed by the Marine Offices and representing all manner of marine interests. In Belfast we organised the Northern Ireland Maritime Safety Committee, which met twice a year in the local coastguard conference room in Bangor. Besides that we had to organise no less than seven sub committees to represent defined coastal and inland waters areas. These had to meet once a year and report to the

Main Committee. Such areas included Belfast Lough, Strangford Lough, Lough Neagh and the River Bann, and Lough Erne. For the areas which included Lough Foyle and Carlingford Lough we invited representatives from the Republic of Ireland. It took a great deal of time and effort to set up all these committees and a great deal of time and effort to keep them going. Indeed for the last two or three years before I retired, I spent more time on this task than anything else! Most of the meetings took place in local council offices or leisure centres and the average number of members was about 20. They would be a good cross section of local marine interests, both official and private, and as more than one delegate remarked to me, it was a nice way for me and the Secretary to get around the country and meet a lot of people! So it was, and I met a lot of people I had never met before, and learned a lot of facts I never knew before! We were provided with a fancy recording machine from which the Secretary produced the minutes. Apart from the minutes there was a lot of following up after a meeting, and since both the Secretary and I had our normal duties to carry out in the Marine Office, we were often into the next meeting before we had cleared up after the last one! We did have a budget, but basically this only ran to light refreshments during or after a meeting. This was unfortunate since some of the delegates at first thought they could get finance for pet projects and arrived with their shopping lists! The best we could do was point them towards other organisations where they could at least ask.

We could certainly find plenty to discuss at all these meetings and plenty of areas where action to improve safety afloat was desirable, but we had no remit other than to encourage others to find the finance and take action. Matters which came up on a regular basis included the dangers of the wash caused by high-speed ferries in Belfast Lough and the nuisance and danger of jet-skis performing close to public beaches. I honestly don't know whether these committees made any difference to the local maritime safety situation but I like to think that in some instances we did some good. I am sure that the Larne Lough Committee played some part in persuading the RNLI to establish a lifeboat station at Larne Harbour and I am equally sure the Belfast Lough Committee had some hand in getting the high-speed ferries to slow down within the confines of Belfast Lough!

One of the many miscellaneous tasks assigned to the Marine

Offices concerned what was referred to as "Works in Tidal Waters" and this was covered by one or two statutory instruments. Our basic concern was to protect the public right of navigation in tidal waters and while this not very onerous work used to be dealt with by the coastguard, it was transferred to the Marine Offices while I was working in London. I remember being sent all the way to Maidstone in connection with a proposed new bridge across the River Medway. I was assigned a Government Car Service car with one of the "Girls in Green" and I had to buy a local map to find out where we were going. On arrival it did not take long to discover that the bridge in question was upstream of a set of locks and therefore not in tidal waters, and also therefore not in our remit! I think the driver and I had a pleasant lunch in a nice pub and then drove back to the office. A phone call would have dealt with this case, but who was I to argue!

Nearly all the cases I got in Belfast were dealt with without leaving the office, since I knew the coast of Northern Ireland pretty well and had all the large-scale Admiralty charts and Ordnance Survey maps to hand. The local Department of the Environment were the planning approval authority and nearly all cases came from them. Most of the proposed works concerned features such as new piers and harbour extensions which could only improve the public right of navigation. However, I also dealt with "dumping at sea", under other legislation, and this mostly concerned dredging spoil. There were a number of long established spoil grounds around the coast of Northern Ireland, all marked on the Admiralty charts, but sometimes there was the need to dump dredging spoil elsewhere and this required consultation with interested parties. There were always loud objections from the fishermen's representatives, no matter where a dump was proposed! In severe weather we sometimes got complaints that dredgers were dumping short of the designated area but it was hard to prove anything. Until quite recently there was also daily dumping of sewage sludge from Belfast by m.v. "Divis II", the local "honey boat". There was a designated area to the East of the Copelands and out in the tideway of the North Channel. Dumping of a load took only a few minutes and resulted in a large brown stain on the water for a while. We quite often got reports from overflying aircraft that there was oil pollution off Belfast Lough!

However, the big excitement came when we started getting applications for the establishment of fish farms. The proponents of various schemes for salmon and trout farms looked around for a suitable site and inevitably came up with Strangford Lough! One plan I received even had the cages located right in the middle of the starting line and the moorings at the Strangford Lough Yacht Club! Of course the objections to such schemes came in thick and fast from all quarters and eventually a high-powered conference was set up by the Local Dept. of the Environment and the Fisheries Division of the Dept. of Agriculture. The star speaker at this was the Head of the Queens University Marine Biology Station at Portaferry. He described in some detail the amount of waste matter that would emanate from a fish farm and the effect it would have on the sea bed for a long way around the farm. That was enough for all but the proponents at that conference and the whole idea was totally shot down!

The yacht clubs and other interests did not even have to say their piece! Since then, Strangford Lough has been declared an area of Special Scientific Interest and a Management Committee of sorts has been set up. There are some fish farms but only for shellfish, which involve no obstructions on the surface. The Northern Salmon Company, which had some powerful interests behind it, eventually established salmon cages off the East Antrim coast near Glenarm and Carnlough with a large hatchery ashore in one of the Glens. Once they got cages that could stand up to the strong tides and sometimes very severe weather in this exposed location, the operation was apparently a commercial success. Because of the strong tides there was always clean water in the cages and the effluent was swept well away. Also the fish had to swim hard to stay in one place and were much healthier and more marketable than those farmed in sheltered waters with little or no tide! Driving up the coast road, you would hardly notice these offshore farms unless you knew they were there but there were numerous objections for all sorts of reasons before they were established.

The most enjoyable "job" I ever had under the heading of "Works in Tidal Waters" had to be the construction of Bangor Marina, although I think my input to the scheme was virtually nil! In July 1976 I was invited to a meeting at Queen's University where a fine model of the proposed marina was on display, and all the technicalities were explained. A lot of research had gone into this and I returned to the office with a thick book full of diagrams, drawings, artists' impressions and explanatory text. Work started in 1980 when the old and derelict wooden part of the existing North Pier at Bangor was demolished. In April 1981 the then Mayor of Bangor tipped the first lorry-load of rubble into the sea to mark the start of construction on the new north Pier and there was a splendid reception to follow, which I attended. From then it was eight years until the whole job was completed since finance had to be raised for each separate stage. On completion of each of the many stages there was a splendid reception, all of which I attended! (I think the consultants and contractors paid for these events, not the ratepayers!) The final event was in April 1989, when Bangor Marina was officially opened and by 1990 it was fully operational. It is a splendid big marina and rates five "Gold Anchors", which I suppose is equivalent to a five-star hotel. My own boat, "Melandy", was berthed there soon afterwards and I have had a boat based there ever since.

In early July 1991 the Tall Ships visited Belfast, and the preparations for this went on for months beforehand. A large number of ships and crowds of visitors to see them were expected and so it turned out. Most of Pollock Dock in Belfast was reserved for these ships and their crews and the Harbour Commissioners provided excellent shore facilities, with a large transit shed being turned into a reception area. To control the number of yachts and other craft wanting to visit the harbour and view the fleet, permits had to be applied for at the Harbour Office and my own boat happened to be issued with Permit No 1! (The total number ran into hundreds.) More than a few private and commercial craft, other than the regular small passenger vessel, wanted to carry passengers and so our office examined these craft. If they were suitable and had the necessary safety equipment, we issued short term Passenger Certificate Exemptions.

All went well during a week of fine weather and there were no casualties or even "fallings in" that I heard of. Our own office staff got a free guided tour of Belfast Harbour in my boat and this included refreshments! The big event afloat was on the last day when the whole fleet set sail for their next port, which was Aberdeen. The shores of Belfast Lough were lined with crowds of people and I have never seen such a huge assortment of small craft afloat on the Lough before or since. No doubt many of them were carrying passengers when they should not have been but there were no accidents. Anyway, I was now off on three weeks' leave and our annual family cruise in "Melandy". We accompanied many of the fleet up the North Channel and met up with some of them in ports on the Scottish coast. Most were headed for the Caledonian Canal but the larger ones were too big and had to go round the top of Scotland.

Reverting to the Deck Officer examination scene, the Marine College at the University of Ulster had virtually run out of marine students by this time and closed down a year later in July 1992. All the overseas students must have found a better deal elsewhere, but I know not where! The peak had been in 1985 and 1986 and one week in March 1985 we dealt with a total of 46 candidates – unheard of for Belfast! Fifteen fishermen were accommodated in the Custom House, while 18 Class 1 and 13 Class 2 were accommodated in two separate rooms at the college. The logistics and organisation of this lot strained our resources, especially the staff, to the limit! In May of that year there were 13 Class 4, of whom I noted one had a white face! With all the changes that have taken place since, the local examiners have nothing left to do except a few oral examinations and the occasional sight test.

Finally, a couple of miscellaneous incidents may be of interest. One very wet winter day a very scruffy Cypriot ship of about 5,000 grt arrived in Belfast loaded with rice bran from an Indian port. We visited her for a general inspection and many serious defects came to light. These included the anchor windlass, main and emergency generators, corroded and leaking hatch covers radio equipment and of course safety equipment. The lifeboats were virtually frozen to the chocks and the equipment rotten or missing. She was called "Lory T" and was registered in Nicosia, in the "Turkish" part of Cyprus. The Turkish owner had apparently purchased her in India and she was next bound for some Turkish port supposedly for drydocking and repair work. She was in such a state that we immediately detained her and since she was "classed" with Germanischer Lloyd we called in the local GL surveyor. He had a look and called in one of their senior surveyors from London. We couldn't do much more until the cargo was discharged. It was unloaded by grab into hopper lorries in between rain showers but the whole ship and the adjacent quays and sheds were soon coated in a sticky mess of rice bran! When we did get to inspect the ship properly we found even more serious defects such as badly wasted hull and deck plating. We insisted on essential emergency repairs in Belfast and she was then given what is called an "Interim Certificate of Seaworthiness" by GL for a single voyage to Rotterdam and further repairs. We let her go and about a week later I telephoned Rotterdam to find out if she had arrived. No news! Some time later I found out that she had appeared off the Hook of Holland, anchored for a while and then disappeared. Germanischer Lloyd put in train a search for her and she was eventually found in some small Turkish port, but now named "Nisa" and registered in Istanbul! I never heard what happened to her eventually.

When there was severe weather in the North Channel or Irish Sea, very occasionally a RoRo ferry would meet a rogue wave and heel over to such an extent that heavy lorries or trailers on the vehicle deck would break their lashings and end up on their sides or leaning on other cargo units. Off Corsewall Point near the entrance to Loch Ryan seemed to be a prime area for occasional rogue waves.

The "Darnia", on the Larne-Stranraer run, was an odd ship and certainly looked "top heavy". Without any cargo at all on board she also had a slight permanent list but numerous calculations had shown her stability to be more than adequate to meet the various rules and regulations. In fact she was perhaps a little too "stiff" and had a short rolling period. One winter Saturday night I was at home when the telephone rang and I found the Sealink Superintendent at Stranraer on the other end. The "Darnia" had hit a bad wave off Corsewall on the way into Loch Ryan and several cargo units had broken loose when she heeled over. These were now being unloaded by the local crash and recovery specialist but most of the crew had made their minds up that the ship was unsafe and had in effect staged a "sit in". Would I mind coming over to try and convince them otherwise? I therefore set off for Larne and crossed to Stranraer on one of the other ferries.

It was about 0300 on Sunday morning when I boarded the "Darnia" to find the Sealink Chief Naval Architect in the crew messroom talking to crew members, most of those present being catering staff and the appointed spokesman a junior one at that! I think most of the regular deck crew were too embarrassed to be there. By now all the damaged and other cargo units had been landed ashore but I gathered all the necessary information and re-worked the stability calculation for the voyage in question. It was perfectly satisfactory. None of the cargo units which had broken loose had shifted much due to other units stowed close beside them but I did note that one heavy trailer had fallen on top of a nearly new Jaguar alongside it and had certainly given it a different profile! I don't imagine the owner was best pleased! We convinced the crew that the ship was perfectly safe but the Naval Architect and I agreed to sail with the ship to show our confidence in her! I had already made many crossings in this ship in the course of official business and also privately, in various states of weather, and had no doubts about her safety! The ship was eventually loaded with a cargo for Larne and we had an uneventful crossing. The Naval Architect returned in her to Stranraer but I went home, arriving in time for a late lunch. Most of the trouble with RoRo cargo in bad weather was due to badly-stowed cargo within the cargo units themselves, over which the crew had no control.

One morning one of our surveyors went to Londonderry to inspect a Russian or other East European ship which had just arrived from some port in North Africa. When he went into the forecastle space to inspect and try out the emergency fire pump he noticed some black plastic bags on the deck of this compartment. When some crew members came in and tried to furtively remove these bags he began to wonder what was in them. When he demanded that one be opened he found it was full of mostly live tortoises, now an illegal import to this country and no doubt regarded by the crew as a source of ready cash! HM Customs were advised of the find and several hundred small tortoises were removed from the ship by the RSPCA. I sometimes wondered if we would come across smuggled drugs in any of our shipboard activities, but in my time we never did.

In October 1995 I retired from what was now called the Marine Safety Agency, whereupon my wife returned to work and I found that I had plenty to keep me busy at home. There were also preparations for some longer cruises in "Melandy" since the time limits were now only dictated by school holidays. I undertook a few private survey jobs and occasional consultation work until I became an old age pensioner and then virtually retired completely from paid employment.

Launch of "Pleiades" at Holywood, 1966

"Safari" at Kircubbin Regatta, 1966

"Sarita" in Gott Bay, Tiree, 1969

"Samphire" racing in the North Channel, 1969

"Ruffian" racing in 1973

"Golden Delicious" in Ballyholme Bay, 1976

"Golden Leigh", 1977
Racing off Bangor during Comet Wheel Event

Photograph by courtesy of "County Down Spectator"

"Golden Leigh", 1977
A happy crowd aboard during Comet Wheel Event at Bangor
Photograph by courtesy of "County Down Spectator"

"Golden Leigh", 1977
The Admiral's Cup racing crew on board at Cowes

"Golden Leigh", 1977
On a run during Cowes week racing

The Squib "Chance" off Cultra, Belfast Lough, 1977

Squibs in the Sixmilewater, Lough Neagh, 1977

"Melandy" in Belfast Lough, 1981

"Melandy" on the slipway at RNIYC, Cultra

"Melandy" in Loch Sween, Scotland, 1981

"Sundowner" on Lake Vanern, Sweden, 2000

At a lock on the Gota Canal, Sweden, 2000

Sundowner's Family Crew, 2000

CHAPTER 15: SAILING DAYS, 1965-1968

Between coming "ashore" in March 1965 and starting work with the Marine Survey Service in July, I put in my time helping out with backstage work at the Circle Theatre, including three visits to local drama festivals, which involved long hours and late nights but it was all good fun. However, once the sailing season started at Holywood Yacht Club I was very active there. I raced "round the buoys" at Holywood or went to Belfast Lough regattas in either an old and heavy GP14 "Gazebo", owned by my friend John Olver, or in "Safari", a big Rambler dinghy owned by Fred Duffin, an older member of the Club. He enjoyed sailing and racing but would not helm the boat himself! The highlight of the season was Strangford Week in July, when John and I sailed "Safari" with Fred in a week-long series of races at various Clubs in Strangford Lough. We won virtually everything in the handicap class, which included dinghies, keelboats and assorted cruisers and this included one heavy weather race when we broke the rudder and had to finish the race steering with an oar! Fred was delighted!

Meanwhile, I had ideas for a small boat that could be lived on and taken for modest cruises. At that time "pocket" cruisers between 17 and 22 ft in length were very popular and there were numerous designs and production models on the market, such as the Silhouette, Lysander and the Westerly. I found a small firm in Bungay, Suffolk, which was producing basic plywood kits and ordered a kit for one of their designs called the Ibiza, 20-ft long and fitted with bilge keels. When it was delivered in October, I took some time off to check out the contents, and construction work started almost immediately. We had already reserved our neighbour Mahoods' basement as a building site and Dad couldn't wait to get going!

Construction continued all winter in the evenings and at weekends, and when I was away in London on various official training courses, Dad continued with the building. The design called for twin bilge keels of sheet steel but we were not keen on this arrangement and Dad produced a wooden plug for cast-iron keels, which were then cast at the Grosvenor Foundry in Belfast. I think their main line of business was manhole covers and such like. My fine Sunbeam Rapier car was somewhat neglected during this period and even grew moss on the roof! We constructed a trailer for the boat using the front axle and wheels of an old van or taxi, and on 12 June, 1966, "Pleiades", as I called her, was towed behind my car to Holywood and launched at the club slipway.

"Pleiades" was probably as good a performer as most boats of her type, though of course not very good to windward. Her accommodation consisted of two forward berths and two quarter berths with a simple galley arrangement amidships. The toilet was even simpler – "bucket and chuck it"! Mechanical power was provided by a long shaft Seagull outboard which was fitted down a trunk at the after end of the cockpit. I think the total cost was about £500.

In my new boat, I sailed in some local races in Belfast Lough without much success but at the same time my friend John and I were still successfully racing in the Rambler "Safari". In July we sailed "Pleiades" round to Strangford Lough with a night stop at Donaghadee on the way, in time for Strangford Week. The arrangement for this was quite good and a lot of fun since "Pleiades" was our accommodation boat while we raced in "Safari", which we towed behind us to the various events around the Lough. We were able to enjoy all the parties without having to drive home afterwards! "Pleiades" remained in Strangford Lough thereafter, an area for which she was well suited, and I was able to lay a mooring for her at Ballydorn. This was before the Down Cruising Club got properly established and there was any control over the moorings there. There were numerous trips to remote and interesting parts of the Lough, and drying out then walking ashore at low tide was the norm! However, Strangford Village was a favourite spot, afloat or aground, and the "Lobster Pot" a favourite watering hole. At the end of the season we pulled "Pleiades" out on her trailer and towed her up the road to spend the winter in a barn at the "Beeches" where I had been a happy evacuee for two years during the War.

For the 1967 season I had "Pleiades" in Strangford Lough but was still racing in "Safari" quite successfully at Holywood. In early June "Pleiades" had an offshore trip when John and I plus another friend, Tom McFarlane, sailed her to Port St. Mary on the Isle of Man. This took five days, since we spent a night at Strangford village going out and again coming back, plus three nights on the island. We hired a car to tour the island, went fishing very successfully on Wort Bank and really enjoyed the trip. We had a flat calm going over under engine and a fresh south-westerly wind coming back under sail and there were no problems. I was unable to get off work for Strangford Week in July but "Pleiades" was there with John and another friend, David Grime, on board. I was able to join them on the Friday and it was some time during this weekend that we happened to be tied alongside an old classic 39-ft cutter called "Sarita", whose base was the Strangford Lough Yacht Club at Whiterock.

Conversation and hospitality ensued and thus we got to know George Lennox, the owner. He was only there for the "beer" and the partying with no intention of racing in anything. The outcome of this meeting was that we went sailing in "Sarita" several times before the end of the season, the most notable trip being from Whiterock to Portpatrick and back one weekend. This happened to be the weekend of the Royal Ulster Yacht Club's Portpatrick Race, always noted for the heavy partying after the race. This occasion was no exception but we did make the dinner at the Portpatrick Hotel and we even sailed for home at 0130 on Sunday to make the tide in Strangford Narrows. "Sarita" had been built in 1910 in Southampton as a "gentleman's yacht". She had a splendid wood panelled saloon and large quarter berths for the owner, plus crew quarters and galley in the forecastle. She had been altered somewhat over the years and the galley was now aft, though the saloon was still basically the same. I had actually met this boat many years before when I was in the 59th Belfast Boy Scout Group. Two of us were doing our Oarsman's Badge and to this end a kind gent called Ronald Green took us to Strangford Lough Yacht Club to demonstrate our skills in "Sarita's" dinghy on Whiterock Bay. He treated us to tea in the clubhouse and then showed us his yacht which was in a shed at the nearby boatyard. At some much later date he sold her to George Lennox.

At the end of the sailing season "Pleiades" was brought home by road for some modifications and spent the winter back in George Mahood's basement while "Sarita" was sailed round to Cultra, close to Holywood on Belfast Lough, and was hauled out at the Royal North of Ireland Yacht Club yard for the winter. George was a member of the Club. By now it had been agreed that there would be a West Coast of Scotland cruise in "Sarita" the next summer, for two weeks in July. John was married with two small children and so was David Grime. David was a marine engineer who after doing his "time" at Harland & Wolff had been at sea with the Cunard Line but was now back in the "Yard" as a manager. His brother Charles was the English Master and Deputy Headmaster at Sullivan Upper School. George was married to long-suffering Pat and had four children. This did not deter his other activities. I was the only bachelor and, apart from my work for the Marine Survey Office, had no such commitments! Obviously we turned out to work on "Sarita" during the winter and more so in the spring leading up to her relaunch. George put both John and I up for membership of the Club, someone seconded the proposal, and we were both elected members of the Royal North of Ireland Yacht Club. In later years first John and then I served as Commodore of this Yacht Club.

At the end of April 1968 "Pleiades" returned to her mooring at Ballydorn. John and I spent one enjoyable weekend on board, which included a night at Strangford Village. "Sarita" was launched at Cultra on 9 May and the delivery trip to Strangford Lough at the weekend included all day and all night Saturday spent at Peel on the Isle of Man. Due to an onshore gale and heavy swell we had to go into the inner harbour where we dried out alongside the wall. On Sunday it was a nasty beat across to Strangford Lough and we didn't reach Whiterock until 2200.

The year 1968 was a very active sailing season since I was the Sailing Secretary at Holywood Yacht Club and still racing sometimes in "Safari", both at Holywood and at Strangford Lough regattas, but more often in the Fairy Class at RNIYC Cultra and in particular in "Titania". These old keelboats were built early in the 20th Century and now, into the 21st century, they are still thriving and sailed enthusiastically, mostly by syndicates at the club whose members enjoy good sailing at a very modest cost, and a satisfactory social life to go with it! "Titania" was owned and raced by one Alec Jamison, who could best be described as one of the club "characters". Alec was a "natural" helmsman who had a natural feel for a boat under sail and could tell when it was going at its best – when he was with it enough to know what he was doing! The boat was not in the best state of repair and had serious leaks at the gunwales when heeled over, but still won races. One Saturday we went to Whithead Regatta at the north side of the mouth of Belfast Lough in a near calm and got a tow there behind a Cultra motor boat. A breeze filled in later so that we were able to race and won in our class, following which there was a monumental party ashore in the Yacht Club. By the time we got back aboard "Titania" early on Sunday morning there was again no wind so we just bedded down on the floor boards with the spinnaker sail to cover us until the Yacht Club opened again at lunchtime for another party. In the afternoon we got another tow back to Cultra.

Another boat I got involved in this season was "Vandara of Arklow", owned by the then Hon. Secretary of RNIYC, and I was invited to crew in her for the North Channel race in June. At that time the North Channel race and the Blue Water Trophy were the two most popular offshore races in local waters. While the North Channel was a straight run from Belfast Lough to a destination in the Firth of Clyde, the Blue Water took in a course round the Isle of Man before heading for the Clyde. These two races were run on consecutive weekends, one out and one back with the direction changing each year. For boats whose crews could take a week off there was the opportunity to cruise locally or just socialise in the yacht clubs between the two races. Anyway, the North Channel started from RNIYC, Cultra, at 2200 on Friday 14 June, following a fairly heavy reception in the Clubhouse. Some of the crews being ferried out to their boats did not appear to be in a fit state to "drive"! "Vandara" was a comfortable motor sailer built by Tyrrell's of Arklow and was certainly no racing machine, but neither were many of the boats that went racing in those days! I was intrigued to note that the owner took virtually no part in sailing the boat. His wife appeared to be the driving force while the chief helmsman and tactician was the most eligible and well-heeled young bachelor in the club. In light winds we made slow progress up the North Channel and were off Pladda and the Isle of Arran at 0600 when it became flat calm. After drifting about for some four hours we gave up and motored to the finish at Tighnabruich on the West Kyle. These races were social events as much as anything and the most important thing was to get to the destination in time for the party! Despite a plague of midges it was an enjoyable party and went on in various locations until early Sunday.

Since "Vandara" was now going cruising on the West coast of Scotland, I had to get home by other means and was put on board "Juffra" at about 0730. She was a virtually new Nicholson 32 and had won the race. The crew were all from Royal Ulster Yacht Club and were not known to me yet. I assumed that from such a prestigious club they would be a very competent and conscientious crew. Anyway, a young man appeared on deck, hove up the anchor and got us going towards home. Once settled down and with sail up in a fair breeze, he gave me the helm and disappeared down below again. It was a fine sail down Kilbrennan Sound until lunchtime when the wind died away and the engine went on. The rest of the crew appeared at about this time and set about "nooners". There was something to eat but mainly it was more liquid refreshment followed by more sleep.

As we passed Sanda off the Mull of Kintyre and got out into the tideway of the North Channel, I was aware that we were being carried well to the north and west of the course line to our destination, which was Donaghadee. No one seemed to realise this and eventually I woke one of them up. "Call Billy" was the response. "Billy the Navigator", as he was called, was a mathematician of some note at Queen's University. He managed to get into an upright position and open Reed's Almanac, presumably to look up the tides, but promptly fell asleep again, face-down on the book! At this stage I got to the chart and did something myself but we still ended up near the Maidens' Rocks off Larne instead of following a direct line to Donaghadee. We eventually arrived at 0100 on Monday morning and I got a lift home by 0400. I did not reach the office until lunchtime. Some of that crew are still good sailing friends of mine and, after all, with an ex-Shell Tanker Captain on board, how could they go wrong!

At the end of the season I had another trip in "Vandara" and this was to an Irish Cruising Club rally in Carlingford Lough. A number of boats sailed from Belfast Lough on Friday 6 September to Portavogie, down the County Down coast, here to be joined by more boats from Strangford Lough. There was then an overnight race to Carlingford Lough which again fizzled out due to lack of wind, but as we motored into the Lough we met up with a large contingent coming in from the Dublin area and by the time we all anchored off Rostrevor there were some 40 boats in the fleet. It was an interesting morning since the Flag Officers inspected every boat, particularly for safety equipment. Each crew was also required to carry out a "man overboard" drill using a lifelike dummy, for which points were awarded, resulting in a prize which was not won by "Vandara". I thought this was a splendid idea but I have never seen anything like it at any ICC rallies I have attended since.

In the afternoon the whole fleet locked into the Newry Ship Canal and proceeded to Newry Basin for the party. On "Vandara" we found a following wind in the canal and hoisted the spinnaker. A number of boats following us did the same with the result that an approaching car on the canalside road ended up in the ditch. The poor motorist came round a bend to see what must have seemed like something from outer space coming towards him and got a fit of the wobbles! The weather deteriorated that night although the party went on until early on Sunday. The trip down Carlingford Lough in pouring rain and crossing the Bar with wind against tide was not pleasant, nor was it pleasant after that even with the south-east wind behind us. I had taken a day's leave on Monday which was just as well since we didn't get back to Cultra until 0300. Not very long after that a commercial vessel hit the canal gates with disastrous results and the canal was closed for some time. Then came the "Troubles" and the canal was closed altogether to traffic, so this trip was in fact a unique experience.

The highlight of 1968 was "Sarita's" west coast of Scotland cruise, which took place in mid-July. It was a new experience for my friend John and me, and I don't think George had been very far in that direction either, due to lack of crew. It was not going to be a "dry" cruise by any means since George had a friend in the wholesale drinks trade! Thus "Sarita" was stored with three full kegs of beer, together with the dispenser, piping and gas cylinder to go with it. This lot was rigged up in the forecastle and was mainly for lunchtime "nooners" consumption since we also shipped a full case of Bushmills whisky and another of Gordon's gin, plus the necessary "thinners" for serious evening consumption. I organised the dry stores and all the essentials were put aboard the boat at Whiterock in good time.

On Thursday 11 July I happened to be in Portaferry on official business, which was to keep an eye on the ferryboats operating between Strangford and Portaferry. This was before the RoRo ferry came on the scene and the privately operated open boats were prone to overloading with passengers. Strangford Week was well underway and that day was Portaferry Regatta, so there was some pressure on the ferries. By 1900 I could change my "hat" and crossed over on a ferry to join "Sarita" where she was anchored off Strangford. Most of the four crew for this cruise were already on board, including John, David and, of course, George. John and I went across to Portaferry later for the Regatta dance and I recall that we arrived in our seaboots but had a happy time nonetheless.

The next morning we woke up late and there was a "nooners"

session at the Lobster Pot while we were waiting for the tide to turn in the Narrows. We departed for Scotland at 1530 with the first of the ebb and a little wind which soon ran out and so on went the old petrol engine. Through Donaghadee Sound by 2330 we motored on and had a quiet night at sea, heading north to enter the Sound of Islay and reach Port Askaig by 1500. We moved on to Colonsay for the night. The next day we sailed on through the Torran Rocks and into Iona Sound, where we visited Iona and its abbey, then Staffa, where we rowed the dinghy into Fingal's cave. We reached Tobermory late on 14 July.

The next day saw the end of the Clyde Cruising Club's race to Tobermory and there were many yachts in port. There was some socialising and that evening we attended the dance at the Aros Hall, getting to bed at a late hour. Despite this, John and I were up at 0430 to find a not very bright morning and freshening Northerly wind. We weighed anchor and sailed for Castlebay, Barra at 0500! As we cleared the Sound of Mull the wind freshened more and we encountered a heavy confused sea in the Minch. However, well reefed down, the old boat was comfortable and sailed well on a reach. Some dolphins that came to visit were leaping out of the waves about the level of the cockpit. George woke up at some stage, looked at the situation from the hatchway, made some unprintable remarks and went back to his bunk. We saw nothing of David until after we reached Castlebay at 1630, when he emerged, ashen-faced, from the forecastle.

After calls at Loch Boisdale and Loch Tarbert, we reached Stornoway on Friday and here there was a disaster in that the gas for the beer system had all escaped. There was plenty of beer on board but we couldn't get at it! George found a small mineral water plant in the town and chatted up the owner; our gas bottle was refilled and we were back in business! David had to leave us here to fly home for a family holiday but the rest of us enjoyed a Stornoway Friday night, which is wild – made up for on Sunday, which is dead! This was our turning point and we headed South the next morning to pick up a friend of George's at Portree on the Isle of Skye. Heading on, we passed through the Narrows at Kyle of Lochalsh to spend a pleasant night at Isle Ornsay and then called at Armadale and the island of Eigg before another night at Tobermory. Here we somehow ended up at a party on board a motorboat called "Devorgill" and I was interested to note that they were navigating by means of a road map pinned up in the hatchway! Then it was on down the Sound of Mull the next day to reach the famous anchorage at Pulldobhrain for the night, and we went ashore to walk over the hill to the pub at Clachan Bridge – the "Bridge over the Atlantic". Here we also made friends with David Rombach and family on a fairly old wooden yawl called "Lola", on their way home to the Clyde after the Tobermory Race and a few days on the west coast. As a result, the next morning, after sorting out engine problems on both boats, we followed "Lola" through the Cuan Sound to reach the anchorage at Ardinamar, there to visit the famous Irene Maclachlan and sign her visitor's book. On then to Crinan with "Lola" to lock into the canal and spend the night in Crinan Basin.

There followed a very pleasant trip through the Crinan Canal in company with two other yachts, including a lunchtime stop at the Cairnbaan Hotel. With so many people, working the locks was easy and we were out of this short canal by 1800 to reach East Loch Tarbert for the night. Here we anchored off for the night and after our usual excellent meal on board, launched the dinghy and went ashore for a couple of hours. I remember on the way back climbing down a vertical ladder at the fish quay to reach the dinghy in the dark and suddenly realising that I had climbed down too far and was waist-deep in water! After calls at Lamlash on the Isle of Aran and at Portpatrick, we duly got back to Strangford Lough on Saturday 27 July. It had been a splendid two-week cruise.

Sailing in various boats continued until the end of the season, including another trip to Portpatrick in "Sarita" at the time of the Portpatrick Race, although we only went there for the party! Despite all this activity I still had "Pleiades" in the water and she was duly hauled out and parked in the barn at the "Beeches" for the winter.

CHAPTER 16: SAILING DAYS, 1969-1970

Early in 1969 a member at RNIYC, Gerry Harrison, was changing boats and upgrading from a Folkboat to a Nicholson 36 with the intention of doing some serious offshore racing, and getting to the party in time! I was invited to join the crew and naturally jumped at the chance. At that time offshore racing yachts, certainly locally, were traditional cruising boats with sensible and seaworthy hulls. There was some very competitive racing and the then Northern Ireland Offshore Champion was a Tyrell built traditional wooden boat called "Maid of Mourne". The Nicholson 36 was the first boat designed by Camper & Nicholson for construction in GRP and had the same traditional lines as their wooden boats of the same period. In fact only the hull was GRP, the deck and coachroof being wooden, and I think only about 30 of these boats were built before Camper & Nicholson produced the very successful Nicholson 32, their first all GRP production boat.

Anyway, mid-March saw a pleasant weekend car trip to Wicklow, South of Dublin, where "Samphire" was laid up under cover at Neil Watson's Yard. The boat and all her equipment were fully checked out in the presence of her owner and before we left for home Gerry had done the deal and bought the boat. Originally "Samphire of St. Osyth", she was now renamed "Samphire of Cultra". On 8 May a delivery crew went down to Wicklow and we had a very pleasant weekend sailing the boat home to Belfast Lough, with calls at Dun Laoghaire and at Peel on the Isle of Man. We were very impressed by her performance, especially to windward. Down below she was quite comfortable with seven comfortable berths but a rather poor galley and no chart table. I later made a removable chart table which fitted over the quarter berth, adjacent to the main hatchway. The engine was a Coventry Victor 12 hp petrol engine which gave lots of problems and was later replaced. However, it was obvious that this boat was going to be competitive on the local racing scene. The basis of a competitive racing crew was assembled and surprisingly this basic crew held together for the next nine years and sailed in five different boats under four different owners. The driving force was David Kensett, together with some of his friends from the Royal Ulster Yacht Club. I found my forte as a racing navigator and purser/chief cook!

After a shake down "round the buoys" race in Belfast Lough, our first offshore race was the RUYC feeder race from Bangor to Ramsey on the Isle of Man, a popular event at that time. It started from Bangor on a Friday evening and this time it was a dead beat most of the way into a strong SE wind and a rough sea. "Samphire" stood up well to the conditions and made splendid progress to reach Ramsey at 1230 on the Saturday morning. We were first to finish by over half an hour, with the stragglers not arriving until late that evening – late, of course, for the party. Besides being first home we also won the race easily on handicap, so there was some celebration to follow. Ramsey Harbour dries out at low tide, which is a nuisance and we had to be up and out by 0700 the following morning for the start of the Round the Isle of Man race, another popular event with entrants from all over the Irish Sea. We had a splendid start with a fresh beat up to the Point of Ayre and this got rid of any cobwebs and hangovers from the night before. There was a good run down the West side of the Island before the wind died away off Langness and the whole fleet was becalmed that evening. It was a miserable night with only occasional light airs but a nasty confused swell. We did eventually finish the race at 0630 on the Monday morning. I don't know where we finished but we certainly didn't win!

That week, after the Bank Holiday, I was due to attend an official fire-fighting and damage control course at HMS "Phoenix" in Portsmouth. I shifted my gear to a yacht from the Ribble Cruising Club and got a lift across to Lytham St. Annes. From there I travelled south by train and got to my course in good time!

In early June we went to Rothesay with a number of other boats to take part in the North Channel Race, this year it being from Rothesay to Cultra. Light winds and calms made for a very frustrating race back and we took 36 hours to sail 80 miles. After all the effort we finished 15th out of 26 starters. The next weekend it was the Blue Water Race back to the Clyde, including round the Isle of Man, and was about 200 miles from start to finish. The wind varied from calm to quite fresh and we finished this race in just 48 hours. We finished third and most importantly beat our great rival "Maid of Mourne". There was obviously some leave taken by the crew since we spent two days getting back to Cultra! This included a late night party ashore at Lamlash on the Isle of Aran in company with the crews of "Ain Mara" and "Dinah". Both of these boats were ancient even at that time but they had very competitive and determined skippers! Towards the end of June there was the Ailsa Craig Race which took in the Skulmartin Light Buoy down the County Down coast and Ailsa Craig in the middle of the Firth of Clyde, about 80 miles in all. It was not very interesting to my mind, since it started and finished at Bangor and involved only local boats. We were third boat to finish and were also third on corrected time.

Looking back, this was a very hectic time. I had a full-time job with the Marine Department; I was racing in "Samphire" either offshore or locally every weekend, and in the Fairy Classkeelboats at Cultra during the week. I also still had "Pleiades" afloat at Ballydorn and occasionally got out in her but she was mostly lent to friends to enjoy some sailing on Strangford Lough. Social life ashore was also quite busy, mostly at local yacht clubs. I was, after all, still a happy bachelor with few commitments! In addition I went off on another cruise to Stornoway and back in "Sarita" with George Lennox and my friend John for two weeks in July. We followed much the same route as last year but apart from Stornoway and Tobermory called at different ports and anchorages. At Stornoway our friend in the soft drinks factory from last year lent us a car and we were able to tour the Isle of Lewis while the boat was stormbound. In fact we had quite a lot of adverse weather on this cruise and when it did improve towards the end we had to put in some night sailing to get home in time.

There were two more offshore races in "Samphire" the first being from Portavogie on the County Down coast, round Carlingford Lough Whistle Buoy, and across to Port St. Mary on the South coast of the Isle of Man. This race was notable for very light winds and very poor visibility and more than once we were about to give up and retire since it eventually took us 35 hours to cover only 90 miles and in the poor visibility our little hand-held radio direction finder was in near constant use. At that time the only navigational aids permitted on racing yachts were an echo sounder and a radio direction finder. Such delights as radar and the Decca Navigator were forbidden and in any case the equipment then available was too heavy and cumbersome, and too expensive, to be suitable for small boats. The now ubiquitous Global Positioning System was mere pie in the sky. Nowadays serious offshore boats have everything that is available in the way of navigation and communications equipment, not to mention being fully computerised. I think it was more fun and more of a challenge in the 1960s and '70s. The last offshore event of the season was the Portpatrick Race at the end of August and this was definitely a heavy weather trip with a very strong NW wind. There were only 20 starters on the line at Bangor and the first leg was through Donaghadee Sound and down to the South Rock Lightship. We blew out the big running spinnaker before we got to the Sound and soon after that blew out the No. 1 genoa as well, also developing a split in the mainsail! From the South Rock it was a long hard beat north to Portpatrick with a smaller headsail and a well reefed main. We were first to arrive at 0930 on Saturday morning and with only four boats finishing the race, we won it easily. The wind continued to blow hard and by Sunday morning was round to SW with a horrible sea coming into Portpatrick Harbour. We waited until late afternoon but it was still a struggle to get out and clear and we were certainly touching bottom at one stage! It was another hard beat in rough conditions across the North Channel and we ended up in Donaghadee at 2100 where we picked up a mooring. Home by about midnight and back to the office the next morning!

There were one or two more local races in "Samphire" and even a weekend cruise to the Isle of Man before she was hauled out into the club yard at Cultra for the winter. "Sarita" joined her there while "Pleiades" was towed up the road from Ballydorn to her winter storage in the barn at the "Beeches". While there was still a paid yard crew at RNIYC, under the well known Billy Wilson, much of the work was already DIY and one Saturday we organised a gang to lift the masts out of both "Samphire" and "Sarita". This was done using old-fashioned sheerlegs, various guy ropes and a heavy six-fold tackle, and was very labour intensive. It involved recruiting volunteers from the club bar to lift the sheerlegs, man the guys and heave on the tackle, and to complete the operation without damage to boat, mast or even people was always a relief! Nowadays a mobile crane is used! In fact the whole system in the yard of hauling out boats, moving them around and chocking them off was very old-fashioned and remained so until very recently. Nevertheless, the yard filled up every autumn and could accommodate around 14 boats of up to about 40 ft in length. At the prize distribution dinner at RUYC, "Samphire" collected five or six cups and certainly won the Northern Ireland Offshore Championship for 1969. The owner of "Maid of Mourne" was not best pleased! During the winter I did quite a lot of work on "Samphire" and enjoyed it. Not least was making and fitting a decent chart table.

A nice Christmas present was the news that I was to be transferred to the London Marine Office, though this could not happen until the Department found someone to take my place in Belfast. (As it turned out, I did not transfer until early August.) I advertised "Pleiades" in the local newspaper and she was sold in March to a man in Killyleagh. Meanwhile, fitting out proceeded on "Samphire" for another season and she was launched early in May. The engine was sent for overhaul but continued to give endless trouble throughout the season and whatever could possibly go wrong with it did so frequently. In April there was a pleasant surprise when I was invited in my official capacity to be the principal guest and speaker at the RUYC offshore dinner. After the last season I already knew nearly all the offshore racing fraternity and about this time I was also elected a member of the club.

The first race of the season was a short one in Belfast Lough. The owner of "Maid of Mourne" had not taken his defeat in the Offshore Championship lightly and now had an Sparkman & Stephens designed 36-ft boat which he called "Cygnet of Mourne". This boat had a more radical underwater shape than anything yet seen in local waters, although such boats were by now quite common in the south of England, and she was perhaps a foretaste of what was to come everywhere on the racing scene. Anyway, she won this first race of the season which must have been satisfying for owner and crew. The race from Bangor to Ramsey on 22 May was one of light airs and a lumpy sea in which "Samphire" finished third but the subsequent Round the Island Race turned out be a heavy weather event. This time, because of the tidal situation at Ramsey, we did not start until 1200 on the Sunday. It involved a run-up to the Point of Ayre and then a heavy beat down the west side of the island. The seas at the Calf of Man were quite ferocious but we then had a fast run to finish on 0100 on Monday. Out of 48 starters, 23 retired and there were three boats dismasted! "Samphire" finished second and I have no record of "Cygnet" even being at this event. However, we beat her into first place on an inshore race in Belfast Lough the following weekend.

For the Ailsa Craig Race in early June, conditions were generally light and we only finished in third place, being beaten by an Excalibur 36, "Eevin", who was first, and "Cygnet of Mourne", who was second. This race finished back at Bangor at 0240 on the Sunday morning after which we tied up at Bangor North Pier and turned in for a few hours. After that it was up to RUYC for breakfast, followed by "nooners"! The North Channel Race this year was from Rothesay, on the Clyde, back to Cultra. Due to light winds and a continuing sick engine we only reached Rothesay in time to turn round and sail home again! The race was a bit fresher and we finished at 1730 on the Saturday, third boat home out of 36 starters with "Cygnet" close behind us. However, when the handicaps were worked out she was placed first. That evening there was the usual party in the clubhouse at RNIYC and after the bar closed this continued on various boats out on the moorings off the club. I found myself on board David Rombach's "Lola" from the Clyde where the party was based around haggis and scotch! At least the haggis must have soaked up the scotch since I got home safely at 0600 on Sunday.

The big event this year however was the Blue Water Trophy Race, run for a change from Bangor to Cork to be followed by a week of racing at Cork. It started from Bangor at 2200 on Friday 26 June and was a beat all the way with light to moderate winds down to the Tuskar Rock but strong SW winds and big nasty seas thereafter. Conditions on board became uncomfortable and wet, and cooking anything was almost impossible! We had six crew and worked three-hour watches with three on each. We crossed the finishing line off Roche's Point at 0120 on Monday 29 and, after handicap corrections, were placed third while "Cygnet of Mourne" was the winner in our class. We were all well received at the Royal Cork Yacht Club at Crosshaven on Cork Harbour but the following morning four of our crew had to depart for home, leaving only David Kensett and myself. With only two of a crew we did take part in the Cork races but without being placed at all. ("Cygnet" did very well!)

There were interesting diversions, however, including two trips across Cork Harbour in company with other boats to Passage East and "Dirty Murphy's pub. The series ended on Friday 3 July with a race along the coast to Kinsale, another pleasant spot with a hospitable yacht club but here David also had to leave. It was surprising that he was able to stay so long since his wife was about to produce their first offspring! This left me and the boat alone at Kinsale and while I had another week's leave left, I was not going to try and sail home single-handed. She still had a sick engine and no self steering gear! Endeavours were made at home to find someone to come down and help but meanwhile I hired a car and went travelling to visit many of the well known yachting spots of south-west Ireland. As it turned out it was nearly 30 years later before I got to visit many of these places by sea!

The following Tuesday a young lad turned up from RNIYC who sailed with his father in the Fairy Class but had no experience of anything bigger. The next day was exceedingly wet and windy so we stayed safe at Kinsale, but on Thursday made it to Dunmore East at the entrance to Waterford Harbour in a fresh but favourable wind. This place reminds me that at this time there was a seemingly never-ending Irish Bank strike. It lasted for about six months, during which pubs, hotels and other businesses were happily accepting cheques without the benefit of a cheque card or identification. I had run out of cheques by this time and the yacht club at Dunmore East advanced me money on the strength of my "promise to pay" and a signature on a scrap of plain paper! The next day we made it round Carmsore Point and north to Arklow, and the day after that on to Howth. At this point the forecast indicated winds of up to force 8 in the Irish Sea and I was not keen on that. The Howth Yacht Club were very helpful and provided a mooring for "Samphire" and when all was secure we returned home on the train. A few days later four of us returned to Howth and got the boat back to Bangor, in light conditions and in time for the RUYC Regatta, where "Cygnet" beat us into second place. However, we beat her at Whitehead Regatta two weeks later.

On Monday 10 August I started work at the London Marine Survey Office in Seething Lane, near the tower of London, but my sailing was still not entirely finished for the season! At the end of August I took a couple of days' leave and motored up to Stranraer overnight, parked my car, went over to Larne on the ferry and thence home by train. I sailed in "Samphire" in the Portpatrick Race, in which we came third while "Cygnet" was second. It was then a 450-mile car trip back down to London and out to Billericay in Essex, where I had decided to "settle" and was temporarily living in the Railway Hotel. In the evenings I went exploring and by English sailing standards I was very close to Burnham on Crouch. Here there were three yachts clubs and in one of them I found an advertisement seeking crew for a new Swan 43. While "Whirlwind II" had spent the season based at Burnham she was now at Port Hamble on the Solent for an autumn series of races. Thus I spent three weekends in October racing on the Solent!

The boat was a big powerful machine and way ahead of anything in Northern Ireland at the time but the fun and conviviality normally present in sailing and racing at home was just not there. The owners were the founders and directors of the MFI furniture firm and the crew of about ten were from all over the place. One was an RAF officer based at Catterick in Yorkshire and he travelled down by car. My travelling was bad enough since I drove up to the office in London on Friday morning – about two hours for 30 miles, plus parking problems – and then drove down to Port Hamble that evening – about three hours. Driving back to Billericay via the Dartford Tunnel on the Sunday evening took up to four hours! We reported aboard on Friday night or early on Saturday morning to go racing around the Solent on Saturday and at least the race usually ended up at somewhere like Yarmouth IOW. Another race on Sunday brought us back to Port Hamble and then we all went home! There was little or no socialising ashore or with other boats and we didn't even do very well in the races! Some change from Belfast Lough, and any further sailing I did while based in London was mainly in boats I knew from home or from the Clyde.

After one more season, "Samphire" was sold and so was "Cygnet of Mourne". Both owners virtually gave up any interest in sailing and certainly in racing! In Billericay I bought a maisonette which had its own garden and here I developed an interest in horticultural matters.

CHAPTER 17: 1971 TO 1976 – SOME SERIOUS RACING

Early in the season of 1971, I spent two or three weekends on the Solent racing in "Whirlwind II" but with all the effort of getting there on a Friday night and back on Sunday night, I decided it wasn't worth it. The owners were not very competitive and there wasn't much camaraderie among the crew or with the crews of other boats. If they'd had any plans for any of the well-known offshore races and especially the Fastnet, I would probably have stayed with them. I was back home in Belfast for a week at Easter and spent much of the time helping to get "Samphire" ready for launching. Then at the end of May I took two weeks leave and again went back to Belfast, where I arrived on a Friday morning. That day "Samphire" was stored up and taken to Bangor for the start of the Bangor to Ramsey Race. We had most if not all of the original crew on board and the race started at 2100. Light winds and calms all the way meant that we did not reach Ramsey until 1500 the next day, but we didn't have to wait for the tide to get into the drying harbour. I did not record our place, so we certainly didn't win! We had a "session" ashore and a splendid Chinese meal but sensibly we returned on board at a reasonable hour.

The start of the annual Round the Isle of Man Race depends on the tide because of the drying harbour at Ramsey and this year it started at 0600 on Whit Sunday morning. The race attracts entries from all over the Irish Sea and this year was one of the best with ideal weather conditions. In "Samphire" we got round in 14 hours and finished in fourth place at 2000. We then ran aground, trying to enter the harbour between the two breakwaters before the tide had risen enough, but someone was sent ashore in the dingy to obtain essential liquid supplies before the pubs closed. The drying out business at Ramsey could be quite interesting with a large fleet in the harbour, especially if boats of different sizes and draughts were moored alongside each other. If it occurred late at night after the crews had been ashore for a while, it could be even more interesting, with some boats lying over at crazy angles.

On the Monday afternoon we departed for Donaghadee with a dead beat in light conditions and with a sick engine, so that we did not arrive until 0600 the next day. Here we landed four crew members and two passengers, leaving two of us on board. Gregg

Matthews was a Bangor man and an army officer, and like me based at that time in London. He had also taken some leave and the two of us set off for the Clyde, reaching the anchorage at Lamlash on the Isle of Arran by 2130. The next day we struggled to Tarbert, Loch Fyne, in very light conditions and with a very sick engine. It was the original Coventry Victor 12 BHP petrol engine, with twin opposed cylinders and gave constant trouble until it was replaced by a Perkins diesel shortly before the boat was sold. We ended up being towed into Tarbert by "Aeolus", another Bangor boat, and the two crews had a pleasant evening ashore together. The next day we sailed in company with "Aeolus" through the scenic Kyles of Bute to reach Rothesay by 2000 and where we spent Friday 4 June waiting for the rest of our racing crew to arrive from home. That evening saw the start of the Clyde Cruising Club's Blue Water Race, which took a fleet of 16 boats south to round the Isle of Man and then to finish at Bangor. The early part of this race was frustrated by light airs and calms but the front runners made it round the Calf of Man with the tide while the later boats, including "Samphire", missed this tidal gate and were virtually out of the race! The first boat finished at 0800 on Sunday 6 June while we got in at 1600 after 42 hours for just over 200 miles. At least we made the party at the Royal Ulster Yacht Club that evening! This was the end of my sailing activities in 1971 and I returned to London the following week after another few days at home.

An even worse year was 1972, when it looked as though there would be no sailing at all! "Samphire" had been sold, so there was no sailing in her, but I was still in touch with David Rombach in Glasgow whom I met at many Clyde Cruising Club events and who still had the old yawl "Lola". I phoned him and got a berth on "Lola" for the North Channel and Blue Water races. Thus on Friday 9 June I travelled up to Glasgow by train and on to Rothesay on the Isle of Bute in plenty of time to join "Lola" for the start of the race to Belfast Lough at 2210. It was a fast run straight to Cultra, with a fair and fresh breeze which suited this old boat. We crossed the finishing line at 0852 and won our class, which was very satisfying! I went home for a rest and then back to the Yacht Club for the party that evening. It finished off with a "whisky and haggis" party on board "Lola" after the club bar closed, but I actually made it home by 0330!

At that time there were some well-known old boats in the Clyde

Cruising Club fleet and most of the owners were well-known "characters". The Commodore at that time was still, I think, Ian P. Young and his distinctive boat was "Arcturus". A close friend of his was David Reekie of "Dirk II" fame and this boat spent the following week at anchor off Cultra with a huge Scottish flag flying aft and a banner slung between the two masts proclaiming "Home Rule for Scotland". The bar takings went up considerably during the days between the two races! I spent most of the week at home doing some gardening and other chores for my Dad but Friday evening saw me back on board "Lola" for the race back to the Clyde. This time the start was off the Royal Ulster Yacht club at Bangor and the course included rounding the Isle of Man. For this race we had every kind of bad weather, including fog but mostly a force 7 to 8 SW wind with heavy seas and heavy rain in the North Channel and Firth of Clyde. Apart from David and myself, the crew were all keen young men in their early 20s, and they were keen to win! The old boat was pushed hard and we finished off Rothesay at 0430 on the Sunday morning only to find we had been beaten into second place by an even older boat – "Ainmara" from Bangor! I spent a pleasant night with the Rombach family and returned to London the next morning. End of sailing for 1972!

In the spring of 1973 David Kensett, who had skippered "Samphire", telephoned to say that he had chartered "Ruffian" for the season and the intention was to take her south for the RORC Channel Race, Cowes Week, and the RORC Fastnet race. He had recruited many of the old regular crew in "Samphire" and wondered, could I join them for some of the intended races? The answer was an immediate *yes*! "Ruffian'" was built and owned by the Brown Brothers of Portaferry, who have various business and academic interests, and who at that time also had a boat-building business known as Wetherly Yachts. She was about 36 ft in length and probably fell into the "one ton" class for offshore racing. By Northern Ireland standards at that time she was certainly a "racy" boat with a shallow cold moulded hull and a bolted on fin keel of solid lead.

On 22 June Gregg Matthews and I met up at Euston Station and travelled to Holyhead to join the boat for the RORC Irish Sea Race. This started at 0900 the following morning, a Saturday, and the course took in the Morecambe Bay Lightship and Strangford Lough Whistle Buoy to finish at Dun Laoghaire. Conditions were ideal and the sailing was most enjoyable. Rounding Strangford Whistle Buoy on Sunday lunchtime we came across owner Dickie Brown, out in an outboard runabout to cheer us on our way! We crossed the finishing line at 0120 on the Sunday, third boat to finish out of about 30, winner of our class on corrected time and second overall. Not a bad result. After that it was back to London until early August.

    I next joined "Ruffian" at Camper & Nicholsons' Gosport Marina, where she had recently arrived from Bangor and on the afternoon of Friday 3 August we joined about 200 other starters for the RORC Channel Race. This took us from the Solent along the coast to the Royal Sovereign Lightship, across the Channel to a buoy off Le Havre and back to the finish off Southsea. This started as a moderate weather race but finished as a heavy weather race in a full gale of wind. We finished at 2345 on the Saturday night but I have no record of our placing so it cannot have been very good! There followed four days of "round the buoys" racing in the Solent but one day's racing was cancelled for all but the Admiral's Cup fleet due to very severe weather. We did go out to spectate for a while and watch some of them get into spectacular difficulties on a spinnaker run! I think "Ruffian" mostly finished in the first half of the fleet, which wasn't bad considering we were now up against the World's best. The sailing, in competing with so many other boats of different nationalities, was most enjoyable and the social life ashore was pretty good too!

    The Fastnet Race, which started off at Cowes on the morning of Saturday 11 August, was a light weather affair and it took us almost six days for the 650 miles. There were about 300 starters including the Admiral's Cup fleet, and we were never out of sight of several other boats except in fog, of which there was quite a lot! Anyway we made it out past Portland Bill, Start Point and the Seven Stones Light Vessel to round the Fastnet Rock at 0415 on the Tuesday. There were not many spectator boats out from the nearby Irish ports at this hour. This was also in the days before such navigational aids as Decca and the later GPS were allowed on offshore racing boats, and the only navigational aid out here other than the Fastnet Lighthouse itself was the radio beacon on Mizzen Head, about five miles to the West. Careful "dead reckoning" was all important and I was pleased when we picked up the Rock dead ahead, where I expected it to be, and passed it on the correct side!

Very light conditions and poor visibility prevailed all the way back to the finish at Plymouth. Bishop Rock Lighthouse was passed quite close to but not seen and likewise at the Lizard. We reached Rame Head in the approaches to Plymouth by 2200 on the Thursday, with only a few miles to go, but it then took us until 0400 the next morning before we drifted across the finishing line. This was definitely the "Slownet" Race, but the party that night in the Royal Western Yacht Club perhaps made up for it. On corrected time we had finished fifteenth in Class III, out of perhaps 50 boats so I suppose that wasn't a bad result! On the Saturday it was another train trip back to London and that was the end of sailing for 1973. However, in November I was transferred back to Belfast by the Marine Survey Service and the prospects for the next year looked brighter!

A well-known yachtsman in Bangor was Desmond Irwin, who had owned and raced a French-built Arpege class boat called "Aeolis", followed by the Nicolson 35 "Pampero of Down". His son John was also active on the racing scene and they decided to "upgrade" to a Swan 38. This brand new boat, "Dictator", was built at the Nautor yard in Finland and was due for delivery in the spring of 1974. The intention was to race her seriously. The crew was recruited early in the year and the core members included the original core crew from "Samphire", with David Kensett as the "racing driver". Meetings were held and a programme worked out for the coming season. Since at 38-ft the boat fell into the "one ton" class and since there was an International One Ton event at Torquay, Devon that year, she would be entered for that. A local delivery crew was recruited and I would have gone like a shot had I been able to get the time off work. One of them, a very competent and well-known yachtsman, managed to fall down a stairway on a Baltic ferry on the way out and broke his collarbone. He never made it to the boat but the rest of this crew had an enjoyable passage home, which included several Scandinavian ports and a transit of the Gota/Trolhatte Canal system across southern Sweden.

"Dictator" reached Bangor on Sunday 19 May, 1974, and was met by a reception committee. On going aboard we soon discovered that some crew members had managed to pick up much erotic reading material in Sweden or Denmark and this was promptly hidden from Irwin Senior's gaze. It might entertain the off-watch crew during some of our future efforts! The boat herself was beautiful and beautifully finished, with a teak laid deck and plenty of solid wood furnishings and trimmings down below. It was also obvious that for a serious racing boat she was somewhat heavily built!

The following day, Monday 20 May, saw the start of the Ulster Workers' strike, which was politically motivated and severely disrupted just about all activity in the province for nearly two weeks. On some days I didn't make it to the office and other "Dictator" crew members had similar problems, so we went sailing for crew training instead! The following Friday evening saw us off to Ramsey, Isle of Man, on our first offshore race. With light winds we didn't perform very well and were beaten by "Myth of Mourne", also by some of the smaller boats on corrected time! On Whit Sunday we were off on the Round the Isle of Man Race and this time the tide dictated that the start be at 0500, sore on the head after some jollying ashore the night before! Conditions must have been ideal because records were broken. "Dictator" went round in eight hours 54.5 minutes for the 64 miles, but we were beaten by "Myth of Mourne" by a few minutes on corrected time.

Whit Monday was a tourist and party day and some of us even got as far as Douglas on the electric railway. The passage back to Bangor the next day was a nasty beat into force 6 and 7 from the North West. We sailed at 0300 and were back on our mooring in Ballyholme Bay, Bangor, at 1530. During June there were several local inshore races in which we did quite well, plus the Howth to Holyhead Race in which we were second and the Blue Water Trophy Race from Rothesay to Bangor via the Isle of Man, which we won. In early July the boat was dried out alongside the Central Pier in Bangor for some serious work before she went south for the One Ton Cup. David Kensett went to work to try and lighten the boat, much to the dismay of Irwin Senior! Well, he could do nothing about the heavily built hull, nor could he strip off the beautiful teak laid deck, but out came the cabin table and the doors to various compartments, including the loo! A cross linking system for the two main sheet winches was fitted and this involved some serious butchery. Electricity for power tools was obtained by breaking into the bottom of an adjacent lamp post on the quay. Most of the crockery was taken off and we would survive with paper plates and plastic mugs, all of which were light weight and disposable. We even missed racing in Royal Ulster's Annual Regatta over this work and on 7 July, "Dictator" departed for Torquay with a delivery crew of three on board. The racing crew turned up there a week later by various means and I got there by ferry and train via London.

The first two or three days were taken up with the scrutinising of the boats, which was carried out meticulously by measurers who had all the hallmarks of retired Army or Naval officers! We also got to sea for trials but never really got to try our paces against any other boats. There were plenty of out and out racing machines among the fleet of about 35 and one even had twin dagger boards in lieu of a keel and which could be raised or lowered as required. One very racy boat I remember was "Mezzanine", which may even have won the event. The first day of racing was round an Olympic-type course and the start was delayed due to lack of wind. There was never more than a light breeze so that the lightweight boats "cleaned up" and "Dictator" finished 25th out of 33 starters. The next day was worse, with very fluky conditions, and we finished last! Next was a passage race along the coast to Lowland Point Buoy and back, a distance of 150 miles, in which we again achieved 25th place! In two more Olympic-type races, and another passage race which took in CH1 Buoy in the middle of the English Channel and the Owers Lightship, we did no better! Our final placing was 26th out of 33 competitors. I don't think there was anything wrong with our crew but in the generally light conditions our heavy boat just could not keep up with the lightweights! However, the sailing was enjoyable and there were plenty of social activities ashore. With my interest in railways I also found time for trips on the Torbay Steam Railway and the Dart Valley Railway! I remained with the boat for the return passage to Bangor, with calls at Plymouth, Falmouth and Arklow. We picked up our mooring in Ballyhome Bay, Bangor late on 2 August, having taken four and a half days for the trip.

The only other race of note that season was the RUYC Porpatrick Race at the end of August, for which there were very light conditions and I did not even record the result! In between racing in "Dictator", I had still been sailing in the old Fairies at RNIYC, Cultra, and more recently also in the Squibs. These are 19ft 6-inch GRP keelboats which had become very popular nationwide and of which there was now quite a fleet at Cultra. When racing they carry a crew of two.

One Friday night in August I went down to the club for a drink and found two members arguing about the best way to tie a bowline knot. It has always surprised me how many people, even experienced sailing people, who have difficulty tying this knot. It is probably the most important and useful knot used at sea, whether in large commercial craft or small pleasure craft, or anything in between! Being an instant expert in such matters, I was soon able to put them right! One of these members was a young lady, Susie, who I gathered was a graduate of Queen's University. The Queen's Sailing Club had a number of small boats, including two Squibs called "Night Before" and "Morning After". Susie had the use of one of these boats for the summer and indeed it was on a mooring at Cultra. Saturday was Regatta Day at the nearby Holywood Yacht Club and she wanted to race the Squib there, but had no crew. Thus I sailed as crew in "Night Before" at Holywood Regatta the next day and the outcome of this chance encounter was quite surprising. I subsequently sailed in this boat on and off for the rest of the season and also during the following winter at the Antrim Boat Club on Lough Neagh. Susie and I seemed to get along together very well and she was certainly an able helmswoman in small boats. She has now been my wife for well over 20 years!

The Fastnet Race only takes place every second year and 1975 was one such. Despite our poor showing at Torquay the crew of "Dictator", with few changes, were still keen and a programme was worked out for this season to include another trip to the south of England. We started the season by winning the Opening Day race at the Royal Ulster Yacht Club. There followed the passage race to Ramsey and the Round Isle of Man Race in which we were well placed. There followed the Howth to Holyhead Race in which we finished first and were second on corrected time. This ended up a heavy weather race and for the return from Holyhead to Bangor we had force 7 to 8 from the north-west, which meant an unpleasant beat to windward. After some 17 hours of this we made it to Ballyholme Bay and were lucky to be able to pick up our mooring in the prevailing conditions, with heavy seas piling into the bay. This was about 0700 and we then spent the whole day pitching and rolling at the mooring! The weather worsened for a while and it was a disastrous day for many of the boats moored nearby. Some broke their moorings and ended up on the beach or, worse still, on rocks. Smaller keel boats with open cockpits simply filled up and sank but there was nothing we could do to help. Had we let go the mooring we could well have ended up on the beach ourselves and as it was the heavy stemhead fitting was distorted into a most interesting shape! There was no question of attempting to launch a dinghy or of anyone attempting to reach us from shore, so we could only sit in the cockpit with the engine on stand-by and watch the devastation going on around us!

It was late that evening before there was much moderation and a club rescue boat was able to get out to us! Ballyholme Bay is very exposed to the north but it was the only mooring place for local yachts until Bangor Marina was built and commissioned. Every few years there would be a severe northerly summer gale with predictable results and I think latterly insurance premiums went sky high, or became impossible for many owners. Now the bay is devoid of moorings and the boats lie safely in the nearby excellent marina!

There followed the RORC Irish Sea Race, which we won outright and the Blue Water Trophy Race, which was sailed in very light conditions and in which we didn't figure in the placings at all! On 17 July "Dictator" sailed for the West Coast of Scotland and the Comet Wheel series of races. I was not on board since it was just impossible to take all the time off work to do everything on the programme! However, on 24 July I departed for Mallaig in John Irwin's car, together with Susie, and Ken Cooper from the Holywood Yacht Club. We had to spend a night at Mallaig and most of the next day was spent at Armadale on Skye waiting for the last race of the series to finish. We put the time in touring around in the car, until "Dictator" turned up that evening. I cannot remember where she was placed in the event but it cannot have been spectacular! There were an awful lot of people sleeping on board that night but in the morning there was a sort-out and those who had to get back to work for a week departed by car.

There were four of us left to make as fast a passage as possible from Armadale all the way to Lymington on the Solent, the fourth being John Thompson, who was a trainee barrister and had been aboard for Comet Wheel. After a call at Mallaig for stores, diesel and water we were underway in miserable wet weather by 1200 on Saturday 26 July. We motored and motorsailed to keep up speed and made it round Ardnamurchan Point, down the Sound of Mull and the Sound of Jura to pass the Mull of Kintyre by 1130 the next morning. The weather cleared during the night and we managed not to hit any rocks along the way! Monday morning saw a brief call at Howth for more diesel and stores, and welcome showers at the Yacht Club. A fresh Southerly wind then gave us a beat down inside the various banks off the Irish coast but we were out and clear by nightfall and motor sailing in light airs. The Smalls, off Milford Haven, were abeam at 1130 on Tuesday and we passed the Longships Lighthouse at 0715 on Wednesday to round Land's End. Our last call was a one-hour stop at Newlyn for more stores and diesel and we passed the Lizard at 1400. Progress continued at a satisfactory rate up the English Channel and we reached the Berthon Boat Company's yard at Lymington at 1600 on Thursday. This passage had taken five days and four hours for about 650 miles and the average speed, including the stops, was 5.25 knots. The rest of the racing crew were waiting for us and within half an hour of arrival the boat was lifted out of the water for some attention to the bottom!

The next morning Susie and Ken Cooper left us, Susie to visit friends and Ken to return home. We were refloated and got across to Cowes in good time for the start of the Channel Race at 1350. As usual the course took in The Royal Sovereign Lightship and CH 1 Buoy off Cherbourg and despite light conditions we managed to finish sixth in our class out of 36 starters. The total number of boats racing was more like 200! Conditions for the inshore races in the Solent during Cowes Week were very light and the weather was hot and humid. However, we managed to keep somewhere in the middle of the fleet, even though we were once again up against top International competition! The Groves & Guttridge Marina at Cowes was absolutely packed out by evening and on the Monday night we were about the tenth boat from a pontoon. Returning after a "jolly" ashore, including showers and a meal at the Island Sailing Club, it was quite an obstacle race to climb across all the boats in the trot. On the foredeck of one boat there was an open hatchway but this was hidden by a loose spinnaker. I stepped on to what I thought was solid deck and went straight down the hatch, hitting my chest on the edge of it on the way. The result was extremely painful and the next morning, instead of racing, I had to visit the local hospital at Newport. The diagnosis was two broken ribs and I was told to go home and not go sailing!

Well, the light, hot and sunny weather continued and the next day I was back sailing. I was no use on deck but I could sit at the chart table to navigate and produce hot food from the galley immediately opposite! The last day of inshore racing was lighter than ever and none of our class made it to the finishing line before the 1800 deadline. After a layday on the Friday we were off on the

Fastnet Race at 1210 on Saturday 9 August, 1975. It was very similar to the race of two years earlier, with mainly light winds and slow frustrating progress. In these conditions, even with my broken ribs I was no passenger! We rounded the Rock at 0620 on the Tuesday and then had a pleasant spinnaker run for a few hours towards the Scilly Isles before the wind died away again. Most of Wednesday was spent in the sight of the Bishop Rock Lighthouse but we finally made it across the finishing line at Plymouth by 0930 on Thursday. We were placed well down the fleet.

On returning home I visited the doctor, was admonished for having gone sailing and given a sick note for a week. Well, there was no more Squib sailing at Cultra that season but I was back on board "Dictator" for the last local offshore race of the season, the RUYC Portpatrick Race. The wind for this was a persistent Northerly, force 7 to 8, and I took little part in the goings-on on deck! We flew along the first leg from the start to Donaghadee Sound on a broad reach, very much over-canvassed but leading the fleet. Into the Sound and it was a dead run down the coast to Strangford Whistle Buoy. Nothing would satisfy the crew on deck until the big running spinnaker was set, and the boat really flew – off the top of a wave out of control and into a spectacular broach. Recovering from this took a long time but, having recovered, they had to set the spinnaker again, with the same result! This time the spinnaker ended up around the keel and trailing astern in the water. Recovery took a long time and I reckon had we not tried the spinnaker and lost so much time we would have won the race! After a long hard slog to windward from Strangford to the finish off Porpatrick, we finished in second place. In fact only six boats finished out of about fifteen starters. "Dictator" was subsequently sold, to where I cannot remember, and Irwin Junior went looking for something lighter and faster!

In mid-October I spent ten days at Portsmouth at HMS "Phoenix" my third visit to this establishment and this time it was the full NBCD Course (Nuclear, Ballistic and Chemical Defence), including my third session at their Fire Fighting and Damage Control Course, with all its discomforts! It so happened that Irwins had now bought a used Nicholson 31 yacht, called "Golden Delicious" and took delivery of her at Camper & Nicholson's Gosport Marina while I was in the area. I went to visit her on a Saturday morning with Desmond (Irwin Senior) and I think this was his first look at her. She had won the Fastnet Race outright this year, which was about the only thing good about her. After "Dictator" she was an unattractive boat, roughly finished and poorly fitted out down below. Poor Desmond was nearly in tears! The core crew for this boat would be virtually the same as in "Dictator" but I don't recall that Desmond ever sailed with us! She fell into the ¾-ton class for level racing and in 1976 the International ¾-Ton Cup Series was to take place at Plymouth. That, therefore, was to be our highlight for the next season.

I cannot remember whether she was delivered by sea or road but "Golden Delicious" was afloat on a mooring in Ringhaddy Sound, Strangford Lough by 9 November, when I had my first sail in her. Thereafter there was sailing and crew training on several Sundays during the winter, and in early spring 1976 the RUYC organised a series of races on Strangford Lough which were quite well supported. We soon discovered that she was a very wet boat and when driving hard water would leak in through the bolted on keel connections. With her very shallow hull any water that did come in soon found its way up the sides of the boat and into the berths, lockers and everywhere else! When I was not sailing in her on a Sunday I was up at the Antrim Boat Club on Lough Neagh, racing in the Queen's University Squib "Night Before" with Susie. This partnership was really taking off and before the end of the winter season we had bought our own Squib "Chance". After some attention this boat then spent the summer racing at RNIYC, Cultra, and I was certainly aboard for most of the mid week races and some of the Saturday ones.

"Golden Delicious" performed well in the Strangford Lough Series but certainly didn't win every race! On 8 May there was a passage race round to Bangor in which we only finished fourth, but we did better in several local races to follow, including a level rating series organised by RUYC, where we won the 3/4 Ton Class. We were second in the annual passage race to Ramsey, Isle of Man, during the Whit Holiday and won the Round the Isle of Man Race the same weekend.

The Irish Sea Offshore Racing Association (ISORA) was by now well established and this year the big event was a series of races organised by the Royal Cork Yacht Club, for which we were entered. There were feeder races to this event from Falmouth, Holyhead and Bangor. Thus at 2000 on Friday 9 July, 1976, "Golden Delicious" set off on the 230-mile race from Bangor to Cork in a fleet of perhaps six boats. It was a fine night to be at sea, with a fair breeze but later the next day the wind freshened and went into the South with poor visibility. This gave us a nasty beat down inside the banks off the South East coast of Ireland during the hours of darkness. The tidal streams set quite strongly across the banks and careful navigation was all important! On the Sunday morning we were South of the Blackwater Bank, not far from Rosslare, when we saw a red distress rocket go up somewhere behind us. We turned back and shortly found that "Ruffian", our steed from 1973, had run aground on the Blackwater Bank, not far from Rosslare, "Ruffian" now belonged to a dentist from Killinchy, Co. Down, and he had mainly a family crew.

Another boat, "Fantan", which was the Brown brothers' latest racing machine, was already on the scene with Dickie Brown in command. The Rosslare Lifeboat also showed up and attempted to tow "Ruffian" off but the tide was falling and I think the pounding on the bank had also caused the lead fin keel to smash up through the hull. The crew were taken off by "Fantan" but shortly after that the boat sank and that was the end of "Ruffian". Dickie Brown must have been heartbroken but at least there were no injuries or loss of life. On "Golden Delicious" all we could do was stand by in case we were needed and we lost over four hours of racing time over this event. The next day we finished the race off Roche's Point at the entrance to Cork Harbour, and three days later, after the race committee had considered all the facts, we were deemed to have won the race. There followed an inshore race off Cork Harbour, which we won, and then a short race along the coast to Kinsale in which we were sixth, on the Wednesday. The same evening the fleet set off on a 120-mile mini Fastnet with a hard beat to windward in very fresh conditions. The boat got into quite a mess down below but at least we had an easy run back to Cork. We finished second in this race and a win in another inshore race on the Friday resulted in our winning the series overall. In between the races there was of course the usual socialising ashore and on other boats, with the prize-giving party in a local ballroom on the Friday night. Saturday afternoon saw our crew heading for home by car and the boat remained on a mooring off the RCYC at Crosshaven for nearly three weeks.

The next and final event on the agenda was the ¾-Ton Cup Championship in Plymouth and I was designated to find a crew to deliver her there. I was able to take sufficient leave to cover this and the event itself. I was also determined that the delivery would be a pleasant cruise rather than a race to get to a race, as had been the case with "Dictator" the previous year! Susie, being a schoolteacher, was on leave and a friend of hers, Jenny Murdoch, who apparently had sailing experience, was in between jobs and willing to go. I was able to hire a car from Avis for a one way trip from Belfast to Cork and on Thursday 5 August, 1976, the three of us set off early, to reach Crosshaven by 1700 that afternoon.

We soon had "Golden Delicious" alongside a pontoon at the RCYC. I thought we had left the boat reasonably clean after the Cork races but apparently not so, and there was even the remains of stew stuck to the deckhead near the galley – must have happened on the beat to the Fastnet! The girls set to on a monumental cleaning session while I went off in the car to buy stores and diesel. We had supper on board in very hygienic conditions! The next day we took the car to Avis in Cork and returned to the boat on the bus. The weather was hot and sunny, and had been so for some time with a big high stationary over the British Isles. That was the summer of the big drought, especially in the south-west of England, with all manner of restrictions on the use of fresh water. That afternoon we had a short shake-down trip along the coast to Kinsale and a pleasant evening ashore there.

On Saturday 7 August, we sailed for the Scilly Isles in calm and light airs so the engine was in use for some time. The engine was in fact a little single cylinder Yanmar of about 5 bhp, with the small fuel tank mounted on top of it. Spare diesel was carried in cans. The throttle cable had also broken recently and speed was controlled by pulling on a string led into the hatchway. During the night however the wind filled in a bit and we even had to reduce sail. In the resulting motion poor Jenny was seasick but soon recovered.

At 1400 on Sunday we made a good landfall at Round Island and then just motored round the islands to reach Hughtown on St. Mary's by 1600. The anchorage was very crowded and most of the boats flew French tricolours. Had we come to the right place! On going ashore we found that the large fleet of French boats were on a rally. At that time the French seemed to all have small boats with large crews and watching them going ashore in small, heavily overloaded inflatable dinghies could be quite amusing! That evening we found that the local pubs were very lively. It was in the Atlantic Hotel that we came across Harold Wilson, who either was or had just been

British PM. He had a holiday home on St. Mary's and I remembered some fuss in the press over his getting planning permission for same!

On the Monday morning we motored over to Tresco and anchored off a secluded beach. We went walking ashore to visit the famous gardens, where the plants were all wilting for lack of water, and the adjacent collection of figureheads. We spent another night at Hughtown (where it proved virtually impossible to get a shower!) and on Tuesday we visited St. Agnes, anchoring in the gut between the island and Gugh, which becomes a bay when the tide recedes. Back at Hughtown again, Jenny got chatting to a local fisherman, who must have fancied her since we ended up with a bucket full of crabs in the cockpit! Susie knows how to deal with crabs but we didn't have a large enough pot to take a whole one. I took no part in the messy business of preparing supper but the result was quite satisfying!

Thick fog on Wednesday morning delayed our departure for a while but we made the Helford River by 1900, where we anchored in the Pool, a delightful spot. The weather continued hot with little wind. Next day, after a trip ashore for shopping, we motored around the Helford River and then went on to nearby Falmouth to do the same thing. We went as far up the river as Malpas and then returned to Mylor, where we anchored off for the night. There were facilities ashore (including showers with water!) and we went ashore in the dinghy to make use of these. The dinghy we had was a last-minute addition to meet the racing rules and was a cheap and nasty thing, more like a child's toy. We parked it against a hedge and it must have met a spike or thorn for it was flat when we came to return to the boat. After a while another yachtsman who was returning out to his boat gave us and the flat dinghy a lift out.

Friday 13 saw the last leg to Plymouth, with a call at Megavissey for lunch. This was a picturesque place but not a friendly harbour for yachts. At Plymouth we berthed at the pontoon in Millbay Docks reserved for the ¾-Ton fleet, with six days in hand before the start of racing. The racing crew showed up over the next few days and apart from activities ashore, we went sailing, including an interesting trip some way up the Tamar River. We also dried the boat out one day for cleaning of the bottom. Susie and Jenny eventually departed to visit friends in England on their way home. Both of these girls would have loved to go racing but at that time, the offshore racing scene was very much male dominated, certainly in Northern Ireland. Some of our crew were married to non-sailing wives and really just didn't want any females on board!

The first race of the series was on Thursday 19 August on an Olympic course and with a very pleasant force 5 from the East. We distinguished ourselves by coming 22nd out of 31 starters! The next day we did even better, on a similar course and in similar conditions, when we came 27th out of the 31 starters!

There followed the first offshore race which took us 150 miles round the Wolf Rock, East Rutts Buoy, and back to Plymouth. There was a fast run outwards and a long beat back into force 6/7 with the result that we finished seventh and felt rather better for that! Monday was a layday, which we needed to clean the boat up after the weekends efforts! The third inshore race started in very light conditions which became a flat calm with thick fog. This race had to be abandoned and like many other boats we got lost in the fog and had some difficulty finding our way back to Plymouth! The second offshore and last race took us to East Rutts Buoy and then across the Channel to Guern Bouy, near Roscoff on the French coast. Conditions could be described as light to moderate. We had a beat to East Rutts, a run to Guern and a reach home to Plymouth, finishing in 8th place at 1800 on Friday 27 August. Our overall result was 12th out of the 31 starters, which was not too bad! I think the boat was as competitive as any and our crew as good as most but I think we were just not aggressive enough in close quarters situations, especially on the short inshore races. The French, we noticed, were always very aggressive and also very prone to lodging protests even when they were obviously in the wrong. At this level of competition one just has to be very aggressive to have a chance of winning!

The next day we cleaned the boat out yet again and she was left at Plymouth for a professional delivery crew to take her to Lymington. Here she was put on the market and that was the end of our sojourn with "Golden Delicious"! The crew returned home by car and ferry and on the Monday morning I was back in the Office. The following season, I think Irwin Junior got involved with some other local racing boat while at a later date Irwin Senior bought a new Nicholson 30. These boats were probably the last production yachts designed by Camper & Nicholson, had their traditional lines and were built for comfort and good looks rather than racing ability!

For what was left of the summer season, Susie and I raced our Squib "Chance" at RNIYC, Cultra and then in October she was taken to the Antrim Boat Club on Lough Neagh, where we raced in her most Sunday afternoons through the winter. However, on the offshore scene, no sooner was "Golden Delicious" out of the way than the next ambitious project surfaced. This time it was nothing less than to get a boat into the highly prestigous International Admirals Cup Event in 1977. I don't know who thought of this but no doubt David Kensett, our racing skipper since "Samphire" days, had a lot to do with it and I'm sure it was he who persuaded Norman Cordiner to provide the boat! Norman had built up a very successful business from scratch called Cordiners' Kitchens and which had a large and well equipped factory in Bangor. It is still very much in business. Norman had apparently been interested in racing cars and was now interested in big racing yachts! Anyway I was approached at an early stage and was only too pleased to join the potential crew!

CHAPTER 18: A NEW BOAT AND MORE SERIOUS RACING

In mid-December, 1976, a bare hull arrived in Bangor on a low loader and was immediately taken into the kitchen factory for completion and fitting out, which proceeded forthwith. The boat was one of three built to a very recent design by the up-and-coming New Zealand yacht designer Ron Holland, and at about 41 ft in length, it was designed to fall into the Two-Ton Class for level racing.

The Admiral's Cup Series was probably at its zenith in the 1970s and took place every two years at the same time as, and as part of, the Cowes Week goings-on. It included the RORC Channel Race and Fastnet Race, with a number of inshore races during Cowes week in between. The racing took place on a handicap system under the now almost universal "International Offshore Rules" or IOR, and each participating country had to enter a team of three boats. To select the best boats for the team, most countries had to run extensive trials over several weeks and in countries such as the UK and the USA these trials were hotly contested. To get on the British trials we would have had to take our boat to the south of England for several weeks, never mind the time required for the actual event. With our amateur crew, who all had full-time jobs, this would be impossible and with such fierce competition our chances of making the British team would have been pretty slim!

However, in Northern Ireland we have always been in a peculiar position, as we could be either Irish or British, or both! I well remember a time when the UK was in some financial difficulties and there were severe restrictions on the amount of money one was allowed to take out of the country. Such restrictions did not apply in the Republic of Ireland and I knew of more than one hard headed Protestant/Unionist "Not an Inch" and "No Surrender" businessman who applied for Irish passports and thus became citizens of the Republic! On the sporting scene rugby football had always been played on an All-Ireland basis and yacht racing was much the same. We could sail for Great Britain or sail for Ireland, whichever seemed the most advantageous at the time! Even at RNIYC, with our Squib and Dragon Class fleets we could run the Irish National Championship one week and the United Kingdom Championship the next! It was therefore obvious that the new boat should be entered for the Irish Admiral's cup trials, which is what happened. In any case, there were other anomalies in this event and it was well known that the Hong Kong team consisted of three boats that had failed to get on to the British team!

During the winter, work proceeded apace on the new boat. The fitters in the Kitchen factory worked on her during the day while David Kensett and others of the crew worked in the evenings and at weekends. While Norman may have been keen to win races, he was also keen to have a beautiful and well fitted-out boat. Therefore beautifully made berths, lockers and other items of furniture were produced and fitted during factory working hours, only to be ripped out again when David got on the scene in the evening. The final berths were no more than lightweight aluminium frames with light canvas over them and the crew lockers were no more than PVC pockets attached to the insides of the hull. Internal lining of the hull was totally unnecessary for racing purposes but she did end up with some internal PVC lining. One item which Norman did get away with was a beautiful teak laid veneer deck and an expert from somewhere on the Shannon spent a long time carefully fitting this. It was, of course, extra unnecessary weight but Norman did want the boat to be saleable at some future date!

The final layout down below was that forward of the mast was a completely bare open space for the stowage of sails. Immediately abaft the mast were the loo and galley, both of which, while fairly basic, were in fact luxurious compared with what is found on a modern racing boat! Aft of this were two double berths, one above the other on either side, to sleep eight people with the engine casing amidships aft of that. There was a "tunnel" either side of the engine casing leading to the "navigatorium", which was arranged athwartships together with a narrow athwartships bench for the navigator to sit on – and sleep on! It was barely long enough for my modest length! There was a window in the athwartships bulkhead for the navigator to communicate with the helmsman and aft of this was again open space except for the steering gear and the heating unit of a central heating system. Soon after the boat was in commission this unit got so soused in water that it failed completely. There were faults in the navigation instruments for the same reason. Indeed, like "Golden Delicious", this was a wet boat and the water came from all directions, including the keel bolts! Outside, she was flush decked with two cockpits aft, one for the winch winders and one for the helmsman.

On 14 May, 1977, "Golden Leigh", as she was now called, was

rolled out of the shed and the bolt on lead keel fitted. On 18 May she was taken on a low loader to Bangor Central Pier, lifted into the water by a mobile crane and the mast stepped. On 19 May the crew assembled and we had a busy morning preparing the boat for sea. A short trial showed something seriously was wrong with the engine, or the propeller or both, since she just would not drive properly and the engine, a Perkins diesel, was labouring to the point of stalling. We thought the wrong propeller must have been fitted but there was no time to make a change and by 1500 we were underway for Dun Laoghaire and the first Admiral's Cup selection race. We only had light airs for this passage and after the propeller fell off and was lost during the night progress was very slow.

We reached Dun Laoghaire with only an hour to spare before the start of the race on Friday morning. Sailing conditions were actually ideal for this first inshore race but we only finished fifth out of I don't know how many starters. However, our boat had only been launched for the first time less than 24 hours earlier and we'd had no practice at all! The next day we were fifth again, but very much closer to the first boats. On the Sunday we finished fourth and would have been second but for a mix up at a leeward mark. It was undignified having to be towed to and from a mooring in the harbour! The logistics involved in getting crew to and from the boat for the trials took some organising and this time two family cars came down from Bangor to take us home.

The following weekend there was to be a passage race from Dun Laoghaire to Cork and for this we hired a minibus. Susie came with us to drive the bus between Dun Laoghaire and Cork and was able to visit friends in Youghall on the way. The race got underway at 1200 on the Saturday in light conditions which unfortunately became a flat calm by Sunday afternoon. The race had to be abandoned and we reached Crosshaven on Cork Harbour under tow at 1900! The bus departed north at 2330 and reached Bangor by 0730. We wasted an hour by getting lost in the dark in the Knockmealdown Mountains, not far from Cork. Like the telephone system, Irish sign-posting was long overdue for a serious upgrading!

Friday 3 June saw the crew arriving at Crosshaven by various means for a long offshore race, which started that evening. I travelled down with another crew member in his old Citroen CV2 car and we were lucky to get there an hour before the race started. "Golden Leigh" carried a crew of nine for offshore races and sometimes more on short day races, when virtually the whole crew would be on deck. When close hauled everyone, when not doing anything else, and except the helmsman, would sit along the weather gunwale with their legs over the side in the form of movable ballast. This was by now common practice in racing boats. On long passages there was a simple two-watch system of four on-watch and four off, usually for three or four hours at a time. The four off-watch had to occupy the four windward berths when the boat was close hauled and in the event of a tack had to shift berth to the other side – again movable ballast! As Navigator, I did not keep a watch but spent most of my time in my "hole" aft, but it was far from restful since, apart from plotting our position and courses and considering tactics with the Skipper, I had to listen to every available weather forecast.

On the Admiral's Cup offshore races there was also for the first time a twice daily radio check with a guard ship. I came out of my hole to produce meals for all of us, sometimes with help and sometimes not, and also had to help out on deck when necessary! The rest of the crew thought I had an easy time of it but I rarely got more than two hours' sleep at a time on my narrow bench! However, the worst job in this boat was acting as Purser and while Norman Cordiner had provided the boat, he had not provided anything else. At this level of racing, even before it became virtually fully professional, it was common for well-heeled owners to feed the crew and pay their expenses. Not so with us, and I had to keep wheedling money out of the other crew members to keep the kitty afloat and pay for food if nothing else! At the end of the season I figured I was considerably out of pocket!

Anyway, this trial started at 2100 and the course took us from Cork to the Seven Stones Lightship of "Torry Canyon" fame, thence to the Fastnet Rock and back to Cork. The weather for the whole of this race was gale force NW winds, rain and poor visibility! I forget how many starters there were but certainly all the top Irish offshore boats were there, including Dennis Doyle's "Moonduster", Archie O'Leary's "Irish Mist II", and Harold Cudmore's "Big Apple". We all had a splendid fast run across to the Seven Stones and our boat rounded at 1730 the next day, Saturday, in very close company with two other boats, which I think were "Irish Mist" and "Moonduster".

It was then that the fun started, for it was a long hard and most unpleasant beat from there to the Fastnet Rock. We hadn't been going for long when the boat hit a nasty steep sea like a brick wall.

The off-watch crew were in the windward bunks and suddenly the two in the upper bunks found themselves keeping company with those below as the lightly built and secured bunks collapsed! Later on there were other problems such as when the cooker broke adrift from its gimbals. Proper feeding was just not possible and in these circumstances Mars Bars and such, plus a common mug of strong orange juice to pass around, do just fine! (This is known as "sippers".) However, at some stage we did manage to secure the cooker and roast a large chicken. I remember that it took two of us on the cabin floor to hold this beast and a third to hack at it with a knife. The rough pieces were just passed around and up to those on deck!

Actually, it was lucky the boat held together and nothing important broke because she was being driven really hard. Needless to say, it was very wet, both on deck and down below! Sheets of kitchen roll, known as "broadarse", were much in demand for wiping salt out of eyes and cleaning glasses.

We rounded the Fastnet Rock at 2230 on the Sunday and, believe it or not, after 29 hours of hard beating to windward, the same three boats rounded the Rock together and set spinnakers for a fast reach to the finishing line at Cork. It was still very close when we approached the line but unfortunately "Irish Mist" ran into a fishing net and spent some time getting it cut away from around the keel and rudder. We were second boat home, at 0630 on the Monday behind I think "Big Apple" which was a much bigger boat, but how we were placed on handicap I cannot remember. We might even have been first! This was the end of the trials and it was gratifying to learn some time later that the Irish team for the Admiral's Cup would be "Big Apple", "Irish Mist II" and "Golden Leigh" – two boats from Cork and one from Bangor.

We spent much of the day cleaning up the mess down below and drying the boat out followed by a splendid meal at the Grand Hotel, owned by Dennis Doyle. Later that evening we dried the boat out alongside a quay and fitted a new (and hopefully right) propeller which had been sent down to us. On Tuesday a delivery crew arrived by car to take the boat back to Bangor and the racing crew departed for home in the same car, plus the CV2. I had three days in the office that week and even went racing in "Chance" with Susie at Cultra! On the Friday morning David Kensett telephoned to say that the delivery crew on "Golden Leigh" were exhausted after windward work all the way from Cork, and that the new propeller was useless! Could I meet them at Dun Laoghaire and let two of them get home for urgent appointments? Other racing crew members were earning some plus points with their wives or had other urgent commitments!

That evening Susie and I drove down to Dun Laoghaire in one of the delivery crew's cars and on checking at the Royal Irish Yacht Club, we found that the boat had only got as far as Wicklow. There we arrived to find "Golden Leigh" moored alongside a quay in the river. The two crew concerned left for home in the car at once and I think that left four of us on board. It was a dirty wet windy night and we remained stormbound for most of the next day. However, there was a lull in the evening and I persuaded another Bangor Yachtsman who happened to be in Wicklow with his boat to tow us out of the harbour. He would only use his inflatable dinghy and outboard, which at least got us out of the river and into the outer harbour before he ran out of steam or the towrope broke! We got a headsail set just as fast as if we had been racing and managed to tack the boat out through the pier-heads into a Northerly force 7. If nothing else, "Golden Leigh" was highly manoeuvrable under sail!

We headed out through the nearest passage in the off-lying banks in view of the engineless situation, but after beating for a while the wind veered on the Sunday morning and we ended up with a pleasant run to Bangor, where we berthed alongside the North Pier without difficulty. Because of possible vandalism here we arranged for several of our crew to take it in turns to do nightwatchman and sleep on board! Later that week the boat was lifted out on to the pier and the engine problem finally located. When originally fitted there should have been a reduction gear between the main gearbox and the propeller shaft, but this was omitted! With a reduction gear fitted the problem was solved and thereafter we had plenty of power under engine.

On 23 June it was off to Holyhead for the RORC Irish Sea Race which was sailed in light conditions and was complicated off Chicken Rock, south of the Isle of Man, when the Belfast to Liverpool ferry "Ulster Queen" reported a man lost overboard. We cannot have been well placed at the end of it all since I did not record the result.

The next race was a feeder race from Gourock, on the Firth of Clyde, via the Isle of Man to Bangor for what was known as the Comet Wheel Series of races. This year it was staged at Bangor and the feeder race was so slow, in light conditions, that we barely finished in time on Tuesday 12 July to sail in the first inshore race of the series. The owner was on board for this race, one of the few times he actually sailed with us!

There were various races during the week with boats from all over the Irish Sea and Scotland. These included a middle distance race taking in the South Rock Lightship and Milleur Point Buoy at the entrance to Loch Ryan. The weather continued light all week and at the end of it all "Golden Leigh" was placed second, having been beaten by a one-tonner called "Prospect of Puffin" from North Wales. There was plenty of social activity ashore during this week, especially in the local yacht clubs and our crew were involved in most of this. It was, after all, prime holiday time in Northern Ireland!

The next week I had two days in the office and then was off for almost a month. The first task was to get "Golden Leigh" down to the Solent and for this there was a delivery crew of four. I had Susie plus the youngest member of our racing crew and his girlfriend, who was not much help as she was sick for much of the time! We sailed from Bangor at 2100 on 19 July and in light conditions all the way we made a non-stop passage to Lymington, using both sail and engine to keep up speed. We rounded Land's End at 1600 on the 21st and berthed at Lymington by 1900 on the 22nd. This passage was 450 miles in two days and 22 hours, giving us an average speed of 6.4 knots – the fastest I have ever done this trip, before or since! There followed four days at Lymington, where the boat was lifted out for final preparations and polishing of the bottom. We had quite a number of people living and sleeping on board and those with no bunk simply stretched out on sail bags in the large forecastle space!

On 26 July the boat was relaunched and we immediately sailed over to Cowes and our reserved berth at the Groves & Guttridge Marina. Already there were "Big Apple" and "Irish Mist" and we tied up astern of them. Both of these boats were flying huge Irish tricolours from their sterns, plus "Battle flags" forward, and there ensued a debate among our crew as to what we should fly! To my knowledge the boat had never been officially registered as either British or Irish, since there just wasn't time to go through this tortuous procedure before the serious action began. We could hardly fly a Red Ensign since we were on the Irish team and the matter was settled quite categorically when at least two of our crew stated that if the boat flew an Irish tricolour they would simply go home and take no part in the event to follow! We flew only a large "battle flag", decorated with a shamrock, from the forestay and nothing else. Of the 19 national teams in this Admiral's Cup Series (including, for the first time, a Japanese team), we must have been the only boat in the entire fleet not proudly flying a national flag! But nobody seemed to notice, or at least no comment was made.

The following day was fully taken up with scrutineering, with just about everything on the boat measured and checked by the Royal Ocean Racing Club (RORC) scrutineers. We went out for some practice that evening, during which one crew member fell overboard with a winch handle in his hand. We were relieved that when we recovered him he had not let go of the winch handle! Thursday 28 was the first inshore race, in which the Irish effort was not bad and we were fourth at the end of the day. Next followed the weekend Channel Race with about 200 yachts, including the Admiral's Cup fleet. The course this time was from Portsmouth, round the Isle of Wight to the Needles Buoy, then across to CH1 Buoy off Cherbourg, thence to a buoy off Brighton and back to Portsmouth. This was a very light weather race but we managed to keep going fairly well and the Irish team was well placed.

The following Monday the second inshore race was cancelled due to lack of wind, but all the other Cowes Week events took place. The starting line used for all classes was off the Royal Yacht Squadron at Cowes and extended a long way out into the Solent. With such a large number of boats and so many different classes one wondered how the Race Officers ashore managed to keep track of anything that was going on! Even if there was no wind there was still plenty of tide across the starting line and this particular morning there was a huge fleet becalmed on or near the line, some of them making very good progress backwards with the tide. Into the middle of this lot there arrived the supertanker "Esso Northumbria", inward bound to the Esso refinery on Southampton Water. Well, the starting line extended right across the deep water channel and there must have been some confusion both afloat and ashore, since half the fleet was out of sight from the Battery at the RYS, on the far side of the tanker. There was certainly much hooting of sirens on the tanker and much trying to get out of the way by boats in the deep water channel. The comment in the Daily Telegraph the next morning was that the only boat to make a good start that day was the "Esso Northumbria"! On Tuesday we did race and all three boats did quite well, resulting in the Irish team getting up to third place, but that was as high as we got! After the last inshore race on Thursday we were down to fifth place.

For Cowes Week, while these inshore races were taking place the boats were back in the marina every evening and the crew of every Admiral's Cup boat except one were staying ashore in various hotels or rented houses. On "Golden Leigh" we spent the nights on board and each morning a mountain of sleeping bags and other gear was taken ashore and stowed in a station wagon belonging to one of the crew! There had however been no expense spared on the sail wardrobe and we had the latest in racing sails from Hoods, which warranted two of their expert staff being in our crew. While their services were free, they did not expect to have to pay for their food and it was embarrassing to have to ask them to contribute to the kitty!

Friday was a layday when all the boats made preparations for the Fastnet Race. On our boat we reckoned that in average conditions we should finish this race in four to five days and that we should store accordingly. Any more stores would be unnecessary weight and of course we took the minimum of water and diesel. Washing was unnecessary except for the occasional tooth clean and face wash! As it was, our provisions were more limited by lack of cash than by the possibility of excess weight!

The 1977 Fastnet Race had to be The Slownet Race! We crossed the starting line at 1600 on Saturday 6 August and the whole fleet of 300 or so boats, including the 57 in the Admiral's Cup fleet, made slow progress out of the Solent and down the English Channel. On our boat we did manage to get past Portland Bill against the tide by crawling so close inshore that we could almost touch the rocks! There followed two days of almost flat calm and it was sometime on Monday before we even got past the Scilly Isles. If nothing else it was hot and sunny and all the crews got well sunburned! Light fickle airs only got us out to the Fastnet Rock by 1500 on Wednesday and progress back to the finish at Plymouth was equally slow. The whole of Friday was spent becalmed between the Lizard and Plymouth and we only struggled across the finishing line at 0700 on Saturday 13 August, after just a few hours short of a week at sea – some Fastnet race!

All of the boats were running short of food by midweek and some of the comments on the twice daily radio check-in were interesting! Many of the foreign yachts carried British navigators (for obvious reasons) and this included the Japanese trio. One of them remarked that he was down to a cupful of rice a day and he never, ever wanted to see rice again. On "Golden Leigh" the situation was particularly grim since, due to our financial situation, we had barely enough provisions for four days, never mind a week! We were on very strict rationing from Wednesday on and some most peculiar dishes were served up. One supper was tinned peas and gravy with nothing else, since we had almost run out of meat and were right out of potatoes and bread! I well remember opening the last 12oz tin of corned beef, which I did in full view of the whole crew. There were four faces peering down the hatchway and another four peering out of the bunks in eager anticipation! Tinned corned beef comes in a wedge shape and trying to divide this into nine equal portions to satisfy everyone was almost impossible!

It is indicative of the conditions on this race that there was time to read books and I personally got through two lengthy popular novels!

Once the race was over it was straight ashore for monumental meals and equally monumental showers! Susie was in Plymouth to meet us and remarked that we all stank to high heaven, but since we all stank the same we had never noticed! Later we met up in the RWYC with a delivery crew who had come over from Bangor to sail the boat back home, and who were looking forward to a pleasant cruise. We had not seen anything of the owner the whole time of the Admiral's Cup Event but now he showed up to tell us that the boat was only to be taken to Lyminton and put on the market! The only cruise the delivery crew got was from Plymouth to Lymington, after which they returned home! I cannot remember where "Golden Leigh" was individually placed in the Fastnet Race but so far as the Admiral's Cup was concerned the Irish Team were placed joint eighth with Spain, which I suppose was not too bad out of 19 teams.

After a night ashore in Plymouth we departed for home by car and the Holyhead to Dun Laoghaire ferry. I was back in the office on the Monday morning! The only sailing during the rest of the season was one or two "round the buoys" races in "Chance" at Cultra.

Having sailed in three consecutive Fastnet Races in 1973, 1975 and 1977, the next time I sailed round the Fastnet Rock was over 20 years later, when a family cruise in our boat "Sunddowner" took us right around Ireland. The three races in which I took part were all "soft" as far as the weather was concerned, especially the last one! This was more than made up for in the next race, in 1979, which was "Fastnet Force Ten"! The whole fleet was decimated, with many boats being abandoned or lost, or both, and unfortunately there was loss of life despite a huge search and rescue operation.

The inquiry into this disaster was more than the government marine surveyors could possibly handle and it was passed over to the Royal Yachting Association to organise. They produced a detailed questionnaire which was sent out to the owners of all the boats involved. They then collated all the replies and produced a report.

CHAPTER 19: TWENTY YEARS WITH "MELANDY"

With Norman Cordiner's sudden sale of "Golden Leigh" in August 1977, a decade of sailing and racing in various offshore yachts as one of a team came to an end for me. The 1978 season was virtually boatless except for the 19ft Squib keelboat which Susie and I owned and raced mainly at RNIYC Cultra. We were even reduced to going on a motoring holiday in Scotland! We did, however, have one or two short trips with a friend who had bought a Nicholson 32 yacht called "Jacana" of St. Mawes at the end of the previous season, mainly for family cruising. These boats were built between the mid-'60s and mid-'70s on traditional lines and are splendid small seaworthy cruisers, many of which have done long ocean passages and round-the-world trips.

This boatless situation was most depressing and we resolved somehow to get a boat of our own. What we wanted was a sound, safe and well-proven cruising yacht, easily handled by a man and woman. Since finance was a problem, we also wanted a well-known class of boat which would at least hold its value. What better than a Nicholson 32! There was nothing available locally so we scoured the advertisement pages of every yachting magazine, looking for something within our price range. As a result, one very cold and snowy Saturday morning in January 1979 found me at the Universal Shipyard on the Hamble River near Southampton, surveying a very shabby and rundown Nicholson 32. This was "Melandy", a Mark IV model built in 1965.

Examination showed that she had been badly neglected over the past several years but that the hull, spars, standing rigging and most other important items were sound. All equipment other than the cooker appeared to be original – and thus 14 years old – and the engine was certainly the original Watermota Seawolf petrol engine. The coach roof windows when the boat was built were secured by rubber mouldings. The four large ones had since been fitted with rough metal surrounds but the six smaller ones still had the original rubber which was badly perished and these windows could be pushed out with one finger! The on-deck varnish work was in very poor condition and down below all the woodwork had been coated with ordinary teak oil. It was unsightly and in places just a sticky mess. One thing I liked, though, was that she was already fitted with Aries self steering gear. Obviously there would be a great deal of work to do to bring this boat up to a standard which would satisfy us, but basically she was sound. The topsides had originally been dark blue but some previous owner had made a poor job of painting them a bright red while the underwater was light blue.

Needless to say, the price being asked for "Melandy" was the lowest for any Nic 32 we had seen advertised. When I returned home, Susie and I discussed the matter, then made an offer considerably below the asking price. After some arguing with the owner, we agreed a reduced price in view of her condition and then went off to talk to the bank manager. A month or so later I was back in Southampton to complete the deal and "Melandy" was ours. I instructed Universal Shipyard to give her a coat of antifouling and launch her for Easter. Back at home we began to gather all the things we would need for the delivery trip, some bought and some borrowed – inflatable life-raft, inflatable dingy and second-hand Seagull outboard engine, an unwieldy portable VHF radio discarded by Belfast Harbour, lifejackets and much, much more. Not least was a length of window rubber and the tool to fit it with. No way were we going to sea in a boat where the windows could be pushed in or out by finger!

On the Wednesday before Easter my car was loaded to the gunwales with all this gear and there was also a lot of deck cargo on a borrowed roof rack. It was then driven onto the Belfast Liverpool ferry and the cargo unloaded into a baggage locker. That night Susie and I crossed to Liverpool as foot passengers and next morning the reverse process took place with a car hired for a one way trip to Southampton. We had a pleasant run south and reached the shipyard just before they closed for the holiday. "Melandy" was out on a pile mooring but we soon had her alongside the only pontoon and got our gear on board. Susie had seen photographs that I had taken, but even so she was nearly in tears when she saw the state of the boat.

The next two days were very busy but by the end of Easter Saturday I was satisfied that the boat was in a fit state to go to sea. We went for a trial trip down the river, filled up with petrol and that was us ready. We sailed on Easter Sunday, 15 April, and except for a call at Newlyn for petrol, we made a non-stop passage home. The weather down the Channel to Land's End and on the long open stretch north to the Tuskar Rock was mostly light and fortunately the old Watermota kept going. Thereafter the wind freshened from the west and we had a splendid beam reach up the Irish Sea with the Aries gear doing all the steering. It was still very early in the season by northern standards and so we went into the shelter of Strangford Lough and put the boat on a friend's mooring for a few weeks. The passage home from Southampton had taken five days. Later on we sailed round to Belfast Lough and put her on a mooring off RNIYC at Cultra, which was only a few minutes, drive from our house.

Since we had very few commitments other than work at this time, "Melandy" was well used and we were away somewhere most weekends, plus we got in at least one decent cruise during a season, sometimes two. We found that we could go anywhere within about 50 miles of our base on a normal two-day weekend and be sure of getting back in time for work. For many boats based in Belfast Lough the most popular weekend haunt is Portpatrick, across the North Channel on the Scottish coast, but this is only 25 miles away. We frequently visited such places as Port Ellen and Bowmore on Islay, Gigha, Campbeltown, the Isle of Aran, Girvan, Loch Ryan, Isle of Whithorn on the Solway Firth and, of course, the Isle of Man. In our first season we had two longer cruises, the first being to North Wales. Since a number of our local Squib Class keelboats were competing in the National Championships at Abersoch on Cardigan Bay, we sailed over there to cheer them on! This involved two nights and a day at sea to get there and an exposed anchorage when we got there so we had to sleep with the leeboards up to stay in our berths! First visit for me since the "Garibaldi" in 1949! Two days at Pwllheli saw us doing the tourist bit, including the Ffestiniog Railway.

Our return home was via the Menai Strait which proved as fascinating as I had expected. It resembles the narrows leading into Strangford Lough but is about five times as long and has equally fierce tides. It is only a matter of arriving at the Swellies, the rocks between the two bridges, at High Water slack to make for an interesting and scenic passage. One night was spent dried out alongside the wall beside Caernarvon Castle and another at anchor off Beaumaris where we also visited the Castle. Later we made a modest cruise on the West Coast of Scotland which included circumnavigating the Isle of Mull. The whole season was dogged by engine problems but we managed to keep it going. Replacing a core plug at the back of the cylinder block was interesting, to say the least! Of course the whole bell housing had to come off but it was done without removing the engine and took a whole weekend of contortions on my part while Susie read a book and provided me with sustenance. After that the valve springs started to break and by the end of our Scottish cruise I had replaced all eight. By the time I did No. 8, I had it down to about 20 minutes' work. It can be done without removing the cylinder head and the only special tools were a few bits of wood and a bent 6-inch nail!

In the winter, "Melandy" was laid up in the yard at Cultra and major work took place. Every piece of wood down below that could be unscrewed we took home for stripping and revarnishing and the spare bedroom became a workshop. What we could not take off, we dealt with on board. The engine was lifted out and taken home, where it was completely dismantled and rebuilt, including a rebore and new pistons. There was much else and all this effort involved work at home most nights of the week and work at the boat almost every weekend through the winter. Except for the specialised work on the engine, we did it all ourselves – I might add that at this time we had no family!

In 1980 our main cruise was for three weeks in July when we beat our way up the West Coast of Scotland against cold Northerly winds and reached the Orkney Islands, a fascinating place. Our return home was via the Caledonian Canal. The following winter the financial situation improved and this resulted in new power both on deck and down below. We invested in new mainsail, working jib and heavy genoa by Ratsey and Lapthorn and a multi coloured cruising chute by Bruce Banks. The old engine was replaced by a Watermota Seapanther diesel engine and this included a whole new exhaust system, controls and more new electrics. By opting for the Seapanther the actual amount of butchery in the engine space was minimal and also it was lighter and cheaper than anything of comparable power we considered. Even so it was quite a task and I think the original engines in these boats must have been installed before the lid, i.e. the deck/cockpit/coachroof moulding was fitted! An Autohelm tiller pilot made life easier when under power since normally there were only the two of us on board. The Aries gear was fine in a breeze but no use in a flat calm or anytime with the engine running. The Autohelm was known as "George", the Aries gear as "Charlie" and both were reliable helmsmen!

In 1981 we spent part of the summer in the USA and our main

cruise was limited to two weeks in August, again on the West Coast of Scotland and in mainly poor weather. We did visit some new anchorages including the island of Gometra off the West coast of Mull, the island of Rhum and Loch Dunvegan in a gale of wind. Here we visited the Castle, entering from seaward by the back door! We got as far as Stornoway before turning for home and called at a fascinating and landlocked remote anchorage called Acarsaid Mhor on the Isle of Rona, which itself is off the East coast of Skye. One memorable passage on this cruise was a beat into SW Force 6 with rain and poor visibility from Isle Ornsay on Skye, down the Sound of Sleat and round Ardnamurchan Point to sight the lighthouse and make sure of our position before turning into the Sound of Mull.

The 1982 season was splendid and in three weeks we visited the Outer Hebrides, the Northern Orkney Isles, Fair Isle and Shetland, again returning home via the Caledonian Canal. In late August we made a ten day trip back to North Wales going as far as Pwllheli and returning via the Menai Strait and the Isle of Man. This was a summer of generally good weather and light winds. 1983 was another satisfactory season with good weather and our main cruise was three weeks up the "West Coast". This included a trip out to St. Kilda via the Sound of Harris and returning via the Butt of Lewis and Stornoway.

However, during one severe gale towards the end of the season "Melandy" broke free from her mooring at Cultra and ended up aground close to the sea wall. Fortunately the tide was still rising and we got her off under her own power despite the onshore wind and sea. On hauling out we found the lower part of the rudder quite badly damaged but fortunately little else other than scratches and scrapes on the bottom of the keel. Removal of the rudder involved digging a pit underneath the boat so that it could be dropped down and clear. Apart from the necessary rudder repairs there was only routine maintenance this winter, which was just as well since there were developments on the domestic front. Son number one, Geoffrey, was born in March 1984 in Portland Oregon. Geoffrey went sailing with us from the age of three months and this first season with a child on board was quite easy since he was not very mobile and spent a lot of time in the carry cot. As usual we were away somewhere virtually every weekend and enjoyed a very good cruise in August, in mainly light airs and brilliant sunshine. We made a first visit to Kildalton and the Ardmore Islands on Islay, a beautiful place, though only in fine weather. On then to the outer Hebrides via Canna and we got as far North as Loch Skiport on South Uist. Our return was via the west coast of Skye, including the famous Loch Scavaig.

Two pieces which I wrote for the Yacht Club magazine during this time may be of interest to the general reader, so here they are!

"MELANDY'S" NEW DEVICE

For some years now Susie and I have been trying to obtain a device for "Melandy" which is to be found on board a number of cruising yachts but which is more commonly found on shore. Many people have one and indeed quite a number of people have two or more! Despite all our efforts it looked as though we were going to be unsuccessful. Some people have no trouble at all obtaining them but others like ourselves are not so lucky. After exhaustive enquiries and a great deal of effort, quite suddenly out of the blue we were advised that one was available in Portland Oregon and that we should get out there immediately to collect same. Hence our sudden departure for the USA at Easter. All went well and eventually the device was brought home and installed on board "Melandy". After launching towards the end of May, our first trial trip was across to Portpatrick and back in fairly fresh conditions, and all went well.

The device now weighs 15 pounds and fully extended it is about 18 inches long. It has many of the characteristics of a small diesel engine but for such a small one it has a remarkably high fuel consumption. It requires refuelling about every four hours, although with the increasing size of its fuel tank it should go for six hours or so without too much attention. The injectors have to be cleaned at frequent intervals and one or two spare ones have to be kept at hand for immediate insertion into the combustion chamber when called for.

Like the inlet end the exhaust end also requires frequent attention but in time it should be able to exhaust directly overboard. As it is at present we have to carry a large stock of disposable effluent containers which if they are fitted correctly usually prevent the exhaust escaping into the cabin. Cleaning up after an exhaust leak can be a messy business so it pays to be careful and methodical.

Like most engines it makes quite a lot of noise when all is not well but even with my lack of previous experience it seems to produce less noise than many of its type. Attention to either the inlet or the exhaust or more often both ends at the same time usually stops the noise. I have also noticed that even when all is well at both ends it sometimes makes gurgling noises but I am assured that this is only the sign of a well tuned and cared for device.

Near the top end there are two appendages which quite frequently go round and round in circles. It has occurred to me that in due course this device can be attached to the winches so that we will have self winding and self tailing winches. If these parts can also be induced to work backwards and forwards, then together with the sensor unit on top when it is more fully developed it can be attached to the tiller and we will have a third method of self steering. At the lower end there are two further appendages and from their motion it looks as though they have been designed for a certain type of coffee grinder winch fitted on some large racing yachts. In any event I gather that these together with the two upper ones will shortly enable to device to propel itself about the boat without assistance. Actually I can see problems here and it may have to be secured to the deck!

All in all this new device has many exciting possibilities. When we were considering it initially I was not one hundred per cent sold on the idea but now that we have it I would not part with it at any price. We already have Charlie (the Aries gear) and George (the Autohelm) who are not quite so demanding of time and attention. This new device is in fact a Waters Junior Mark I and we have called it Geoffrey Keith!

A SAD STORY

One Sunday evening in June three yachts were returning to Cultra from Portpatrick in quite fresh conditions, the wind being Southerly 5 to 6. On board "Jessie May" were John and Eileen Heyes together with Eric and Liz Allen. "Kittiwake" had the whole Aston family on board while on "Melandy" there were four of us, Susie and I plus the Reverend Doctor ER, who was visiting us from Washington DC and of course our new device. Approaching the moorings we chatted on the radio and it was agreed that I would pick up the Club launch from its moorings and ferry everyone ashore in greater comfort and safety than would be possible in our various dinghies. Having picked up our mooring and stowed the sails on "Melandy" we then launched our inflatable dinghy and I set off towards the Club launch leaving Susie to pack up our gear and tidy the boat. I would be back later with the launch having first picked up everyone from the other two boats. The sequence of events was then as follows;-

1. The wind being offshore the water close inshore was smooth but out at the moorings there was quite a lumpy little sea. About halfway to the launch the Seagull outboard shipped some water in the air intake and stalled. I therefore shipped the oars and pulled for the nearest moored boat before being driven out to sea by the wind. This happened to be the Dragon "Souwester" and I tied on while I attended to the engine.

2. On board "Jessie May", John Heyes saw what had happened and launched his own inflatable dinghy. He got to the launch and brought it over to see if I needed help. His own dinghy was left on the launch mooring. By now my Seagull was running and I told John to go round the three yachts and pick everyone up, while I headed for the slipway, pulled up my dinghy and stowed it away at the back of the Clubhouse. The launch duly arrived at the pier with everyone else on board and all the gear which was taken ashore.

3. I was now informed by Susie that in the rush to pack up and leave "Melandy" she had forgotten to turn the main battery switch to off. John and I therefore returned to the boat in the launch where indeed the main battery switch was still on. This fixed, we returned the launch to its mooring and embarked in John's dinghy to get back ashore. His Seagull outboard refused to fire or show any sign of life.

4. After trying everything we could think if we gave up and started to row for the slipway. Rowing an inflatable dinghy into a fresh breeze is hard work and we made slow progress, but we were getting there. Meanwhile, on shore, another Club member who had been watching the goings on decided we needed help and very kindly launched the rescue boat to tow us in. On hauling out the rescue boat we discovered that its cradle had a flat tyre which might well be damaged beyond repair.

5. With everything stowed away I now went to "Melandy's" bags at the head of the slipway to get my keys, the car being parked

a little way up the road. I soon discovered that my Henri Lloyd jacket in the pocket of which were both my car keys and house keys was not there. I therefore went into the Clubhouse where Susie and the Rev. Dr. E.R. were enjoying a drink and the device was making anxious noises about his supper. No she had not packed my jacket. She didn't think I needed it and didn't know all my keys were in the pocket!

6. Never mind. At home I had spare car keys and Susie had her house keys. John Heyes kindly ran me home in his car where, with Susie's keys, I gained access to the house and her car. I then returned to Cultra and parked her car behind mine. However, on opening the door of my car, I realised that I had Krooklocked the steering wheel before going to Portpatrick and where was the only Krooklock key? In my jacket on board the boat – great!

7. Returned to the Clubhouse where Susie and Rev. Dr. were still consuming alcohol. The device was receiving an advance instalment on his supper but urgently required attention at the other end. I therefore ran them all home in Susie's car before returning for the next stage of the game.

8. Returned to Cultra, retrieved the dinghy from behind the Clubhouse, launched it, rigged the engine and proceeded out to the boat where I removed my jacket and all my keys. Back then to shore, carried the dinghy back to where it lives, stowed engine etc., and drove home.

9. Returned to Cultra with Susie and all necessary keys and was at last able to get my car moving. Bar shutters in the Club were now in the closed position so no hope of a refresher there. Both cars returned home and supper very late!

10. End of story. We do not usually have this trouble when we return from a trip in "Melandy" and in fact this was the first time. The Rev. Dr. E.R. was definitely not to blame, nor was the device, but the fact that we now have a lot more gear to transport back and forth to the boat may have had something to do with it!

Son number two, Robert, was born in June 1985, also in Portland Oregon. Between our trip to the USA and making a necessary large extension to our house there was no time for sailing. In fact "Melandy" spent some weeks at the local Bangor Shipyard where she had the full works of anti-osmosis treatment. The summer of 1986 was dreadful in our part of the world and our main cruise was confined to the Firth of Clyde in August. This included five days stormbound in Kip Marina and with this particular gale, the further south one went the worse it was. There were countless boats damaged or lost in Belfast Lough and further south, and if I remember right the beast was called Hurricane Charlie.

Our domestic arrangements on board were now somewhat changed; indeed, with two children the whole scene was changed! Before their arrival, we used to go to sea in quite dreadful weather but with two babies to cope with there would be no pleasure in that. In port or at anchor at night we used to share the big triangular berth in the forecabin, with two sleeping bags zipped together – very cosy! At sea and especially on night passages we used the pilot berth in the main cabin on the "hot bunk" principle. "Melandy" had the traditional five berth layout of the early Nicholson 32s and we made no changes. The infill to create the big triangle forward was there when we bought her.

The arrangement now was that the children had a berth each forward with the leeboards up and the space between them made a good play area. Initially I fitted a wooden grill to prevent them falling out into the loo and also for obvious reasons I had to fit isolating switches to the two berth lights. Back in the main cabin Susie had the pilot berth – the most comfortable berth in the boat, while I made do with the starboard settee berth. While it *was* narrow, I never had any difficulty sleeping there so long as I kept the leeboard up.

By 1987 the new marina at Carrickfergus, across Belfast Lough from Cultra, was open. This was the first proper marina in Northern Ireland and was designed for 300 boats. We still had our chain mooring at Cultra but "Melandy" spent various short periods at this marina during the season. Despite a 20-mile drive in the car to get there it was just so much easier to walk aboard with all our gear, provisions and children rather than ferry everyone and everything out to an exposed mooring more than half a mile from shore. A limited summer cruise took us to Gigha, Loch Sween and the Fairy Isles, Craighouse, Jura and Port Ellen, Islay in very indifferent weather. In 1988 the boat spent the whole summer based at Carrickfergus but again the weather was generally poor. We got as far North as Tobermory, Mull, but a lot of time was wasted there and at Oban, stormbound with gales of wind and much rain. At least Oban is an interesting place for small boys, with so much to see on the quays and adjacent railway station. We were reduced to hiring a car so that we could visit friends further north at Kyle of Lochalsh. On the way home after five days stormbound at Gigha we still had a very rough passage down the North Channel and just made it into Larne before the tide turned against us and the southerly wind reached force 9 with driving rain and almost nil visibility. We left the boat there and went home by car, four days late, and returned for her the following weekend.

In 1989 the summer was generally warm and dry with light winds and we had many enjoyable weekend trips to Portpatrick and the anchorage at Port Logan nine miles south. However, by the time we set off for a two-week cruise in August the weather had broken and I think we got the worst two weeks of the whole summer. We got no further than Larne before we had three days stormbound, followed by five days stormbound at Tarbert Loch Fyne on the Clyde. We eventually transited the Crinan Canal in pouring rain just for something to do and the boys enjoyed helping to work the lock gates and paddles. We did not even lock out at the other end since conditions were so unpleasant off Crinan and we returned home the way we had come – down the Firth of Clyde.

June 1990 saw us move house to Crawfordsburn, a bit closer to Bangor. The "new" house included a flat for Susie's mother, who moved over from the USA to live with us. Despite all the upheaval, "Melandy" spent the summer afloat and we got away for a two-week cruise in the Firth of Clyde at the end of August. The weather was very variable but we got as far as Inverary near the head of Loch Fyne and duly went ashore to visit the castle. 1991 saw an early season trip to Port St. Mary on the Isle of Man with a day there doing the tourist thing. This time we travelled to Castletown on the steam train and visited the maritime museum. We also visited an old colleague of mine from London days who was now working for the Isle of Man Marine Administration and living at Colby.

Our main cruise was in August when once again we headed up the west coast of Scotland. The Tall Ships were in Belfast at the end of July and we accompanied them out of Belfast Lough and off to the North. Belfast Lough had never seen anything like it and it was quite an experience. We got out to Castlebay on Barra and the splendid beach on nearby Vatersay in reasonable weather but there were indications of a longish spell of strong winds and unsettled weather. The result was that we headed back to the Sound of Mull and up Loch Linne to the Caledonian Canal. Here we bought an eight-day pass and spent a pleasant week despite the weather. There were plenty of runs ashore and places for the boys to play. Perhaps the best for them was the Great Glen Water Park on Loch Oich which had a heated swimming pool and other attractions.

For the 1992 season "Melandy" moved from Carrickfergus to the newly opened marina at Bangor and remained based at Bangor thereafter. While the Carrickfergus marina had been perfectly satisfactory, it was a 21 mile drive from home while Bangor was only three, so the move was inevitable. Our main summer cruise in July was back to North Wales. We covered no great distance in the boat but a lot of distance was covered by bus and train! We got to Holyhead via the Isle of Man and there spent a week on a mooring while the wind blew hard from the South. Holyhead, being a busy ferry port, does not sound the best place to spend a week but it was excellent. The Yacht Club ran an excellent launch service and we had the use of the Club for showers and other facilities. The most used chart during this week was the local bus and train timetable and we went somewhere every day, including Conway Castle, Anglesey Sea Zoo and a trip up Snowdon on the mountain railway.

An easy day sail got us to Pwllheli, where by now there was an excellent marina. Our tourist day there was spent on the Ffestiniog Railway and visiting the old slate mines, and another day doing necessary domestic chores. Time was limited and we now sailed round the Llyn Peninsula to reach Porth Dinallen on the north side in beautiful sunshine and little wind to anchor off the beach and the famous Ty Coch Inn. During the night the weather went sour with a strong Southerly wind. We dragged anchor and had to re-anchor closer inshore. It was now a Saturday and by afternoon there were a large number of yachts in the bay to attend an RNLI function on the beach. We went ashore but the barbecue was really a washout. Sunday was no better and I was concerned about getting safely across Caernarvon Bar into the Menai Strait. A motor sailer from the Royal Welsh Yacht Club kindly led the way and while there were some nasty breaking seas we got across safely and on up the strait to the small marina in the old slate dock at Port Dinorwic. Here there were two more tourist days, one to Caernarvon and its castle and one to Beaumaris where, besides the castle, there is the old jail and courthouse, and many other attractions. Our return home was again via the Isle of Man.

Another poor season was 1993 and a two-week cruise only saw us as far as Tobermory on the Isle of Mull with four days at anchor or on a mooring in strong winds and plentiful rain. Return was via the Crinan Canal and the Firth of Clyde. One thing about the west coast of Scotland: there are so many excellent anchorages that, apart from the flesh pots, one can always visit somewhere new. We did so this time as on most of our cruises in this area. Weekend trips included the Isle of Man and of course Portpatrick.

In 1994 we were back up the West Coast and this time we made it north of the famous Ardnamurchan Point and up through the Kyle of Lochalsh to Plockton to visit my old friend John Olver and his wife, who had lived at nearby Balmacara for some years and ran the local post office-cum-shop.

Then, in 1995, we were heading south again, in the hope of perhaps getting as far as the Scilly Islands. It was not to be and for a start we spent three days at Port St. Mary with Susie sick. A visit to a doctor produced antibiotic pills and things improved. I took the boys on steam train rides and visited Castle Rushen at Castletown and the amusement arcades in Douglas. This was followed by three days at Holyhead due to strong head winds and the outings here included a forty-mile train ride to Rhyl to visit the Sun Centre – an indoor waterworld complete with slides, chutes and wave making machines! An overnight passage then got us to Milford Haven, a large natural harbour with many oil berths, which was a new port for us. In the approaches the tide was strong and there was a very confused uncomfortable sea, with only a moderate wind. Our pitching and rolling was such that the wind instrument at the masthead was fatally damaged!

We found our way past all the oil berths to the snug marina at Neyland where we were made welcome. We explored ashore, made use of the Neyland Yacht Club and went for a trip up the River Cleddau in "Melandy" until we ran out of water and turned back. Leaving the Haven to head back north, we had the same wild rocking and rolling for some time. This was another night passage and we were motor sailing towards Pwllheli in a light SE wind when the engine gearbox failed during the night. It looked as though an oil seal had failed and as a result the gearbox was wrecked! We were somewhere in the middle of Cardigan Bay and continued under sail at slow speed. By mid-afternoon the wind died altogether when we were about five miles from Pwllheli and at this stage we lashed the dinghy alongside. The outboard engine pushed us along at all of 1.8 knots but it was a Saturday afternoon and there was a lot of yachting activity in the area. For the last two miles we got a tow in from a sympathetic local boat and made it to the marina. Here we remained for five days while a new gearbox was obtained and fitted. This involved disconnecting the whole engine, getting it out into the saloon to do the job and then the reverse. The weather was hot, humid and calm and I was not in the best of tempers! Luckily, the boys were happy enough playing around the marina and in the dinghy. When we did get away we were running out of time and had to make a non-stop passage back to Bangor instead of going the pretty way through the Menai Strait once again.

In October 1995 I retired from the Marine Safety Agency, which meant that our summer cruise could be extended to two months, the length of the school holidays, rather than the two or three weeks possible while I was working. Thus in 1996 we decided to sail to Denmark.

A CRUISE TO DENMARK, 1996.

The plan for a cruise to Denmark was largely conceived by my wife Susie and Virginia Boyd during the Christmas Holiday in 1995, when Virginia and family were in Northern Ireland for some time. As well as being close friends of ours, Virginia's family is well known in Northern Ireland sailing circles. Some years ago Virginia met and married a Dane, Soren Somonsen, and now lives at Odense on the island of Fyn. Subsequently her young brother married Soren's sister and Soren's brother married another girl from Bangor, Co. Down. The Boyd family boat, "Moidart" was at the time laid up in the garden at the Simonsen's house. We therefore had very good reasons for sailing to Denmark!

Preparations for the trip started immediately after Christmas and a lot of time, effort and money went into "Melandy" to bring her up to Marine Safety Agency standard although being a private boat we were not required to do so. It was just good sense. We also purchased huge quantities of stores and dry provisions for the whole trip since we were advised that the price of virtually everything in Denmark would be about twice the UK equivalents. This turned out to be true and also applied to such essentials as diesel oil, bottled gas, alcohol and tobacco!

I got away from Bangor on 22 June, a week before school ended, with some friends on board, and we made it up the west coast and through the Caledonian Canal to Inverness by the 28th. There were a number of incidents, on the way including alternator failure on the engine and a blocked fuel line but the friends enjoyed it nonetheless! At Inverness there was a crew change when Susie and our son Robert joined, together with two other friends for the North Sea passage. Our son Geoffrey was flown out to Denmark, since we did not want them both on board for the North Sea: they were still too young to be useful crew. Because of bad weather we had two days in the marina at Peterhead Harbour but the crossing to Thyboren in Denmark was in light Westerly winds and the 330 miles took just under three days. We celebrated two birthday parties, our friend Donald's on 5 July and Susie's the next day. Despite our plan to run a "dry" ship, Donald had smuggled on board four bottles of whisky, ostensibly to be used for trade in Denmark. One was broached for these parties and once we had visitors on board in Denmark, the rest were soon demolished!

Navigation was no problem since a couple of years before I had finally succumbed and fitted a Decca Navigator, I might add that I only did this when most of the useful radio beacons were closed down! However, by this time Decca was being phased out and the Danish chain seemed to have closed down already. As a back-up we had a hand held GPS receiver and this proved to be excellent. We also passed a few oil rigs on the way across.

Shortly after our arrival on 7 July, we had the Danish invasion together with our son Geoffrey. Fortunately they came complete with camping gear. For the next two days there was sailing and camping in the Limfjorden, a splendid system of inland lakes and channels between the North Sea and the Kattegat. After that we sometimes had friends aboard and sometimes it was just the four of us. Basically we headed South in the Kattegat, circumnavigated the island of Fyn and worked our way back north to Skagen, the most northerly port in Denmark. Except for three days stormbound at Oerne, while the wind blew southerly 6 to 7, we had fine warm sunny weather and light winds. We were in a very popular sailing area and we were amazed at the number of German boats about for the first two weeks until we learnt that it was the German holiday time!

There were numerous marinas but there was always a race into them at the end of the day to find a berth – led, of course, by the

Germans. Once most of them had gone home it was a lot quieter! This was our first experience of Baltic marinas which, because there is no tide, consist mainly of long fixed jetties with a parallel row of poles on either side. Boats are moored bow on to the jetty with lines out aft made fast to the poles. Berthing in a strong cross wind can sometimes be interesting!

We visited numerous interesting ports and made lots of tourist trips. These included Vejile, from where it was a bus ride to Legoland, and Nyborg, from were we travelled by train and train ferry for a day in Copenhagen. We had two or three visits to the Simonsens' house at Odense where, of course, we were well looked after, and on the way back north we called at the islands of Ballen and Vestero. Skagen is an interesting port with a large section devoted to yachts, mostly Swedes and Norwegians on the "beer" run. While alcohol is expensive in Denmark, it is much more expensive in these countries and anything other than weak beer can only be bought in state liquor stores. Gothenburg in Sweden is only 40 miles away and apart from all the yachts there were also fast ferries bringing day trippers for the same purpose.

We had Soren Simonsen on board for the return trip across the North Sea while Robert flew home to stay with friends. It was our intention to call somewhere in southern Norway on the way, but soon after sailing from Skagen on 9 August we had two days of force 6 and 7 from the south-east, nasty steep seas for which the North Sea is famous, and poor visibility. At least it was behind us and the boat was quite comfortable doing 5 knots under working jib alone, if not particularly comfortable down below! We kept well off the Norwegian coast where the chart bore the legend "dangerous waves"! On the third day the wind died away and we were left with light airs, overcast weather and fog banks before reaching Peterhead again. The return home via the Caledonian Canal was uneventful and we were back in Bangor Marina on 21 August with ten days in hand before school started. The total trip was 1905 miles and we were away for 60 days.

A BAY OF BISCAY CRUISE, 1997

Following our last successful trip, we started planning for the summer of 1997. There was some idle talk of sailing to the Azores and back but in the end we settled for the north coast of Spain. Soren, who was keen to come with us, wasn't able join us until early August and then only for a short time. The insurance company required that we have three experienced adults on board for a Bay of Biscay crossing and since we had only two adults and two children, we got to Spain without crossing the Bay – we sailed round it! Fortunately we had fine weather and generally light winds for almost the whole of this cruise and only one day stormbound in port.

We departed from Bangor on 29 June and headed down the Irish coast calling at Ardglass, Howth, Arklow and Kilmore Quay near Carnsore Point. The latter used to be a place most yachts stayed clear of but now it had a dredged entrance channel and an excellent small marina within the fishing harbour. From here we had an overnight passage to Hughtown in the Scilly Isles, our first visit here since 1976 in "Golden Apple". Another overnight passage got us to Camaret Sur Mer in Britanny and that was us on the Biscay coast. Here it was hot and it remained hot from then on – very much shorts and T-shirt weather! There was more motoring and motor sailing than pure sailing for the next several days, but the weather was splendid.

On the way to Lochtudy we passed through the notorious Raz de Sein with the tide behind us and some swell but otherwise flat calm. On this passage the autopilot failed completely and I broke my teeth on a piece of soft bread! Two days at Lochtudy got us a new autopilot and my teeth fixed before we sailed on to Le Palais on Belle Isle. As it turned out, we could have visited Isles De Glenan and the famous Morbihan, both nearby, but we had to be at La Corunna by early August and we did not know the weather would stay fine for so long. At Le Palais the harbour was extremely crowded due to it being the Bastille Day holiday and along with other yachts we anchored outside – obviously a very popular port! We landed to find a very picturesque town and had supper at one of the pavement cafes.

On we went to Isle d'Yeu in flat calm to find a much enlarged marina and a pilot boat to lead yachts in to a berth – very helpful but the lady with the ticket machine was waiting for us! Port Joinville, where we were, was packed with boats and people and we had to make do with a pizza carry-out for supper as every restaurant was booked out. That evening there was a splendid fireworks display together with bands and other noise until well after midnight.

On then to Les Sables d'Olonne, where there was a huge marina, perhaps 1,500 berths, and all facilities including laundry, post office and bank, Here we spent two days to catch up on domestic chores and witnessed another spectacular fireworks display. Our last French port was Royan on the Gironde Estuary, a big French holiday resort with a long promenade, crowded beaches and a large marina. It is approached by a long buoyed channel from what seemed miles out in the open sea. Despite a moderate following wind there were some big seas and this would not be a pleasant approach in bad weather!

We left Royan by the South Channel and again met steep confused seas until we were well clear and then set course for Bilbao, another quiet and uneventful overnight passage. We thus cut across the south-east corner of the Bay of Biscay but did not think there was anywhere of particular interest to visit. Bilbao is a huge harbour and here we found a brand new marina which had only been officially opened the day before. It was so new that the toilet block was not finished and we had to make do with showers in a workmen's hut.

Having had minimum form filling to do at any French port, we were now faced with a bureaucratic nightmare. A certificate of registry for the boat and passports for all persons on board were necessary, not only at the first port of entry in Spain but at every other major port thereafter! The next morning we motored the short distance to Castro Urdiales, a delightful spot where we anchored in beautiful clear water within the harbour and found the local Club Nautico very hospitable and helpful. A Swiss friend, Elizabeth, on a motoring holiday in the area, finally found us here and later spent a few days on board as we cruised along the north coast of Spain. This is a splendid cruising area and the smaller towns are largely unspoiled by foreign tourists or the package holiday industry. We were also blessed with fine hot weather, and averaged about 30 miles a day, calling at Santander, Vincento de la Barquera, Ribadesella, Gijon, Puerto Luarco, Ribadeo, Ria del Barquero, Ria de Cedeira and finally La Corunna, where we arrived on 31 July. We ate ashore most evenings and although, even with a dictionary, we had difficulties with menus, we never had a bad meal!

Because of the fine weather and no delays we had a week to spend at La Corunna before Soren arrived for the passage home. First we had to lie at anchor among dozens of other transient yachts, many bound for distant places, but later got a berth on the pontoon at the hospitable Real Club Nautico. Corunna is a fascinating city and we were ashore somewhere almost every day. Our longest excursion was a train ride to Santiago de Compostella to visit the famous cathedral. It was a fascinating place but in the boys' opinion it was just a boring old town! Soren arrived on 7 August minus his bags, which had missed a connection somewhere and we were delayed for another day. We then sailed the 50 miles round to Camarinas as our last port in Spain and found a lovely small town and excellent Club Nautico. We had a splendid meal ashore at the usual very late hour in Spain and that night there was a spectacular thunderstorm which blacked out the town for a while!

From Camarinas we made a non-stop passage across the Bay of Biscay to the Scilly Isles which took just under four days for 442 miles. We were so lucky with the weather, having light favourable winds and hot sunshine all the way. There were big long Atlantic swells which were hardly noticeable until we saw quite large merchant ships apparently sinking and then resurfacing! During the first night we crossed the Southbound lane of the Bay of Biscay "M1" and there was a constant stream of ships passing from starboard bow to port quarter for some time. While the days were hot and sunny the nights were generally clear with a beautiful display of stars, planets, waxing moon and numerous shooting stars.

Nearing the Scillies there was a tremendous double bang from somewhere overhead which must have been Concorde passing overhead. We reached Hughtown early in the morning and spent a day there on a visitor's mooring in the crowded anchorage while we ate ashore and arranged for Soren's passage home. Next morning he departed on the first plane out and somehow managed to get home to Odense all in the one day. The remainder of our own passage home to Bangor was just the reverse of the outward one with an overnight passage to Kilmore Quay and then day hops up the Irish coast. We did call at the new marina at Malahide rather than Howth but found that the approaches and the marina were far from complete. We arrived and sailed at high water since at low water there was only a trickle of water in the channel! Malahide itself is a very pretty town and has all necessary facilities. We arrived back in Bangor on my birthday, 21 August, having been away for 53 days and having covered 1979 miles.

In 1998 we spent most of July in the USA on a family-and-friends visit and our main cruise was limited to two weeks in August which once again took us to Stornoway and back. The only notable thing this time was that when motoring out of Loch Harport on the west coast of Skye, into a strong headwind and a nasty sea, the engine stopped due to a choked fuel line. We managed to beat out clear of all dangers and then turned north for Stornoway, some 70 miles away. Fortunately the wind blew force 6 and 7 from the West all day and we had a fast if bumpy passage, during which I did not attempt to clear the fuel blockage. We even managed to enter Stornoway Harbour under sail and dropped the headsail just as we reached the small marina right at the top of the harbour! The following day was Sunday and I spent the morning clearing the engine fuel system in peace and quiet. Stornoway is probably the last outpost of the Scottish Puritan Sabbath and the Wee Free Church rules supreme. While the town is pretty wild on Friday and Saturday nights, on Sunday it is totally dead with everything except churches closed. You cannot even buy a Sunday newspaper until Monday morning and you most certainly cannot use the public toilets!

That autumn, while Susie was doing a check on her financial situation, she realised that she had an insurance policy due to mature in a very few years, and my retirement gratuity from the Marine Safety Agency was still intact. "Melandy" had served us very well for 20 years but we now had a hankering for something a bit larger. After all, the boys were rapidly growing up and taking up more space and also if we were going to change we should do it now before we got much older! Thus the hunt for another boat began!

CHAPTER 20: "SUNDOWNER", A COMFORTABLE CRUISING YACHT

The ideal specification for our next boat was fairly simple. She should be about 38 to 41 ft LOA, have two masts, a longish keel, teak laid decks and roomy accommodation with two loos. This narrowed the search area very considerably! The owners of two local boats, a Halberg Rassy 38 and a Nicholson 39, which more or less met our requirements, were kind enough to let us make an inspection and gave their views. In the end I only went to look at two boats, the first being a Halberg Rassy 41 at Kinsale. She was rather neglected, German-owned, and there was no documentation available. She also had a considerable "walk on" bowspit and a dinghy in davits off the stern. My tape measure showed her to be 49 ft between extremities and this is the length on which one pays marina fees, etc! Manoeuvring in a close quarters situation in adverse conditions and without a bow thrust might also be interesting!

Early November 1998 found me flying to Exeter and thence to Dartmouth by hire car to view a 20-year-old Oyster 39, "Sundowner of Beaulieu". Regional flights are not cheap and one could fly the Atlantic for what it cost to get to Dartmouth! The boat had been laid up ashore for about 18 months at Glampton Greek, well up the River Dart. Here there is an old quarry which has been redeveloped as a boat storage area and it was certainly full of boats! I was quite impressed with "Sundowner" in the limited time I had to inspect her, and she certainly met our basic requirements. Designed by Holman & Pye, she had been fitted out to a high standard by Clark & Carter at Ipswich and the ensuite after cabin with its panoramic windows was a particular feature. Underneath, she had a long keel by modern standards and she was sitting quite happily on the ground supported by only a few props. Having been laid up for so long, there were signs of neglect but nothing serious. I shot off a few rolls of film and flew back home to report to Susie.

The result was that we made an offer which was accepted, and after independent survey and the usual procedures I was back in Dartmouth two weeks later to complete the deal. "Sundowner" was a fully registered British ship and the register was "clean". In early December we became the proud owners of an Oyster 39 and in fact we were now "fleet" owners since we still had "Melandy", laid up ashore at Bangor. This can be an unhappy and worrying situation! We had placed "Melandy" with local brokers, without any result, so on my last visit to Dartmouth I had placed her with the brokers there. Within two weeks there was interest and early in December a doctor from Ballycastle came to have a look – the result of looking for a boat on the internet! In January 1999 he became the proud owner of a 34-year-old Nicholson 32 and we were delighted that "Melandy" was going to a good home in the new marina at Ballycastle.

Christmas presents between Susie and me were obviously items for the boat, such as a new life-raft, echo sounder, GPS receiver, new sidelights and numerous other items. After the Christmas holiday the dining room at home was cleared and became the collecting point for everything destined for "Sundowner". February 5 found us loading all this gear, plus dinghy and outboard, sleeping bags and blankets, plus tinned and dry food, and even oilskins and boots for the delivery trip, into a hired Transit van.

Robert had a week of half-term holiday from boarding school in Dublin but Geoffrey was not so lucky and had to be farmed out to friends. That night the three of us crossed over on the Belfast-Liverpool ferry and the next day drove down to the River Dart and "Sundowner". Susie saw the boat for the first time and any fears I might have had were soon dispelled. We spent one night in a B&B in Brixham and then moved on board our boat in the yard. The weather was kind, for the next two days were fine and dry, and while Susie cleaned out down below, Robert and I emptied the van and got everything lifted aboard with the help of the main boom and tackle. There was a large sail wardrobe on board, taking up a lot of room down below, much of which appeared unused. All but the essentials for the delivery trip were loaded in the van to go home, likewise a number of berth extensions and cushions. Basically the boat will sleep seven, without any doubling up, but with all the possible extensions in place, it would sleep at least ten! We wondered where all the personal gear would go, but in fact in 2000 we had ten men, women and children on board for three weeks in the Baltic!

On 19 February 1999, the boat was launched and we parked her at Noss on Dart Marina for the next few weeks. We returned home until Easter, then as soon as the boys finished school we headed for the boat, flying to Exeter and thence by taxi to Noss on Dart. It was our intention to spend three days preparing for sea, including trial trips, and then sail for Bangor on 1 April with about ten days inhand for this passage. It was nearly midnight by the time we got on board the boat and long after that before we were sorted out. I started the engine to charge the batteries, having checked oil, water, etc. but after running for a while it started making serious noises and I stopped it. I thought perhaps there was a broken valve spring, of which I have some experience. A further attempt to start it the next morning resulted in an explosion and a wrecked engine, with holes on both sides of the crank casing – great! I may have missed checking something, I just don't know, but certainly there was a fault in the instrument panel since there was no warning of impending disaster, like low oil pressure, overheating or whatever.

The engine was the original Perkins of about 75 bhp and according to the meter had only done about 1,600 hours. There was no record of maintenance but I believe Able Marine, who had checked the engine for me, were honest. The mobile telephone is a wonderful thing and I had one on board, bought especially for use on the boat. I contacted Able Marine and they showed up to confirm my worst fears. A replacement engine was the only solution! Various options were considered but the quickest and easiest was to fit a replacement Perkins, and one could be delivered to Darmouth by 14 April. So much for our planned leisurely delivery trip to Bangor with the whole family on board!

Easter on board the boat was not unpleasant, however. We bent on sails, cleaned all the bilges, fitted new sidelights, GPS and echo sounder, and did numerous other jobs. There were daily trips to Dartmouth in the dinghy for the papers and stores. We had friends to visit on board and visited friends ashore, although we spent most evenings on board, playing Scrabble after supper. Robert, and sometimes Geoffrey, went off for trips in the dinghy on their own and one day Robert got "done" for speeding! He was brought back to the boat in the Harbourmaster's launch in some disgrace and I was duly lectured on speed limits and safety afloat. I omitted to mention my own background with the MSA!

On 7 April Susie and the boys returned home by train and ferry, since they were all due back at school a few days later, and I was left on my own to await the new engine. I spent the time scraping and rubbing down the gunwales and other bright work, of which fortunately there was not as much on this boat as on "Melandy". Able

Marine showed up in good time to disconnect the old engine and prepare for lift out but on 14 April the bad news was that the new one would not arrive before the 23rd. I returned home myself and spent two weeks gardening and doing other neglected jobs around the house. I flew back on May 2, knowing that the new engine was with Able Marine and the following week it was all action. Two trips under tow to Philip & Son's repair berth saw the old engine out and the new one in, but it took two days to couple everything up, line up and get it going. There was now also the problem of a delivery crew for the passage home and at least one potential crew member was unable to come at the last minute.

The saviour was good friend Terry Anderson of Down Yachts who had a week free from his business activities. He flew in on Monday 10 May and the two of us sailed for Bangor the following day. It would have been an easy trip with an autopilot but the Neco auto pilot, which had been working, was not working after the new engine was fitted. During the contortions to fit the new engine some wire or other must have become disconnected but despite the efforts of Able Marine and even an electrical expert, nothing could be found and there just wasn't time for a complete overhaul. It just meant that one of us had to be on the wheel all the time at sea and with the weather we got this was hard work.

We sailed – or rather motored – out of the River Dart at 1200 on Tuesday 11 May into SW force 5 to 6 and quite a heavy sea, dead on the nose! The new engine, while the same dimensions as the old one, was in fact more powerful and produced some 85 bhp. This particular model is known as the Perkins Sabre M90. While I was in no great hurry to get home, Terry was, since he had a booking for his boat the following Monday. As he operated commercially, he was used to keeping to schedules whatever the weather and had therefore become a "hard driver". The idea of going into the River Yealm to visit friends was definitely out, due to the strong onshore wind, but so was the idea of going into Plymouth for the night.

We plugged on down the Channel and past the Eddystone Rock to reach Falmouth by 2300 and eventually found the visitor's pontoon in the dark. Down below there was quite a lot of water where it should not have been and so there was some attention to the stern gland. It was also coming in via the chain locker although I did not realise that at the time. With "Melandy's" very deep bilge this would not have been a problem but I was now reminded of "Golden

Delicious" and "Golden Leigh"! At least the iron keel was encapsulated in the hull so no water came in that way! The following morning we were under way again by 0730 into similar conditions, only this time we set a reefed mainsail to steady the boat somewhat. We kept well off the Lizard and 1330 saw us off the Longships and bearing away to the North, heading for Tuscar Rock with a night at sea ahead of us. We now had wind and sea on the port quarter and while the speed even increased, keeping the boat on course was hard work and demanded constant attention. A two hour stint on the wheel was more than enough and during the night we were lucky to get an hours lie down between spells of steering. I am partial to sardines on toast during a night watch but now the best I could do was put a tin of sardines in my oilskin pocket and eat with my fingers while trying to keep the boat on course. Having a smoke while on the wheel was an impossibility!

At about 0230, when the Smalls light was abeam to starboard, the engine suddenly stopped and the only thing I could think of was a fuel blockage somewhere in the system. With darkness and the motion of the boat I was not inclined to start investigating so we rolled out the headsail and continued on course at a still reasonable speed. Once past the Tuscar Rock, and with daylight, the seas eased and I started disconnecting the fuel supply lines. There seemed to be a blockage somewhere between the fuel tank and the first filter but I could not blow it clear and nor could I get the connection adrift on top of the tank.

Meanwhile we sailed on, mainly with Terry on the wheel, but by the time the Arklow Buoy was abeam to starboard at 1015, the wind was easing and the forecast indicated light Northerlies later. This decided us to head for Arklow and we eventually anchored off the pier at 1315. My morale was at a low ebb and I even envisaged having to send Terry home on the train!

Telephone calls to various available numbers produced no result and I ended up calling "any vessel in Arklow Harbour" on the VHF. As a result of this we were under tow by mfv "Ocean Wave" towards the harbour by 1400 and we were taken to a berth in the basin. A walk around to Arklow Slipway produced "Jimmy", who left what he was doing and came to look at our problem. He got the tank connection adrift and found what appeared to be some kind of broken rubber non return valve down the pipe. A trip to the workshop then produced a modified pipe to push down inside the original and we were back in business! In the circumstances the people in Arklow were magnificent! The Arklow Slipway charge was minimal and the crew of the "Ocean Wave" would not accept any more than the price of a pint of Guinness each.

By this time I felt exhausted and ready for a good sleep but "Terry the Driver" would have none of it. He announced that he had got his second wind, and so after topping up with diesel we headed back out to sea at 1745. It turned out to be a pleasant evening with only light airs and the occasional shower. I even cleaned and tidied up down below before we reached Howth Marina at 2215. Here Terry announced that we would have one pint each at the Yacht Club, followed by fish and chips for supper! I dealt with the marina while he went for the fish and chips and I suppose we were asleep by about midnight.

Next morning Friday 14 May, I was up at 0530 for the weather forecast and we departed on the last leg of the trip at 0625! The wind was Northerly, 3 to 4 all day, and the sky cloudy with sunshine, but more important we hit the tides just right, carrying the flood to off Carlingford Lough and the ebb thereafter. Morale was now very high and there was time for more boat cleaning. We also did a pretty good job of cleaning ourselves and donned clean clothing for arrival! While passing through Donaghadee Sound we telephoned the reception committee (ie, our wives), who were there to meet us on arrival at Bangor Marina at 1730. We had covered the 90 miles from Howth in 11 hours, which wasn't bad, even with the tide helping. Needless to say, the reception committee had thought to buy a couple of bottles of fizzy stuff so we could celebrate our arrival. "Sundowner" was home at last!

There followed some immediate work on the boat, including cosmetics, and the most important item was the fitting of a new Simrad autopilot, which proved satisfactory. The old Neco gear proved to be unfixable! "Sundowner" had many features which we did not have on "Melandy" and with advancing years they were very welcome! On deck there was a furling headsail, slab reefing with lazy jacklines for the mainsail, self tailing sheet winches and a spray hood for the cockpit! The ketch rig makes for easier sail handling by our limited crew and there are some interesting sail combinations. The mizzen staysail is particularly useful in the right conditions. Features down below included hot and cold running water, warm air central heating, a quite large built in refrigerator and two toilet/

shower compartments. With her high topsides there was full headroom throughout, including the ensuite cabin aft. There was also a workshop/storeroom/ oilskin locker with access both from the cockpit and down below. During June and early July we put in weekend trips to Portpatrick and Campbeltown and got to know more about the boat and her characteristics. Then we decided that our main shakedown cruise this first year would be a circumnavigation of Ireland during the school holidays, something we had never done in the 20 years we had "Melandy". Now seemed like a good time for this trip, especially with a favourable pound/punt exchange rate.

Apart from our family crew, we had two older friends with us for the first 11 days. These were Jean McCadden (Geoffrey's music teacher) and her husband Stuart. In view of their seniority we allocated them the ensuite after cabin! Sailing from Bangor on Sunday 11 July, we headed south and spent the first night in the excellent small marina at Ardglass. Then it was on to the not-so-excellent marina in Carlingford Lough, where, however, the marina restaurant was perfectly adequate and good value. We entered this marina at low tide and ploughed a furrow in the seabed in doing so! I had previously contacted Dublin City Moorings and booked a berth for us there for two nights. These pontoons had been put in for the Tall Ships visit the previous year and were now available for visiting yachts. We passed through the East Link Bridge two hours before the advertised opening time and berthed at 1930 on 13 July. This facility is excellent for visitors since it is in the middle of Dublin and close to all amenities. By arrangement, showers were available just across the road at Jury's Hotel. After two nights here it was on south to the new pontoon in the river at Arklow but after that, due to a force 6/7 Southerly wind we spent two nights stormbound in Rosslare, rather than going round Carnsore Point to another excellent small marina at Kilmore Quay.

Rosslare is a dreary ferry port but a good port of refuge in adverse weather conditions. There are facilities ashore if one walks far enough and Robert soon found the local fish & chip shop, while Susie found a shower at the nearest hotel. The McCaddens were good company and while they were on board there were serious nightly sessions of Scrabble, and a game new to us called Rummikub!

A week out from Bangor on 18 July we made it round Carnsore Point in light sunny conditions to pass Hook Head and proceeded all the way in to Waterford. The approaches to this river port are very pretty and the pontoons on the quayside are right in the town centre, with all amenities (except showers) close at hand. For showers we had to take a taxi out to a leisure centre on the outskirts of town. After two nights here the wind went South West 5/7 again but we made it down the estuary to spend two nights alongside fishing boats at Dunmore East and in company with several other yachts, all waiting for better weather. Climbing ashore over the fishing boats was difficult for the less agile but after some effort on the second evening we all made it to the Ocean Hotel for an excellent meal!

Thursday 22 July found us entering Cork Harbour in much better conditions and we berthed at the relatively recent East Ferry Marina. Although a long way from Cork City, this is a very pleasant spot, very pretty and much quieter than the pontoons at Crosshaven. The next morning the McCaddens left us to proceed home by train and we spent a day doing the tourist thing, thanks to a friend of Susie's who lives at Youghal. Our dinghy was in the water and Robert had been exploring extensively. That evening I went with him to take some photographs and view "Dirty Murphy's" pub from the water, last visited in "Golden Delicious" in 1976. I had been advised by a local that this pub was not dirty any more and indeed it had been all modernised with electric light and running water, completely spoiling its old character.

I well remember a lovely story about this place from years ago. An English yacht had arrived at the broken-down pier and the two crew had walked up to the pub for a drink or two. Now Murphy only washed glasses when they were needed and for this purpose he had a bucket of water behind the bar. Obviously as the day progressed the water became browner until eventually it was nearly as strong as what was dispensed from barrels and bottles. The two visitors ordered a pint of Guinness each and so Murphy took two dirty glasses from the counter and gave them a swill round in the bucket. Before he could fill them, the horrified visitors grabbed the glasses and walked all the way back to their boat. Here they boiled a kettle of water and carefully washed and dried the glasses. On return to the pub they set the glasses on the counter and asked for two pints of Guinness. "Sure," says Murphy and, taking the two glasses, gives them a good swill round in the bucket behind the bar!

From here on we visited some of the well-known yachting spots of south-west Ireland, the first being Glandore. Then it was on to

Baltimore, where the harbour was very crowded and we had to anchor off. On a summer Sunday afternoon it was very busy with tourists of all kinds and numerous commercial passenger craft. A short hop took us along the coast to Skull, except that we went out round the Fastnet Rock on the way, my first time round since 1977 in "Golden Leigh". Next day in Long Island Sound the scenery was quite impressive and from there it was round Mizzen Head and across Bantry Bay to Lawrence's Cove Marina on Bear Island. This is a splendid little marina in a beautiful setting and has all necessary facilities, including a spotless toilet block and laundry. There were two expeditions to the nearby village, first to the very old-fashioned shop/post office and later for a very good supper at Kitty's Restaurant. We could have spent longer in this part of the world, but pressed on in case of adverse weather later on, so that our next port was Dingle, another place now with a fine new marina and shore facilities.

On Friday 30 July we motored through Blasket Sound where the scenery would have been very pretty but for drizzle and poor visibility, and reached Kilrush on the Shannon Estuary. Kilrush used to be a tidal creek but a barrage with lock gate has created a lake, with a marina at one end, close to town. We followed the approach channel carefully towards the lock, which appeared to be wide open, and then saw a motor cruiser coming out. We held back and while passing he shouted something about a strong current. We again approached the lock and were swept through it like a ferret down a rabbit hole! We learned that, to maintain the water level inside, the lock is opened at high water, especially at springs, to let some water in. Again there were excellent marina facilities and everything we needed in the town.

We locked out on Sunday 1 August and headed north for the Aran Islands. The run down to Loop Head, at the northern entrance to the Shannon Estuary, was quite scenic and as on the way in we had the company of some dolphins for a while. Loop Head was quite impressive and so were the Cliffs of Moher, further north. Because it was calm we headed close in and could see little ant-like figures moving on the cliff edge! We had previously viewed these cliffs from the shore, and from the air, courtesy of Aer Lingus, but this was the first time from the sea! Because of this diversion we were now East of the Aran Islands and our course took us close to Inisheer and then Inishmaan before closing on Kilronan Bay on

Inishmore. We were surprised at the large number of houses on these islands and the number of people about – obviously a prime holiday area! Here there were neither alongside facilities for yachts nor visitors moorings, so we had to anchor off for the night.

Next morning from an early hour there was a procession of ferries bringing out the multitudinous day trippers, and a fleet of buses on the quay to take them round the island. We were not inclined to join them and after a quick trip ashore for stores and papers we hove up and motored the short distance across to Cashla Bay on the mainland. Here we anchored at Struthan, just opposite Rossaveel, a big new fishing harbour and also the terminal for the ferries to Aran. Careful navigation was then necessary for the 25 miles along the coast to Roundstone, for there is a mass of small islands, rocks visible and invisible and the inevitable fishing floats and nets. The modern GPs system makes such navigation very simple, if used with care! Roundstone, on the coast of Connemara and with the Twelve Pins or Bens seemingly quite close by, is very picturesque. It was a busy little place, well geared up for tourists.

On 4 August it was on to the island of Inishbofin and the main headland of the day was Slyne Head, which is in fact a rock at the extremity of a line of rocks and islets. Boffin Harbour is small, and as we discovered, the holding ground is poor. At the third attempt the anchor stayed put and remained so for the night, but there were frequent checks, resulting in broken sleep!

Proceeding north, the next day we diverted to have a close look at Inishturk and then worked our way past Achill Head and into Blacksod Bay, perhaps well named since it didn't seem very inviting! Here we anchored for the night in Elly Bay off a beach to windward of us but possible shore facilities was so far away that we didn't even launch the dinghy. During the night the wind freshened from the east which meant there was now a long fetch to windward across Blacksod Bay. By morning we were pitching and rolling, with the anchor chain starting to slip on the windlass, so breakfast was expedited and we got underway for Ballyglass in Broadhaven, some 36 miles by sea but only 12 as the crow flies! Here there were visitors' moorings off the fishing pier and we made use of one. There are no facilities at Ballyglass, the nearest shops being at Belmullet, about six miles away. There is, however, a lifeboat station with a modern Seven Class lifeboat out on a mooring. Its area of operation must be one of the most exposed anywhere in the British Isles.

Next morning the engine refused to start and turning the key produced only a click at the starter motor – a sickening feeling! Well, I reasoned, if there was a lifeboat here there had to be a mechanic somewhere close and we tracked him down that afternoon. Joe Murray was an angel and so was his brother, who ran a ramshackle garage in Belmullet. The problem was identified in the starter motor, which was taken ashore to the garage for some emergency attention, and late that evening we were back in business! There was wetness in the starter and my mind went back to the delivery trip when there had been water in places where it should not have been!

On Sunday 8 August we motored the 61 miles across Donegal Bay to Killybegs into ENE force 6 but we made good time and found a berth alongside other yachts at the root of the town pier. Killybegs is a major fishing port and several very large supertrawlers are based there. We spent a day shopping and doing laundry and that evening found an upmarket Chinese restaurant upstairs in a local hotel for a splendid supper overlooking the harbour.

The next call was at Burtonport which has a narrow and tortuous approach through islands and rocky channels. It was however all well marked and the scenery was very pretty on a fine summer evening. Another fishing port, there was however little of interest ashore. Next it was out round Tory Island and then in to pick up a visitor's mooring off the pier at Downings. That day, 11 August 1999, was the day of the solar eclipse but it was overcast and, except for perhaps a little further darkening at about 1100, we didn't notice anything! This was obviously another popular holiday spot but any shops or other facilities were a long way off and only Robert made the effort to walk there. Lough Swilly was our next destination and here we found a berth on the rather exposed pontoon at Rathmullan, well up the Lough. Here the minimarket provided stores, delivered to the boat, and the Pier Hotel provided showers and a very reasonable supper.

The next day we were joined for the rest of the cruise by Elizabeth Rufer, a longtime Swiss friend and who had been driven up from Bangor to meet us. The next day we went down the Louth and out round Dunaff Head, Malin Head and finally Inishowen Head to enter Lough Foyle. I had no large scale chart of Lough Foyle but I knew that some visitors' moorings had been laid off Moville on the Republic side and once into the marked channel we proceeded carefully in a strong NW wind. The scenery to starboard on the way in is very pretty but to port less so, with Magilligan Prison on the skyline. Once past the fishing harbour of Greencastle we were soon off Moville and then proceeded carefully to the location of the moorings. We duly found eight in a row and all being vacant picked the one nearest the town. We got it at the first attempt, despite the fresh NW wind and some twisting of our lines. Robert went ashore in the dinghy to get essential stores but otherwise we all remained on board for the night. A splendid chicken stew for supper and an early night suited us all.

Sunday 15 August must have been the most uncomfortable passage of the whole trip, for once we cleared the Tuns Buoy at the entrance to Lough Foyle it was a humpy bumpy ride along the north coast to Ballycastle, 30 miles away to the east. Between tide and wind this area can be definitely lumpy, and so it was! We were glad to make it into the new small marina here by early afternoon and to find our old boat "Melandy" moored nearby. Like Ballycastle, Rathlin Island, just five miles away, also had a new harbour and the next afternoon we motored over there to spend our last night before the end of the cruise. We proceeded inwards very gently but did not touch bottom, and after turning round moored alongside the old fishing boat "Maud Chambers", which at that time was almost a permanent fixture. That evening we dined ashore at the somewhat Spartan pub/restaurant – three big mixed grills and two big helpings of lamb cutlets, all with lashings of chips!

The next morning the engine refused to start once again, but at least I now knew what the problem was and how to deal with it myself. The girls went off on a minibus trip to the west of the island to view the "upside down" lighthouse and whatever birds were still around at this time of the year while I sorted the engine problem.

On Wednesday 18 August we departed Rathlin at 1000, set all sail and headed for home. The tide was right and with the flood behind us we passed Torr Head at 1100 and the Maidens at 1320. With favourable tide and a fair moderate wind we were back into our birth at Bangor Marina by 1530.

We had been away for 38 days and covered a leisurely 1050 miles in 153 hours underway. The average speed had been all of 6.8 knots.

CHAPTER 21: AN AMBITIOUS CRUISE

During the winter of 1999-2000, while the boat was ashore in the yard at Bangor, there was some major expenditure and work needed, most of which I did myself. All new navigation instruments were fitted, including a new radar, new refrigerator unit, new extractor fans, a new propeller shaft and much else. A major improvement was to fit not just "granny bars" in way of the mainmast but a whole double railing on the foredeck, similar to what can be found on a pilot boat. Susie said this arrangement looked like a cattle pen but it is far less conspicuous than some of the gantry arrangements I have seen at the after end of other boats, for carrying aerials and other equipment! It gives a great sense of security when on the foredeck at sea and inside the pen we can securely stow sailbags, fenders and even Geoffrey's wheelchair in fine weather. Some years ago, Geoffrey was diagnosed as having Friedrich's Ataxia and he is now virtually wheelchair-bound. He is also a diabetic but none of this has prevented us from going sailing as a family. He can steer the boat and perform some basic navigation at the chart table, when he is so inclined, and he also takes a great interest in the weather. He can even get up the foredeck in fine weather, since he has something secure to hold on to, and when we are at sea the wheelchair normally stows in the workshop.

For the year 2000 we had an ambitious cruise in mind and planning for this started even before Christmas. We had been to Denmark four years earlier in "Melandy" and we had friends there only too keen to sail with us in that area. This cruise, however, would be more challenging and, as well as brief calls in Denmark, we would also visit northern Germany, southern Sweden and hopefully southern Norway on the way home. However, as in 1996, severe weather in the Skaggerak prevented our visit to Norway but since Scotland and/or England counts as a country, we still visited four countries! We also transited four canals, these being the Caledonian, which we transited twice, the Kiel Canal, the Gota Canal and the associated Trollhatte Canal. We were away from our base at Bangor Marina for eight weeks and covered almost 2,500 miles. There were no less than 18 men, women and children on board at various stages with a maximum of ten for a period of three weeks in the Baltic and Gota/Trolhatte canal system. Because of having to be at certain places by certain dates for crew changes, we had to work to some sort of timetable. Also, because of adverse winds or little wind, there was little pure sailing and we just sailed, motorsailed or simply motored to keep to our timetable!

We departed from Bangor on 23 June 2000, as soon as the boys had finished school, but Susie had another week to work and was left behind to close up the house and take the cat and dog to their holiday home! The McCaddens were on board for the first leg and I also had Chris McFerran, a friend from RNIYC. We had an uneventful trip north, with calls at Carnlough and Oban before transiting the Caledonian Canal. There followed calls at Peterhead, Montrose and Eyemouth before reaching North Shields on the River Tyne on 1 July. Here we berthed at the recently opened Royal Quays Marina, in the old Albert Edward coal Dock. We were the first visiting boat from another Crest Nicholson-run marina so we got a good welcome and a good discount on the berthing fees! Here Susie joined us and the McCaddens departed for home in her car.

We spent three nights here as there were friends to visit and entertain on board, including my old friend Brimer Dale from my seagoing days. A drive around the area brought back happy memories of time spent in the various Tyneside dockyards on several ships but they were now virtually all gone as were a few famous establishments such as the "Jungle" and "Uncle Tom's Cabin"! We were joined for the North Sea passage by Michael Jamison, one of the Mates on our local Ocean Youth Trust yacht "Lord Rank". He was an ideal watchleader for son Robert on this passage We covered the 330 miles from the Tyne to Helgoland in just over two days of generally light and sunny weather. We arrived on 6 July and celebrated Susie's birthday with a fine meal ashore. We also stocked up on the duty-free, since Helgoland has this status. It is a magnet for German and other visiting yachts, plus passenger ferries and cruise ships. From there it was an easy day's passage into the Elbe Estuary and Brunsbuttel, where we entered the Kiel Canal. Basically the Kiel Canal is a sea level canal across 55 miles of flat country and the locks at either end are only necessary because of the varying sea levels outside

It is very busy round the clock and commercial ships go through in about 8 hours. We moored at the small marina just inside the locks and there was noise and action all night in the big lock just beside us, with commercial ships on the move. Chris McFerran left for home the next morning and we motored along the canal to Rendsburg, about the halfway mark. Apart from the commercial traffic there was a procession of yachts proceeding in both directions! At Rendsburg we were joined by Albrecht Von Bremen, a friend of Robert's from school in Dublin, and his father Thylo. Mother delivered them from Hamburg by car and the car was useful for our re-storing activities! Later that day we had an invasion of Vikings – Soren and Virginia Simonsen, plus three children and dog – a foretaste of what was to come! They had motored down from Odense in Denmark to put some gear on board in advance of their joining us a few days later. The gear included numerous cases of Danish beer in tins, plus soft drinks for the children, bought in Germany. (In Denmark you could only buy drink in bottles and there was a hefty deposit on them. It was also cheaper in Germany.) The workshop ended up stacked to the deckhead with cases and there was almost no room to get at the main electrical switches nor room to stow the wheelchair!

The next day, Sunday, we exited the Canal at Kiel, having paid the equivalent of £10 for the transit, and made our way out of a very busy Kieler Fiord with yachts and other small craft everywhere. In a brisk SW wind we had a pleasant sail to a huge marina at Heligenhafen, as recommended by Thylo and who then treated us all to a splendid meal ashore. Next day it was under the Fehmansund Bridge and on to Travemunde where Von Bremens and Michael Jamison left us for urgent appointments, although Michael's deadline seemed to be with a lady in Amsterdam! Tuesday 11 July was a tourist day and we went to Lubeck on the train, complete with Geoffrey in his wheelchair, and explored this fascinating old Hanseatic town. Wednesday got us to Warnemunde, where we spent a night riding out a local "blow" on a rather exposed pontoon and on Thursday we headed across to Gedser, the most Southerly port in Denmark, an easy 25-mile passage.

Gedser was really the "pits"! Once a busy ferry port it was now much less busy, even with several ferries a day to Germany. There was a one-train-a-day station, no bank, a single small store which would not accept credit cards and a post office open for two hours a day which would not cash travellers' cheques! The marina fortunately had adequate facilities and would accept German cash. The Viking invasion happened the next day when Soren and Virginia joined us, plus Jamie (11) and Nickoli (eight), together with Sarah

(17) and her friend Tanya (also 17). We now had ten people on board for the next three weeks. Susie, Geoffrey and I occupied the after cabin and the rest bedded down elsewhere. The sleeping arrangements seemed to vary from night to night, but it all seemed to work and there were no complaints! On Saturday we had a gentle motor sail to Klintholm on the island of Mon, a Danish holiday resort apart from the yacht harbour. Here the local Spar accepted credit cards and the marina fee included use of the swimming pool and showers. Things were looking up!

Our first Swedish port was Ystad and here it was all very civilised. Marina fees, diesel and stores from local shops were all paid for by credit card. It was also a very pretty place with ample green space by the marina for various ball games. On this Sunday evening there were lots of strollers looking at the boats and they were all very friendly. Things were now settling down on board, especially on the domestic front. Breakfast and lunch were really movable feasts and I was always up first, to beat the rush. Supper however was usually a communal affair, thanks to Susie and Virginia. One huge saucepan was used for variations of Danish/Swedish meat-balls/burgers and another for potatoes/rice/spaghetti and usually carrots. The daily consumption of milk, bread, biscuits and soft drinks was prodigious, requiring frequent re-storing. The two girls were some help on the domestic front but took little or no interest in working the boat. The two small boys behaved just like small boys, although Nickoli was very good at peeling potatoes! Nevertheless, it all worked remarkably smoothly and in three weeks there were no fall-outs or fisticuffs!

From Ystad it was back to Denmark, where we called at the Northern ports of Hammerhaven and Allinge on Bornholm and then the nearby tiny Danish outpost of Christianso, which is not even shown on many maps. It consists of two islets, each about ½ x ¼ mile with a gut in between, which is the harbour. Originally occupied as a garrison it has all the garrison buildings and fortifications, all well maintained and occupied. It is now really an unusual museum and tourist attraction, with frequent ferries from Bornholm to bring out the tourists. Having secured a berth alongside, we remained for a whole day and did the tourist bit!

On 19 July we had a longish passage of 75 miles in fresh conditions north-east to Kalmarsund. Some crew members did not feel well and stretched out both in the cockpit and down below. However, this was our last "open sea" passage for some time and that evening we reached Bergkvara on the Swedish mainland. Then it was on up the sound for an afternoon and a night spent at Kalmar, a major Swedish town and a picturesque and historic one as well.

On northwards and under the Kalmarsund Bridge we spent a night at Byxelkrok on Oland before heading across into the Swedish skerries. Think of Strangford Lough x 1000, plus no tide, and you have some idea of the Swedish skerries. They extend up to and beyond Stockholm and the navigable channels are all very well marked by lighthouses, beacons and IALA type buoys. We had large-scale, up-to-date Swedish charts on board and it was necessary to keep very careful track of progress. Otherwise it is easy to get lost among the multitudinous rocks and islands! The GPS is admirable in this respect! For the two nights we spent in this area we found suitable deserted islands to anchor close to for swimming sessions and barbecues ashore on the rocks. It must have been high holiday time for there was a continual stream of yachts in both directions in the main channels, but the whole area is big enough to absorb them all and to find privacy! On 24 July we arrived at Mem, the Baltic entrance to the Gota Canal and for the next ten days we were in inland waters.

The Gota Canal connects the Baltic with Lake Vanern and is 102 miles long. There are 58 locks and the summit is 100 meters above sea level. However, it is more akin to our own Crinan Canal, rather than the Caledonian, since the locks are only marginally bigger than those on the Crinan. It is purely a leisure craft canal with a very short opening season from mid-May to mid-September. The only commercial traffic consists of a few passenger vessels, including three cruise ships which get from Stockholm to Gothenburg in four days and have preference at all the locks. We took six days for the Gota Canal alone and could have happily taken a lot longer! Surprisingly, there was no charter boat operation, such as on the Caledonian. The locks are all manned, mostly by young people of both sexes, most of whom are students doing summer jobs. Having read it all up beforehand, we expected our boat to be inspected at Mem and for all the toilet seacocks to be sealed, since the Swedes are so proud of their clean water canal. Not so, and the Porta Potty we had on board in case someone was "taken short" between shore facilities was only used twice!

Everyone kept telling us that this was the worst summer in Scandinavia for about 50 years and certainly there was excessive rain and serious flooding further north. After several days of fine sunny weather we now had two days of rain and indeed the first sections of the canal were near to overflowing with dirty brown/green water. A little bit more effluent would have made no difference. That said, the canal is scenically very pretty and, apart from the yachters, it attracts lots of tourists, including hikers, cyclists and campers. To describe it all and our passage would take several pages but young and old we all enjoyed it! Apart from the canal, the lakes are spectacular, the channels well buoyed and some of the passages narrow and interesting to say the least. All the bridges have traffic lights!

We reached Sjtorp on Lake Vanern on Sunday 30 July and proceeded as far as Lacko Castle on the island of Kallandso for the night. Lake Vanern is really an inland sea, some 60 x 60 miles, and even ranks as a sea area in the Swedish shipping weather forecasts!

At Vanersborg we entered the Trolhatte Canal to reach Gothenburg. This canal is in fact the Gotaalv (river) which is canalised in places and extends 47 miles from Lake Vanern to Gothenburg. While not on the scale of the Kiel Canal it is still very commercial and allows ships of about 1,600 grt to reach the various ports on the Lake. It is open year round and with "street lights", as on the Kiel Canal, is available 24 hours a day for commercial ships. There are only six locks, three singles and a treble, but after the Gota they are huge, with a huge and fast fall. We spent one night in a creek, which Susie described as a frog pond, before reaching Gothenburg on Wednesday 2 August. Here there was a big marina right in the middle of town, with all facilities to hand, and huge shopping centre just across the road. Younger crew members immediately noticed the McDonalds sign on it and there they had to go for lunch, including Geoffrey on his wheels. In the afternoon Susie and I went ashore by ourselves. Gothenburg is a tram city with a splendid up-to-date citywide system, but also a few ancient trams (shades of the Isle of Man) and we travelled on one of these for a bird's eye tourist view of the city. We also had time to visit the floating maritime museum close to the yacht harbour.

Thursday found us back at sea for the 47-mile trip across the North Kattegat to Skagen, the most Northerly port in Denmark. We had already been to the most Southerly, Gedser, and the most Easterly, Christianso! During this passage the wind freshened from the West and then settled down to strong to gale force Westerly for the next few days – just what we didn't need! On arrival that evening we found the yacht harbour extremely crowded as expected, mostly Swedish and Norwegian yachts on the "beer run". Berthing outside a Norwegian yacht we found that we were right outside the new marina office and toilet facilities – very convenient. Our Swiss friend Elizabeth showed up that evening, having travelled from Switzerland by train. She had elected to join us for the trip home to Bangor.

Friday was clean-up and laundry/shopping day but some crew went off for a visit to the famous sand spit. That evening Soren's brother, Fleming and friend Jorgen arrived to make up the North Sea crew and on Saturday morning there was a big sort-out, after which Virginia and her children departed for Odense and home. We were now left with eight for the North Sea crossing. We would have departed forthwith, but for the weather, and there was no sign of any improvement. The Norwegian boat moored inside us sailed for home and was back a couple of hours later, reporting strong W to NW winds and big nasty seas in the Skagerrak.

The next day this crew left their boat and went home on a ferry! On Sunday the wind was up to force 7 and only Swedes and Germans heading south departed. Norwegians stayed put and so did we! We were getting frustrated!

Monday morning saw no change or sign of change. Soren and Fleming had a flight booked back from Glasgow the next Sunday and time was getting short! We left Skagen and headed South down the inside of Jutland for the Limfjorden. About one third headsail plus mizzen had us screaming along at 8 knots to reach the Limfjorden entrance in about six hours. After that it was sail off and motoring into a strong headwind and nasty sea until we reached a sheltered berth at Alborg for the night. Next day conditions were the same. The Limfjorden is shallow and strong winds produce very nasty steep seas in the open stretches. We ploughed into it at 7 knots, with heavy spray and some solid water flying aft. We could not make Thyboren at the North Sea end before dark so had a diversion into Struer for the night. Next morning we reached Thyboren by 0900 and went straight to the fuel barge for diesel. This being Denmark it was again cash only and the oil man had to run Susie into town in his car to cash travellers' cheques. We then moved to the North Harbour, which is reserved for yachts, got to the shops, took water and all had showers.

We had lunch and then departed for Scotland at 1430 on Wednesday 9 August. There were some breaking seas in the entrance to the Thyboren Canal, but nothing dreadful, and once well clear we motorsailed off on the starboard tack since we did not want to go near the Skagerrak! Later we tacked to get further offshore and settled down quite well even if the conditions were unpleasant and uncomfortable! Soren went down with some bug and was out of action for most of the crossing, so the watchkeepers were Fleming/Jorgen and Robert/Self. Susie managed magnificently to produce good food, including hot suppers. Elizabeth, who is not a sailor, survived very well and said she even enjoyed it! In the cockpit for much of the day, she was helped into and confined to her "shelf" (the pilot berth) at night. We had two days of beating until late on Friday when the wind died away. We were now SE of the Moray Firth and there was no way we could reach Inverness before late Saturday or early Sunday. We simply motored straight for Peterhead and got there at 0330 on Saturday. Soren and Fleming departed for Aberdeen by bus to catch a train to Glasgow and thence flew home to Denmark.

The remainder of the trip home was uneventful and after the Caledonian Canal transit we made calls at Oban and Gigha before arriving back in Bangor Marina at 1300 on Thursday 17 August.

APPENDIX 1: THE BRITISH MERCHANT NAVY, THEN AND NOW – SOME NOTES

When I went to sea in 1949 the Merchant Navy was still recovering from the effects of the Second World War. All the famous British shipping companies, and many not so famous, were still in business. They were rebuilding their fleets and British shipyards were very busy indeed! Indeed, as one old marine superintendent said to me, We had to go to them on our bended knees and beg them to build a ship for us!" Major shipbuilding by cheaper competitors on the Continent and in the Far East was still a long way ahead! Many companies kept going as a stop gap measure by taking on now redundant American built Wartime ships, such as the "Liberty" cargo ships, and the "T2" tankers, of which I sailed in two under the Shell flag.

These ships had been built in some unlikely places in the USA and I believe the record for building a Liberty ship was four days! The story behind these American War built ships is a legend in itself. The Head Line of Belfast acquired two "Jeeps", of about 1,000 tons dw., the "William Howland" and the "Clement T. Jayne", which were renamed "Malin Head" and "Dunmore Head". These ships were basically timber carriers and fitted into the Head Line's Baltic trade at the time.

At that time the average ocean going dry cargo ship or tanker was no more than about 10,000 or 12,000 tons dw. There were much bigger passenger liners and some cargo liners, and of course smaller ships on coastal and short sea trades. Again the huge tankers, bulk carriers and container vessels of today were away in the future! The "T2" tankers at 15,000 tons dw were considered quite large! British owned ships were still registered in the United Kingdom, flew the Red Ensign mostly, and had all British crews. The exceptions were the companies trading extensively to the Middle and Far East, where Indian (Laskar) or Chinese ratings would be carried. For the "small" ships that they were, the crews were large by todays bare minimum standards, but that was before auto pilots to steer the ship were common and the Unmanned Machinery Space (UMS) was still a dream in some shipowner's eye! The catering department was particularly well manned. On a typical ocean-going cargo ship or tanker the crew list might have read as follows:

Master	Carpenter
First Mate	Bosun
Second Mate	Deck Storekeeper
Third Mate	9 Able Seamen or Efficient Deck Hands
4 Deck Apprentices	2 Ordinary Seamen
Radio Operator	1 Deck Boy
Chief Engineer	3 Junior Engineers (5th Engineers)
Second Engineer	Donkeyman
Third Engineer	Engine Room Storekeeper
Fourth Engineer	Pumpman (peculiar to tankers)
Electrician	4 Firemen/Greasers
Chief Steward	Chief Cook
Second Steward	Second Cook and Baker
Deck Officers Steward	Galley Boy
Eng. Officers Steward	Crew Messman
Saloon Steward	

The total adds up to between 45 and 50, unheard of in today's manning scales and even for much larger ships. With Indian or Chinese ratings there were even more, with dedicated helmsmen or quartermasters, bridge boys and dedicated cooks for the ratings.

WATCHKEEPING AT SEA

The watchkeeping system on deck and in the engine room at that time is interesting. Looking back even further, to the days of the good old sailing ships, the ships were smaller and so were the crews but they did have all those sails and ropes to handle! I think about 30 crew was typical. There was of course a Master but only two mates, perhaps ten sailors on each of two watches. Bosun, carpenter and sailmaker would have been another three but the sum total of the catering department would have been a cook and an officers steward. There might also have been some deck apprentices. Propulsion machinery and radios, and the men that went with them had yet to be invented! It was simply a matter of four hours of "watch on and watch off" for the two mates and the sailors, with the two-hour "dog" watches in the evening to break the monotony. If something serious required doing, like tacking or wearing the ship, then it was a matter of "all hands on deck".

Later, with the steamships came the more civilized three watch system – four hours on and eight hours off. "All hands on deck" was only required for berthing or unberthing the ship!

With this system the first mate kept the 4 to 8 watch, morning and evening, the second mate the 12 to 4, afternoon and night (the "graveyard watch") and the third mate the 8 to 12, morning and night. On deck it required three ratings, or apprentices, on each watch and the system worked as follows:

No.1 Two hours on the wheel

No.2 One hour on lookout, either on the forecastle or the bridge wing, depending on the weather.

No.3 He was known as the "farmer", since he could lie in for an hour and then relieve the lookout for two hours. Also he had no wheel duty.

No.2 Had a one hour break and then relieved No.1 on the wheel for two hours.

No.1 Did the last hour of the watch on lookout.

The duties rotated with each watch, so that each third watch one man was the farmer.

During daylight hours those not on the wheel could be employed on other work, such as chipping and painting steelwork along with the dayworkers.

In the engine room the Second Engineer kept the 4 to 8, the Third the 12 to 4 and the Fourth the 8 to 12. Each had a Junior Engineer and a fireman/greaser on watch with them. In motorships especially, they did not spend their time on watch just looking at dials but more likely were overhauling a shut down generator or at least spent their time "grinding valves". On old ships like the "Spondilus" they were fully engaged in just trying to keep all the machinery running at all!

On most ships we rang "eight bells" on the bridge bell at the end of each watch but during the watch only "one bell", which in fact was rung fifteen minutes before the end of a watch, to remind those about to come on duty to get a move on. In the engineer room there would be length of iron hanging from a beam, which when struck with a heavy boiler hammer produced a very resounding chime, heard all over the ship!

When I was apprentice there were usually four of us on a ship and it was common practice for the Mate to put the three most senior on the 4 to 8 watch. This released three seamen to join the day work squad on whatever project the Mate had in hand, chipping and painting usually. It also enabled him to turn out the three watchkeeping apprentices for a three-hour "field day" after breakfast to help with the task in hand. We didn't get any extra pay on top of our pittance but had he turned out watchkeeping sailors, they would have had to be paid overtime. We called our overtime "scotch" overtime!

NAVIGATION AT SEA

Before the arrival of the now ubiquitous Global Positioning System (GPS), celestial navigation was all-important except when coasting and with landmarks to take bearings of. The GPS makes it all so easy that a child can navigate (and mine do!) but this can be dangerous and unsafe. I have heard stories of some supposedly qualified present day deck officers who are able to do little else but push buttons and read dials! Some of them also have the barest knowledge of the "Rule of the Road". In my day a personally owned sextant was a vital part of any deck officer's possessions and on any ship the all important clockwork chronometer lived in a specially padded compartment, usually at one end of the chart table.

The problems of finding longitude at sea and the eventual development of the marine chronometer by John Harrison make fascinating reading in the book by Dava Sobel. I thought the ensuing TV series was equally fascinating. It was the second mate's job to carefully wind the chronometer at the same time every day, usually at about 0800 before morning sights were taken, and woe betide him if it was ever allowed to run down. However, with the coming of radio and radio time signals this was not the dreadful calamity it once would have been!

On most passages, weather permitting, the ship's position would be fixed three times a day. The Mate would take star sights at twilight, morning and evening, and in good conditions would have a position worked out and on the chart within about half an hour. No pre-programmed calculators or computers in those days; it was all done with pencil, workbook, Nautical Almanac and old-fashioned nautical tables, such as Nories or Burtons. At about 0800 the Second and Third Mates would take sun sights and the position lines thus obtained "run up" to Noon. These position lines were then crossed with the latitude obtained when the sun was directly north or south to obtain the noon position. Unless "apparent time" was being kept, noon was usually somewhere between 1130 and 1230. The noon position was all important and once established there were other calculations to establish the daily run, average speed and other information.

Bad weather, with overcast skies, sometimes for two or three days, could be a problem. Outward bound from say the English Channel into the Atlantic was not a great problem since one could steam for several days quite happily on "dead reckoning" without obtaining a "fix". Coming the other way certainly could be a major problem without a reliable fix and when trying to make a landfall. The only aids were not very reliable bearings of radio beacons which were rarely trusted unless close to them.

THE TONNAGE AND REGISTRATION OF MERCHANT SHIPS

I have included this topic since so many people, not in the "business" but showing interest, get totally confused and quite understandably so!

Merchant ships are normally quoted as being so many tons deadweight or just "dw" and this is the number of tons (or tonnes) of cargo bunkers, fresh water and stores they can carry when floating at their appropriate loadline, as marked on the sides of the ship. To complicate matters there are several loadlines and the one in use depends on what part of the world the ship is in and the season of the year. Most commonly a ship will load to her "summer loadline" and so the deadweight quoted is the "summer deadweight". Displacement Tonnage is the actual weight of water the ship will displace and includes the total weight of the ship herself, plus whatever is in her be it cargo, bunkers stores or nothing at all. In the latter case we talk of the Light Displacement.

We now come to Gross and Net tonnages, which are not tons weight but tons of volume at the rate of 100 cubic feet per ton! Basically the Gross tonnage is the total internal volume of the ship including cargo spaces, machinery spaces and crew spaces. Net tonnage is the same figure, less the volume of the machinery spaces, crew spaces and other spaces which cannot be used for carrying cargo. Net tonnage is therefore the volume of the ship expressed in tons of 100 cubic feet, available for the carriage of cargo.

Gross and Net tonnages are very important because it is on these that a ship pays harbour dues and many other "dues". Also Gross tonnage is used in most statutory rules and regulations to determine the level to which a ship must comply with the various rules and regulations. This covers almost anything to do with the safety of the ship, including the number and qualifications of the crew, the safety equipment to be provided and many other matters. British Tonnage Certificates were always acceptable almost World-wide except for the Suez and Panama Canals, which had their own tonnage rules. Thus British ships trading Worldwide always had three tonnage certificates – British, Suez and Panama. The calculation of tonnage and the issue of tonnage certificates used to be an important part of the work carried out by "Board of Trade" surveyors, but it is now carried out by the various classification societies, such as Lloyd's Register, along with the work of calculating and assigning loadlines and the issue of Loadline Certificates. At least with the advance of the International Maritime Organisation (IMO) many National marine rules and regulations have become International and so we now even have an International Tonnage Certificate. IMO, incidentally, is the only department of the United Nations Organisation which is based in the United Kingdom.

Having digested the above, it is obvious from a shipowner's point of view that basically what he wants in a ship is the highest possible deadweight tonnage, or carrying capacity, with the lowest possible gross and net tonnages, on which he has to pay dues. Clever naval architects therefore exploit the tonnage regulations to their utmost to produce such a ship and there have been some interesting results. Many years ago the rules for calculating tonnage only took into account the beam of a ship as measured at the main deck level and the result was a number of what were called "turtle deck" ships. These had very narrow main decks but below this level the hull was very much wider. These were better known as "coffin ships" and were basically unstable in certain conditions. After a number of casualties the rules had to be changed to eliminate them. Another peculiarity was the "open tween deck" or shelter deck ship, of which I am sure a number are still around today. Above the main deck, which was fully watertight, was constructed another enclosed tween deck, which would extend virtually the length of the ship, but with only "temporary" closing appliances in any bulkheads along the way. It would have normal access hatches but at the after end there was an additional small hatch called the "tonnage hatch". This could only be closed with "temporary" wooden boards and lashings and thus the whole shelter deck was considered open, and not included in the Net Tonnage! Dues were only paid on any "deck cargo" which might be carried in there!

There are also at least two "magic" figures for gross tonnage, one being 500 and the other 1,600. At under 500 tons gross a ship does not have to comply with any International regulations, only whatever National regulations apply to it and these are generally quite modest. At 1,600 tons gross and above all the regulations, National and International, become seriously more onerous than if the tonnage is below this figure. One little quirk is that she now has to carry a fully certificated ship's cook. Below that tonnage anyone can be a cook. There are therefore a great number of ships about which have a gross tonnage of 499,9 but can carry perhaps 1,500 tons of cargo and a great number of 1,599.9 gross tons which can carry perhaps 4,000 tons of cargo!

The tonnage business is really an ongoing battle between the tonnage authorities and clever naval architects. This battle even comes into the design and rating of racing yachts, of which more in Appendix 2. It can in fact be likened to the battle between taxation authorities and clever accountants. The accountants will always try to find loopholes in the taxation laws, to the benefit of their clients, while the taxation authorities will spend a lot of time trying to identify such loopholes and plug them securely!

I am not about to voice an opinion on the subject of "offshore accounts" but suffice to say that in recent years many reputable shipowners have had to transfer their ships to "offshore registries" in order to stay in business and make even a modest profit. For British shipowners the Isle of Man, the Bahamas and the Cayman Islands are among the favourites. There have long been the "flag of convenience" registries such as those of Panama and Liberia, with the dubious standards of the ships under these flags but in recent years these countries have done much to improve their safety standards while still aiming to maintain their low cost registries. Indeed during my time at sea the well known Greek tanker owning families, such as Onassis, Niarchos and Goulandris built up their fleets from old "T2" tankers and such like into modern efficient and well run operations, with sleek modern ships, and all were under Panamanian or Liberian registry.

THE "DECLINE AND FALL" OF THE RED ENSIGN FLEET.

Back in the late 1950s, the British Shell fleet had four 30,000 ton dw tankers under the Panamanian flag. They were the "C" class, with names such as "Capulus", and were built in the USA. The reason for their Panamanian registry was more to do with the financial arrangements for their construction than anything else and they were fully part of the Shell fleet, with British officers, and as far as I remember, British crews. However, it must have been the mid 1960s before there was a hint of what was to come. Perhaps my own first hint was m.v. "Hamilton", which while she was a fully registered British ship, the owners were the Hamilton Shipping Co. of Hamilton, Bermuda. Bermuda was by then I think a desirable offshore haven in which ones money would be safe from the British Taxman!

I suppose it was something that was bound to happen. We cannot stop the World developing the way it will, any more than we can stop it turning on its axis, and we just have to adapt to the changes. Britannia had ruled the waves for a long time and the Red Ensign was to be seen in every port of the World, but not for much longer! The United Kingdom had always practised an "open seas" policy and still does. This is not surprising since the British merchant fleet traded Worldwide and the "crosstrades", where British ships traded between numerous foreign countries were an important source of "invisible" income for the owners and the government. Now, however, other countries wanted to ship their exports in ships of their own flag and more recently, with so-called globalisation, it has been a case of whoever's ships can do the job cheapest gets the work! Some countries, however, have always had restrictions and particularly so the USA, where the Jones Act prohibits any foreign ships from competing in their coastal trades. With their high wage crews and other overheads they can only survive in foreign trade with massive Government subsidies.

In Belfast it was noticeable that as say the local Head Line ships on the Continental trade disappeared they were replaced by Dutch and German registered ships, which in turn were replaced by "Funny flag" ships having two or three German or Dutch officers, the rest of the crew being low cost Filipino or other nationality. More and more ships appeared, even on the cross-Channel trades, which were registered in such places as Cyprus, and had minimal foreign crews.

Major British liner companies were not exempt and except for one or two big players, such as P&O and Blue Star, their ships have all disappeared, if not the companies themselves. My old company, Shell, together with other major oil companies, had a very big "clean out". They relied more and more on chartered in foreign flag tankers, with cheap crews, which were much cheaper to operate than their owned ships under the British flag. The much reduced British fleets were flagged out to the Isle of Man, the Bahamas and suchlike registries and remaining officers were offered inferior contracts with offshore management companies. Filipino junior officers and ratings became the norm. The old idea of being a "Shell" man or a "BP" man for your whole career at sea, with a nice secure pension to follow, went out of the window! However, I believe more recently, because of the loss of the old company "spirit" and the rapid deterioration in the condition of the ships, there has been a move back to direct employment.

For many years there was virtually no recruitment of apprentices, because of the cost of training them, but they are the competent well trained senior officers of the future and it was at last realised that there was a huge "generation gap" developing! Having trained up competent officers in the past, deep sea shipping companies often lost many of them to the cross-Channel ferry companies, and to such shore based jobs as harbour masters, harbour pilots and dare I say it, Board of Trade surveyors! Many other officers also left at some stage to go into non related shore employment, usually on getting married or soon thereafter! However, to my knowledge, there are now some sponsored or subsided schemes and apprentices are again being recruited, but only a fraction of the numbers recruited in my day. There are some sophisticated courses (if you can get on one) for both deck and engineer entrants even leading to degrees and involving part time at sea before sitting a first examination.

It used to be that deck apprentices, or ratings for that matter, if they had ambition and ability, only had to go to sea for four years before sitting their first examination – usually second mate (Foreign Going). Engineers had to "serve their time" in a suitable engineering works ashore. They were then "graded" by a Board of Trade engineer examiner and depending on the quality of the work they had been doing were given a variable length of seatime before they could sit for the Second Class Marine Engineer's Certificate. They went to sea as Fifth (Junior) Engineers. Many were the excellent apprentices from the Harland & Wolff Shipyard who went to sea in ships they had helped to build, such as Union Castle passenger liners, got their Certificates of Competency and then returned to the Shipyard as managers. At the other end of the scale it was said that in times of an engineer shortage you could serve your time in a bicycle repair shop and still get away to sea, albeit with a lot of seatime to put in before the first examination! Some engineers never passed any examinations but they could rise as high as Third engineer without paper qualifications, and were known as "Permanent Thirds"!

With the serious reduction of recruitment into the Merchant Navy, so there was a serious reduction in the number of marine colleges. Today I think there are only perhaps three major colleges in the United Kingdom and one in the Republic of Ireland. There are a few smaller establishments catering for fishermen, where necessary. Our marine college at the University of Ulster is long since gone and any local students have to go elsewhere for training. There are occasional courses organised at Kilkeel or Portavogie for the benefit of the local fishermen.

With the huge reduction in the number of British ships and seafarers the organisation I worked for is a shadow of its former self. When I joined it was the Marine Survey Service of the Board of Trade and a lot of changes took place over 30 years. When I retired it was the Marine Safety Agency and it is now part of the Maritime and Coastguard Agency.

The whole pattern of marine examination work for seafarers has changed as well and all the local examiners are left with are the oral examinations. Everything else has been farmed out to the colleges and most of the examination papers are set and marked by such bodies as Scotvec. It is also now not possible to sit for any statutory examination without having first attended a course. In the days when everything was "in house", anyone could walk in off the street and apply for examination. All they had to do was produce proof of the necessary sea service, good references and watchkeeping certificates before sitting an examination. The proof of their knowledge and ability, or otherwise, was established in the examination. Nowadays, even NVQs have hit the marine scene and it is probably possible for a galley boy to get one, even if it is only for dishwashing!

However, it is probably not all doom, gloom and despair and I would never want to be the old man sitting at the back of the cave complaining that everything in the world had gone "down the drain" since his day! I am sure there was many an old shipmaster who felt that way in the days when sail was changing to steam!

APPENDIX 2: YACHTS AND YACHT RACING, THEN AND NOW – SOME NOTES

When I had my first boat in 1947 or 1948, wood was basically the only material available for construction. Small sailing dinghies were of either clinker (overlapping planks) or sometimes carvel (narrow plank on edge) construction. However, my "Titmouse" was neither and was constructed from quite wide planks in what was virtually a box shape, but pointed at one end and flat at the other! The design came from a small book called "simple Boat Building" by Geoffrey Prout – later famous for his catamarans. The Holywood Sharpies, such as the "Spray", were also constructed by the same simple method but had rather more shapely lines and were much better performers! They were said to have been designed by Fred Steen on the back of a cigarette packet! He owned the pub on the Kinnegar seafront at Holywood and while it had electric light and running water, in hindsight I think the interior decor and cleanliness of this establishment was not dissimilar to that of "Dirty Murphy's" in Cork!

It was not until some time in the 1950s, when waterproof marine grade plywood became available that such sailing dinghies as the GP14 and the Enterprise started to come on the scene. Cruising and larger racing yachts continued to be built to traditional wooden designs and invariably were full bodied with long keels. GRP (Glass Reinforced Polyester) appeared in boat construction probably later in the '50s, first in dinghies and outboard runabouts. Before long, as construction techniques improved, larger boats appeared and perhaps one of the first was the Nicholson 36, designed by Camper & Nicholsons, the famous yacht builders, in the late '50s or early '60s. At least one of these boats did very well on the English offshore racing scene. "Samphire of Cultra" was one of the 30 or so boats built to this design; it was C & N's first venture into GRP construction and the boat had very traditional lines. Also only the bare hull was GRP, the deck, cockpit and coachroof being wooden and indeed the outward appearance was that of a traditional wooden boat. Anyway, in 1969 and 1970 she was a "hot" boat on the Northern Ireland offshore racing scene! Camper & Nicholson next went in for an all GRP boat and the famous Nicholson 32 was born. Again designed on traditional lines they were nevertheless competitive on the racing scene in their early days until beaten by boats of a more radical design. However, they were always sound seaworthy cruising boats and remain very popular to this day. They had very attractive lines and so much wood in the way of gunwales, cockpit coamings and other parts that they could still be mistaken for all wooden boats. Our "Melandy", built in 1965, was Build No. 80. In all there must have been about 300 Nicholson 32s built before they could not compete with more modern (and cheaper) designs.

Pre- and post-War, until perhaps the mid-'50s, there was little change in the design of yachts intended for offshore racing. They had traditional underwater lines and were solid seaworthy boats, still with quite comfortable accommodation. There was a man called John Illingworth who was a successful designer, and skipper of offshore yachts, and he must have been one of the first to produce a forerunner of what was to come. His "Myth of Malham" showed the traditional boats on the English racing scene a "clean pair of heels" and her design became the subject of general attention. Basically hulls became shallower and the keels shorter until they became no more than a bolt on deep fin. Rudders were separated from the after end of the keel and hung on a separate skeg. Then the skeg was removed and the rudder became no more than a blade, depending totally on the top rudder bearing for support. The availability of GRP and indeed other exotic materials made the construction of these extreme designs possible.

To my mind and that of many others, the modern offshore racing yacht is no more than a much overgrown racing dinghy, while down below the accommodation is the barest minimum to meet the racing rules in the interest of lightness! I think for example that a Porta Poti screwed to the deck meets the requirements for a fixed toilet! There have of course been numerous examples of such yachts losing their keels, breaking their rudders, losing their masts and rigging and generally falling apart, even in less than heavy weather. However, if you want to have a hope of winning an offshore race these days that is the type of boat you must go for!

In yacht racing a race can be between a fleet of boats which are all exactly the same or it can be between boats of differing types and sizes, in which case they have to be handicapped according to their potential performance. In the first case the first boat home is the winner but in the second case a boat well down the fleet can be the winner after the handicaps have been applied. There are hundreds of different classes of sailing dinghies and small keel boats which race as a class, with no handicapping, and more recently various classes of offshore yachts which also race as a class. This is even the case with the boats in some of the recent round-the-world races.

Offshore racing, however, is still mainly between yachts of different sizes and characteristics and therefore a handicapping system is necessary. There have been, and are, many systems but perhaps the most famous was that devised by the Royal Ocean Racing Club (RORC) in the early 1900s and known as the RORC Rating Rule. The Rule called for extensive measurement of a boat's hull, spars, rigging, sails and equipment, followed by some detailed and complicated calculations. The result was a rating, quoted in feet, which could be anything between about 19 feet and 70 feet. After further calculation a figure called the Time Correction Factor (TCF) to arrive at her corrected time and this could then be compared with the corrected times of other yachts to establish the order of finishing.

The reader may now realise that there is an analogy between the Rating Rule for yachts and the Tonnage Rules for merchant ships. Yes, clever yacht designers set out to exploit the Rule to the full by trying to produce a big fast yacht having the lowest possible rating! Some very strange-looking yachts appeared on the scene particularly in the lines and shape of the hull and some were definitely not safe! As with the Merchant ship tonnage rules it became an on going battle between the rule makers and the designers and there were amendments to the Rating Rule almost every year to try and plug the loopholes. See Appendix 1! Again there is the analogy with the battle between the taxman and the clever accountant! In the USA there was the Cruising Club of America Rule and in Australia the Cruising Yacht Club of Australia also had their own Rule. All the rules suffered the same problems and in the end became so complicated as to be almost unworkable. Thus in the late 1960s a team was set up, under the direction of the well known American yacht designer Olin Stevens, to try and simplify the whole business. The result was the International Offshore Rule (IOR) which at first was widely acclaimed and universally recognised, but guess what happened. Yes, the battle between clever yacht designers and the rule makers started all over again! I am not quite sure what the present situation is Internationally but in the UK a simpler system known as the Channel Handicap was devised and at the time of writing is used for offshore yacht racing in Northern Ireland.

273

Before I mention yacht tonnage I must mention the "Ton" classes. Like "doing the Ton" along the motorway, with the Police in pursuit, this has nothing to do with tonnage! The Ton classes were devised to allow for more "boat for boat" racing, without the boats having to be identical. In each of the classes the boats had to measure up to exactly the same rating and there evolved classes for ¼, ½, ¾, 1 and 2 "ton" boats, and perhaps more. "Golden Delicious", at about 31 ft in length, was a ¾ tonner, "Dictator" at about 38 ft was a 1 tonner, and "Golden Leigh", at about 42 ft, was a 2 tonner. I cannot remember what the actual ratings were for these classes.

Yachts can be fully registered British ships, although for smaller ones it is not a legal requirement. Registered yachts have gross and net tonnages just like a merchant ship, but because there are no cargo spaces the two figures are often the same. Thus our own "Sundowner" has a tonnage of 14.53, both gross and net. These tonnages, together with the "official number", have to be permanently carved in a conspicuous place and with a GRP boat this usually is on a decorative wooden board secured to a bulkhead.

"Thames Tonnage" is commonly used to give some idea of the size of a boat, but again it bears no relation to the weight of the boat and results from a simple formula which only takes account of the length and beam of a boat. A 5-tonner would be about 25 ft in length while "Melandy" at 32 feet is 10 tons. "Sundowner" at 40 feet, works out at 25 tons. Her displacement, or actual weight, is somewhere approaching 20 tons.

Lastly, I will mention the navigational equipment available for yachts. Up until 1977, when I was involved in offshore racing, the racing rules only allowed the equipment found on the average cruising yacht and this would be no more than a magnetic steering compass and hand bearing compass, an echo sounder and a simple radio direction finder. Some boats would have fairly bulky 2 mhz or "trawler band" communications radios and racing boats would have one or more wind direction and speed instruments, especially useful when beating to windward. Navigational equipment went through a huge development stage thereafter both for commercial vessels and pleasure craft and prices came down so much that such items as the Decca Navigator and radar were affordable by the average yachtsman. The racing rules still however only permitted the basic equipment, the view being that if there was no restriction wealthy owners could so equip their boats as to have an unfair advantage over those less well heeled. In addition, access to all the equipment available would make navigation and tactical planning so easy as to totally remove that element from the competitive equation! VHF radios also came way down in price until very few offshore boats were without one. In the 1977 Admiral's Cup races they were compulsory, since each boat had to report in twice a day to the guard ship.

Needless to say pressure mounted for a change in the rules, ostensibly from a safety point of view, and eventually the flood gates opened! Serious offshore racing yachts these days are full of electronic wizardry, the ubiquitous GPS receiver being the least of it. Computers and satellite communications systems are found on many boats, certainly those involved in the now numerous round-the-world events. Such is progress!

GLOSSARY

While anyone who has been to sea or has connections with the mercantile marine or merchant navy (same thing) will understand most of the terms that occur in the text, there may be others who will not and it has been suggested that I included a short glossary for their benefit. I hope the following list will be helpful.

CREW/OFFICERS AND CREW

In general Crew means the total number of working people on board a ship but the term Officers and Crew is often used and in this case the crew are the petty officers and ratings. A ship which had all British officers and all British crew was often referred to as a "white crew" ship, as opposed to many British ships which had British officers but native Chinese or Indian petty officers and ratings. Nowadays one is just as likely to find a "British" ship with only the most senior officers being British, the rest being from the Philippines or some other source of "cheap" crews.

MASTER/CAPTAIN or SKIPPER (fishing vessels)

Officially, in British merchant ships there is no such title as Captain – it is really just a courtesy title. The "boss" of a merchant ship has the official title of Master, so when the title Master or Captain appears, it means the same person. He is often referred to, especially by the crew, as "the Old Man" The "boss" of a fishing vessel has the official title of Skipper.

DECK OFFICERS/MATES

Again, officially deck officers in merchant ships are known as Mates but while the next in rank below the Master is the First Mate or simply Mate, he is just as likely to be referred to as the First Officer or Chief Officer. In a fishing vessel the next person in rank to the Skipper is officially known as the Second Hand.

Thus when I a qualified as an examiner of merchant navy deck officers and fishermen, the official title for this part of my job was Examiner of Masters and Mates. Further complications in terminology arose with the complete overhaul of the examination and certification system. All the statutory certificates are now graded by number and there are all manner of permutations depending on size of ship and area of trading. Suffice to say that what is now called a Class 1 Certificate of Competency used to be known as Master (Foreign Going). The Extra Master Certificate, while still available on a voluntary basis has largely been superseded by a degree in nautical studies.

APPRENTICES/CADETS

In my day, trainee deck officers were known as apprentices and signed indentures with a shipowner. An apprenticeship was for four years and all but a few months of this time had to be actually served at sea. Apprentices were also known as cadets, especially in the more upmarket shipping companies such as P&O.

BOATSWAIN/BOSUN

In merchant ships there are petty officers, who I suppose could be equated to petty officers in the Royal Navy. The foreman of the deck ratings is known as the Boatswain or just Bosun. In ships which had Indian (Lascar) ratings, this man was known as the Serang.

QUARTERMASTERS

In the Army a quartermaster looks after the stores but on a merchant ship a quartermaster is someone who takes the helm and steers the ship, under orders from the captain or officer of the watch. In the average British ship with an all-British crew there were no dedicated helmsmen but with Chinese or Indian ratings there were usually four dedicated quartermasters. Indian quartermasters were known as Secunnies, certainly a rank above the common deck crew who were known as Kalassies.

PILOTS

Marine pilots are found mainly in local areas such as harbours and harbour approaches and are usually employed by the local harbour authority or are self employed. They are almost all former merchant navy deck officers who have specialist knowledge of the peculiarities of their particular area and the berthing and unberthing of ships therein. They are essential for most visiting ships whose Masters are not familiar with the area. For ships trading regularly to certain ports the Master is examined for and granted a pilotage exemption certificate. Thus after six consecutive trips into Lake Maracaibo as Master of a tanker I was granted such a certificate by the Venezuelan authorities. There are some areas of the World where the navigation and pilotage can be particularly tricky and where a local pilot is advisable for strange ships. The Great Barrier Reef on the East coast of Australia is one such and the pilot can be aboard for five days, between Brisbane and Thursday Island in the Torres Strait.

CERTIFICATES OF COMPETENCY/TICKETS

The official qualifications held by masters and mates and also engineers in the mercantile marine are known as Certificates of Competency but in my day they were commonly called "tickets". Thus having completed an apprenticeship as a deck officer and ongoing up for your first official and statutory examination, you were said to be "up for your Second Mate's ticket".

SIGNING ON/PAYING OFF

Traditionally in official terms a shipowner employs the Master of a ship and the Master employs everyone else, including officers and ratings. When a crew member joins a ship he or she has to "sign on" to the Articles of Agreement, as they are called. These set out the conditions of employment and the rate of pay. When a crew member leaves a ship he or she has to "sign off" or "pay off" and traditionally receives all outstanding pay and other financial benefits due at that time. It used to be that virtually all pay-offs were done in cash and in a UK port this would often be done under the eye of a government official known as a Mercantile Marine Office Superintendent or Shipping Master. In the "good old days of sail" there were innumerable instances of poor sailors being led astray and relieved of their pay-off before they got very far from the ship. It sometimes still happened in my day, but there are now generally more up-to-date arrangements.

The Articles of Agreement were time limited and came in various forms, depending on the ship and her trading pattern. The normal limit for foreign going ships was two years or as soon as the ship returned to a UK port. Sometimes there would be a complete pay-off and a change of articles but more often there would be numerous individual signings-on and payings-off during the currency of a "set" of articles.

Traditionally the Master was responsible for his account with the shipowner and this could be a major headache! After a long voyage or a long period "on articles" there could be a very considerable sum of money involved when it came to sorting out the "portage bill" (the Master's account with the shipowner).

For anyone who is interested, but not familiar with "tonnage" this subject is dealt with in Appendix 1.

REGISTRATION OF SHIPS

With the exception of certain smaller vessels, and in particular smaller pleasure yachts, all ships must be registered and carry a Certificate of Registry. This is the most important official document on board a ship since it establishes the nationality of the ship and the ownership. It can be likened to the deeds for a property or the registration book for a road vehicle and is issued by the government of the country concerned. There is a popular misconception that registration means registry with Lloyds' Register but this is not so. Lloyds' Register and several other similar organisations are called classification societies. Ships entered with them have to be regularly surveyed and maintained to high standards. This means that potential insurers, including Lloyds' underwriters, and charterers can refer to the register and get a complete picture of a ship's state of seaworthiness. The classification societies also carry out some statutory survey work on behalf of various governments, particularly with regard to load line and tonnage certificates.

PETROLEUM TANKERS – BLACK AND WHITE OIL CARGOES

"Black Oil" cargoes include all crude and unrefined oils and the heavier grades of refined oil such as heavy fuel oil. "White Oil" cargoes cover the lighter grades of refined products such as motor gasoline, diesel and aviation fuel.

EPILOGUE

When I first went to sea at the age of 16, I think my immediate ambition was to see a bit of the world and to learn something about navigation while I was at it. This would be useful in future sailing activities! The four years ahead of me seemed an eternity and it would be enough just to "complete my time". In later years at sea depression set in from time to time and any shore job seemed preferable to what I was doing. I did enquire about a number of shore jobs including that of a uniformed customs officer but never went further than obtaining application forms! At the end of the day I am glad I stuck it out at sea!

Yes, in the same circumstances I almost certainly would. But circumstances these days are so different that there is really no comparison.

What were the highlights of my career at sea? Undoubtedly, completing my "time" and passing my Second Mate's Certificate were big highlights. I was now a ship's officer and had some status! The other big moment, was of course, getting command of a modern deep sea oil tanker at the age of 30 in the early 1960s.

One is often asked one's preference in such fields as music and my tastes are very plebeian. Basically, I am musical ignoramus! Like many people I often associate certain music with places or events. For example, thinking of the two months in dry-dock at North Shields on my first ship, I cannot help but remember "Red Roses for a Blue Lady" and "Night Riders in the Sky", played on an old portable and clockwork gramophone.

In the early 1960s the Irish "showbands" were at their zenith and so was I! I had the "Extra" ticket, I was Master of a deep sea tanker and I was a happy bachelor! The world was my oyster! I loved the Irish "showband" music and, like many of my generation still enjoy it. I have numerous tapes of Brian Coll and the "Sundowners", Susan Mc.Cann, Philomena Begley and others. American country and western music also goes down well! I will never forget the pleasures of Caproni's dance hall in Bangor and the Melotones band that played there. The site, and the adjacent Bangor Shipyard, are now occupied by a block of flats and an old people's home. My wife, who is classically inclined, thinks all this is rubbish and so do my teenage sons, who are deep into the latest pop music - if you can call it music. To me, this modern pop music is nothing more than a mind-bending racket!

Having seen something of the World I am often asked where I would like to live other than Northern Ireland and to an outsider that may seem a logical question in view of the situation here. However, it is a case of the other man's grass always seeming greener and the large number of outsiders who have settled here, including my own parents, indicates that it is a good place to live! My wife is American and she has lived happily here for over 30 years! Fortunately she grew up with a love of sailing and had her own Cape Cod cat boat at an early age on Cape Cod itself, which is between Boston and New York on the East coast of the USA.

When I joined the then Board of Trade Marine Survey Service in 1965, I had no idea that I would spend all but some three years out of 30 based at the Belfast Marine Office! Now the idea of retirement to Spain or somewhere outside my present environment has no appeal whatever! Everything I love and enjoy is here.

On the sailing scene, when I had my first little boat, I had no idea where my interest would take me although I was certainly interested in cruising boats because of all the reading I did. On the racing scene the highlight has to be my participation in the Admiral's Cup series in 1977 and on the cruising scene, it must be the present family boat "Sundowner", which continues to give us great pleasure. This despite rebellious teenage sons who now want to "do their own thing" and not be stuck with "fuddy duddy" parents.

There have recently been outstanding achievements in sailing by round-the-World single-handed sailors and dedicated yacht racing types, but I like to think that anything I achieved is well within the reach of the average person.

There is also in some people an addiction to boats, from which they never recover. I have a number of friends, some older than me, who have sold their boats and retired from active sailing, only to discover that life without a boat is impossible! There is something about "boat life" which is hard to define but, once you are hooked it is irresistible! A country cottage or even a caravan is one thing, but a boat is something else!

There is a story of a sailor who got fed up with the sea, retired and then walked inland with an oar over his shoulder. When he reached a place where someone asked him what the oar was, there he settled down.

That sailor is not me!